D1827125

I LEARNED TO FLY FOR HITLER

Joe Volmar

KRON PUBLICATIONS
1864 Irish Road
Dundee, Michigan 48131
USA

First Edition

KRON PUBLICATIONS
1864 Irish Road
Dundee, Michigan 48131
U.S.A.

ISBN 0-9671389-0-6

Library of Congress Catalog Card Number: 99-62464

Printed in the U.S.A.

Prologue

This account has been written with a two-fold purpose in mind. It started as an autobiography for the benefit and enjoyment of my sons, their wives and offspring, but as I became involved with the story and was encouraged by friends, I decided to expand the purpose and try to answer a question frequently posed to me: "How could the German people be led down such a wayward path by a madman?'

At the expense of over-simplifying a complicated happening, I will attempt to explain the basics and then let my personal experiences and state of mind while in Germany assist in elaborating upon the subject. I wish to emphasize that this book does not, in any way whatsoever, intend to glorify Adolph Hitler or to condone any of his Nazi philosophies. I merely want to depict how easily one can get swept along with the masses.

After Germany's defeat in World War I and the subsequent harsh terms of the Versailles Treaty, the country experienced one economic and political disaster after another. The average German's standard of living was at the lowest point ever and within the existing framework of a world-wide depression; there was scant hope of improvement on the horizon.

Along came the unknown little corporal who very cleverly orchestrated German emotions by combining emphasis on the proud and staunch Prussian military tradition and the agonizing restrictions of Versailles. Adding fuel to the fire by blaming the Jews, Communists and Capitalists for all of Germany's ills, Hitler managed to attract a following. By nurturing and making promises to the people, many of whom had a minimum education and were "have-nots", he established an organization of disciples, intent upon improving their own well-being at anyone else's expense. With this beginning and some devious and clever political maneuvering, Hitler created an economic upswing like no other by establishing extensive government construction and armament programs. Factory work and other manual trades were promoted as honorable professions and workers were blessed with benefits galore: health insurance, swimming pools and a fleet of cruise ships for workers' vacations appeared out of nowhere.

Once the recovery was underway, Hitler's support grew at a fantastic pace, as he had kept his promises. Even the doubtful soon joined his ranks, as the new regime had re-awakened Germany's pride and put food on the table.

By this time it was too late in the game for dissidents to remain effective. Using Dr. Goebbels' canny propaganda program and total information control, the Nazi torrent swept through the entire nation. Those who may have doubted were now afraid to express their views, as the threat of being accused of disloyalty by a jealous friend or neighbor was all too real to ignore. Besides, why should one doubt a regime that had restored the Fatherland's honor and prosperity in such a short time?

By the time I arrived in Germany in March of 1941, the die was already firmly cast and there was no turning back. I was an impressionable teenager but still suspicious of the Nazis and was determined not to succumb to this "Nazi propaganda stuff"..............would you believe that in six months I was eagerly using the straight arm salute with the rest of my peers?

I have attempted to describe some cultural traits unique to Germans as well as the hardships brought upon by a war (to ALL those involved, friend and foe). You may wonder about my obvious pre-occupation with food.... in a wartime environment of minimum rations, satisfying your stomach's desires becomes the order of the day! Historical facts have been incorporated whenever interesting or pertinent. I have also included considerable training data relating to aviation and soaring.

Fortunately my mother had saved all of my "war letters", affording me a substantial memory bank of detail. In some cases, I have re-created conversations that may not be verbatim, but are intended to convey the mood and meaning of the episodes involved. Most proper names are authentic, but a few are contrived, as my memory was unable to dredge them up after all these years.

Other assistance and documentation was cheerfully furnished by my *Oberschule* classmates Friedhard Huck, Friedrich Schwarz and Fritz Klein. My sincere thanks to many American friends who gave me the encouragement necessary to complete the arduous task of a "first book". Typical of this fine group is Lt. Col. M.S. Eltzroth (USAF Ret.) whose provocative curiosity while he was my superior (and friend) in Germany greatly challenged my analytical and creative thinking.

Another purpose of this book is to emphasize how asinine wars are, as evidenced by the U.S. Air Force friends I made soon after V-E Day, some of whom had "exchanged iron" with me just months before.

A special debt is owed to my wife Patti, whose critical proofreading helped insure a clean manuscript. The cooperation of Martin Simons in Australia and Peter F. Selinger in Germany as sailplane archivists and positive supporters was invaluable. Thanks to my four sons Mark, Paul, Eric and Kurt for their constant encouragement. The friends and their spouses who read and critiqued the manuscript for me include Tim Bortner, Walter Bouck, Barbara Everal, Pauline Fitzsimons, Mary Gresla, Slim Jost, Reba Sarver, Bob Schmall, Winston Smith, Marianne Szymanski, Davis Toth, and Kelly Vasher. If I have omitted anyone, please blame my senility!

A special thanks is owed to Ned Bechtel, one of the most fanatic World War II aficionados I have ever known. Ned, a fellow soaring enthusiast, is responsible for the hand-lettered sign I affixed to my office clock in January 1994 that reads: THIS IS THE YEAR OF THE BOOK! The sign did the trick in keeping me motivated; I hope you'll enjoy my story.

Since the first version of this book was edited, fate dealt a cruel blow to the Volmar family by letting two of our young sons succumb to heart disease. I hereby dedicate this book to the memory of Mark and Eric Volmar and to their love and friendship we enjoyed while they were with us.

Joe Volmar

1

Leaning over the bow rail of the *SS Veendam* my insides were churning with mixed emotions as I saw the Statue of Liberty in the distance. It was June 5th, 1951 and I had been away from the United States exactly ten years. I leaned toward my travel companion and said:

"What do you think, Richard, will this land of freedom and opportunity accept me again or will I be forever doomed to be a man without a country?"

As the ocean liner plowed through the sunlit waves of the Atlantic toward New York harbor, my thoughts wandered back ten years to the time when I departed from the same harbor. It was in the cold swirling snow of March 26, 1941 and I was a fourteen year old adventurer returning to the *Vaterland*. That passage had also been very emotional; feelings of guilt overshadowed by the exhilaration of adventure and world travel buzzed around in my head during the entire stormy crossing.

It seems that I was always destined to be a person torn between two loyalties. Born in Germany just two months after Lindbergh's renowned flight from New York to Paris, my parents brought me to the United States from Germany when I was a three year old toddler. Times were tough in the thirties and my father, *Fritz*, drifted from one job to another. He worked in positions that ranged from waiter at the Hotel Del Monico in New York City to dairy hand on Long Island to superintendent of a 1400-acre estate at the west end of New York State. His fondness for the bottle didn't help matters any; although he was an expert and university-trained farm manager and increased quality and production by applying his Teutonic thoroughness wherever he went, the owners eventually got fed up with his intermittent boozing and sent him packing. Consequently I attended ten public schools to reach the ninth grade by the time I left the U.S.

Naturally, this moving-about produced a certain amount of insecurity which was somewhat tempered by my active membership in the Boy Scouts of America. Regardless of where we moved, I soon joined the local troop and happily participated in hiking, camping and many other scouting activities. Being a "good scout" gave me a sense of direction; the Scout Motto of *"Be Prepared"* is still my password to this day. The Scout Laws have been the basis of my personal philosophy ever since I learned to recite and abide by them at age twelve.

Although I spent my most formative childhood years in American schools and with American playmates, the German heritage and influence always prevailed. I was brought up to be bilingual from the start, even though I resented it deeply at the time. Only German was spoken at home unless we had company; even then I had to speak "King's English", which meant not rolling my "R-s" the American way. So often, while the other kids were playing, I had to stay inside and laboriously write letters to *Grossmutter*[1] or to *Tante*[2] *Grete*. I hated it at the time and felt abused and overworked, but I certainly appreciated this discipline at a later time when I returned to Germany!

Even the womenfolk also furthered the military heritage. A German friend of my mother's would proudly show me an abundantly illustrated World War I picture book. Even though I was only four

---

[1]Grandmother
[2]Aunt

years old, I have the vivid memory of her saying: "And these are the Kaiser's engineers; they have to dig tunnels and build bridges for the other soldiers."

Another distinct memory is of my peace loving and "anti- war" mother Trudel (called "*Mutti*") making her contribution to my military development. I was around seven years old while she was ironing and listening to one of her favorite radio programs. The U.S. Marine Band was being featured in a weekly music broadcast. I was playing outdoors when she called to me: "*Jochen*[1], come in and listen to this stirring march music! Here, take my yardstick, pretend it's a gun and march in time with the drum beat!"

I remember marching in circles around the living room, my chest swelled with youthful pride, while I imagined being a smartly uniformed soldier.

I suppose the frosting on the martial cake was in the form of a picture book, which my Tante Grete sent me, when I was around 11 years old. It was published by a German tobacco company and was filled with color photographs obtained by redeeming cigarette coupons. It depicted the rise of the Third Reich under Adolph Hitler with heavy emphasis on the Hitler Youth, the National Labor Service, the new *Wehrmacht*[2] as well as many other interesting activities that were taking place in the re-awakened Germany. Every time I leafed through this exiting book it stimulated my young mind into fantasizing exciting adventures. One day I was a sailplane pilot; the next day I pretended to be a U-Boat commander!

My thoughts drifted back to September of 1939 when we heard the announcement that Germany had invaded Poland and practically all of Europe was at war. Fritz was fit to be tied...."I have to get back to the *Vaterland* immediately....my regiment can't get along without me!" He had been a brave and dedicated seventeen-year-old infantry lieutenant during World War I and occasionally, when in a sentimental mood, he proudly showed me his Iron Cross which he had earned during a fierce battle near Lille. Many years later, long after his death, my aunt told me that there had been an article

---

[1] Nickname for Joachim
[2] German Armed Forces

published in a German magazine about "Fritz Volmar, the youngest sub-lieutenant in the Kaiser's army".

Within hours after the stunning news that war had begun, Fritz was on the phone with the German Consul in New York and pleaded: "*Herr Konsul*, please help me get back to Germany right away!"

His persistence paid off; the anticipated call came a few days later when he was assured a berth on the German luxury liner *Bremen*. Frenzied packing, hurried good-byes and he went off to New York. My mother was shaken but resolute and decided to stay in America with me and find a job to support both of us.

We had no word for a week; then Fritz unexpectedly showed up on the farm: broke, dejected and hung-over........the *Bremen* had sailed without passengers! Due to the threat of being stopped by patrolling British warships, the *Bremen* made a hurried departure from New York without passengers or cargo, just to get back home in a hurry. As we found out later, she crossed the Atlantic via the extreme northern route and ended up in Murmansk, Russia; she eventually found her way back to Germany later in the war.

Back to the routine of farm life again; from September 1939 until February 1941 we lived on five different farms and I attended five different schools, each school transfer prompting stronger and stronger taunts of "Heinie" and "Nazi", as my school chums found out that we were German and spoke the language at home. Although the U.S. was still neutral at this time the vivid newspaper and newsreel accounts of Germany's *Blitzkrieg* through Poland, Denmark and Norway as well as the Low Countries and France fueled the anti-German feelings more and more. Stories of *U-boats* attacking and sinking defenseless merchant ships regardless of nationality were the crowning blow; I tried to hide my identity each time I changed schools, but to no avail.

Through regular and persistent contact with the German Consulate my father finally was able to return to his beloved Germany. He was allowed to participate in a special exchange arrangement: A group of German repatriates was channeled back to Germany on a Japanese steamer via Hawaii to Japan; from there to the Chinese mainland, then across Manchuria to Russia where they boarded the Siberian

Express to Moscow; then on the Berlin. How strong his desire must have been to listen to the *Vaterland's* calling to travel three-fourths of the way around the world on small bobbing freighters and slow-moving and poorly heated trains!

My mother and I bade Fritz good-bye, not knowing if we would ever see him again. These were tumultuous times......it seemed that the whole world was about to turn topsy-turvy! It was in this atmosphere that my mother and I decided that we should also return to Germany.

She was somewhat afraid to start a new life on her own by staying in the United States and I didn't really want to see my parents break up, in spite of my dad's drinking....a Dad is still a Dad, you know! I was so tired of being called "Kraut" and "Nazi" that I could scream......might as well see what this whole *Blitzkrieg* thing is all about! It would be an interesting adventure and after being bought up in democratic America, I would never fall for this Nazi *propaganda* stuff anyway!

On March 26, 1941 Mutti and I were included in a group of thirty German repatriates, mostly women and children, that had been organized by the German Consulate in New York. Our cabin was in the extreme forward section of the ship, the 14,000-Ton Spanish liner *SS Magellanes*, which was a combination freighter and passenger vessel. We could hear and feel the anchor chains rattling beyond the front bulkhead of our cabin. The sidewalls of our tiny cubicle were merely sweating steel plates separating us from the cold spray of the Atlantic. We had barely left New York harbor when Mutti crawled into her damp berth with an extreme case of *Mal de Mer*, which plagued her until our arrival eleven days later in La Coruña, Spain. She was one of those pitiful people who get seasick by merely touching the gangplank of a securely docked ocean liner and no type or amount of medicine can cure them; relief can only be found by going ashore.

For me, fourteen year old Joe, the hungry kid, it was quite an adventure. Even though conditions were very poor in Spain due to the after-effects of the Spanish Civil War which had just ended, food on the liner was plentiful and well-prepared, though much different than what I was accustomed to. There was wine aplenty at every meal, generally two main courses and excellent desserts. I really lived it up at the dinner table, as if I had a subconscious foreboding of the meager times ahead in Europe. There were five of us teenagers on board and we spent our days at shuffleboard, Monopoly and even swam in the outside pool on the day the ship crossed the Gulf Stream.

We met a number of other ocean vessels during our eleven-day crossing, but the ships just exchanged radio greetings and continued on their respective courses. One cloudy day, however, a small freighter started heading straight toward us. As the ship plowed closer, we could see the staccato flashes of an Aldis lamp sending us a message across the foaming water. The captain of the *Magallanes* hove-to immediately and the freighter, which meanwhile had uncovered a nasty looking four-inch gun on its foredeck, lowered a lifeboat. As the longboat bobbed closer through the foamy spray, we could make out a boarding party of British seamen in full naval uniform, armed with rifles and Tommy guns. The seas were running about 10 to 12 feet and the Tommies had quite a time boarding the *Magellanes* without smashing their hands or cracking their skulls. They finally succeeded in getting on board and stationed themselves around the various deck stairways and set up an interrogation desk in the First Class Salon.

An icy chill of fear enveloped my youthful heart as the grim looking sailors walked by. What was going to happen to us?....were we going to be taken prisoner? Would we have to get into that dangerously bobbing lifeboat?

Suddenly the captain's voice blared over the ship's public address system, "All passengers will please remain orderly and calm; as the letter of your deck is called, please proceed to the First Class Salon for a passport check!"

In a short time in was our turn; we had to line up and shuffle past the examining officer sitting at the captain's table, displaying our passports and explaining where and why we were going. The officer was courteous but firm and explained that any male German nationals eighteen years or older would be taken away for internment. Luckily all the men in this age category were either Spanish, French or Swiss so nobody was taken away. It was a fortunate thing, since we all wondered if the little British patrol freighter would ever make it back to England through these U-boat infested waters. My first taste of the war......I was amazed at how a single piece of paper showing one's nationality could change a person's entire future!

After the British officer had checked everyone's papers and had received the subaltern's search report that the rest of the ship was OK, the boarding party climbed into their lifeboat again. They took with them two sacks of fresh potatoes, a crate of vegetables and a big stack of current magazines. It was obvious that the British had been at sea for quite some time and were really looking forward to some fresh food and new reading material.

The very next day a storm started brewing. The slate gray sky seemed to drop lower and lower into the water as the huge foamy-green waves reached higher and higher, crashing wildly over the foredeck and swirling around the hatch covers. I was one of the few who really enjoyed the violent motion of the boat. One afternoon I remember distinctly; I was sitting on the afterdeck looking at the turbulent wake and watching the stern-rail ascend high into the sky, pause for a moment and then plunge suddenly downward, way below the horizon. Always looking for new ways to pass the time, one of my teenage friends had a bright idea; we stole several rolls of toilet paper from one of the rest rooms and unrolled the paper, one roll at a time, into the wind blowing out over the stern-rail of the ship. The paper unfurled itself hundreds of feet above and beyond us, swirling around and around like a Chinese paper dragon before it sank slowly into the ship's swirling wake.

That same evening during the storm, only a few of us showed up in the third class dining salon. Special rails were clamped to the tables to prevent plates and silverware from sliding off and we had to keep one hand on our wine glasses all the time as the ship pitched and rolled through the stormy ocean. After eating to our heart's content, we stayed on for the after-dinner movie. When the British Navy was depicted, featuring a yawing and pounding PT boat, another dozen or so passengers hurriedly left the dining salon; this kind of extra motion was not for them.

By the end of the tenth day we were tired, bored and champing at the bit to go ashore and get on with our journey to the *Vaterland*. Land was sighted and the next day we docked at the Spanish seaport of La Coruña. Allowed ashore for a few hours, we wandered around the waterfront, gawked at by countless begging children and gawking back at them, as none of us had ever seen a *real* beggar before. These kids had rags on their bodies for clothes and rags wrapped around their feet in lieu of shoes; they all had one thing in common.....the same pitiful look of despair and hopelessness in their sorrowful eyes.

My companion, *Günther*, said: "I've never seen anything like this......is all of Europe going to be the same way?"

2

Later that afternoon the *Magellanes* headed out to sea again. We traveled eastward through the Bay of Biscay on the final leg of our ocean voyage that would end the next day in Bilbao, Spain.

It was almost nightfall when the tugboat finally nudged the ocean liner up against the decrepit quay. A reception committee from the German Consulate met us at the gangplank with some bad news: the hotel rooms they had reserved for us had been released to others, as the ship was several hours later than anticipated. Disappointed and travel-weary, we trudged through the dark and frightening waterfront alleys of this strange city, where everybody spoke Spanish and just shrugged their shoulders when we addressed them in English or German.

Finally one of the Consular people beckoned to us with his flashlight, "Hey folks, I found a place where some of you can spend the night!"

Four of us--Mutti and I, together with another lady and her teen-age son were led into a drab looking old building and up a narrow spiral stairway to a room on the third floor. The room and its tattered furnishings were illuminated by a single, naked light bulb hanging from a wire in the ceiling. We were made to pay cash in advance and were given a pitcher of water and a ragged towel for our morning toilet. We weren't sure that we would ever live to see the morning light, as everything seemed so sinister and frightening, especially since the rooming house proprietor had become quite bug-eyed at the sight of our green American dollars. We slept with our clothes on by the light of a solitary bulb, which we left on all night in fear of being robbed. Before I finally nodded off to sleep, I unclasped my trusty Boy Scout knife and laid it on the rickety night stand beside our bed. In retrospect, I wonder whether this little knife would have done more harm than good for an innocent fourteen year old, who was most certainly a novice at hand-to-hand fighting!

The next morning the Consulate messenger found us alive and well, although not very well rested, and guided us to a small restaurant for breakfast. What new customs we were to learn! First of all, the coffee: the waiter brought each one of us a tall water glass, filled it one-third full of the blackest, most syrupy coffee I had ever seen. He then filled the glasses to the brim with milk; the sugar we added to suit our own tastes. To go along with this brew, we each received a small slice of hard bread and some awful tasting jelly. So much for that....maybe lunch would be better!

Lunch was not better at all, maybe even worse. The guide from the German Consulate took us to another restaurant near his office. Since the consular employees were regular patrons here, maybe the food would be good......It was, by Spanish standards, but not by ours; we were offered the same kind of concentrated coffee that we had for breakfast. Then came a thick bean soup, laced with large strips of red pepper that looked very much like Santa Claus's socks floating in the large bowls brimming with the brownish-colored concoction.

The afternoon was reserved for sightseeing; Bilbao was a beautiful city, but our impressions were marred by the constant presence of beggars....young, old and very old....the Spanish Civil War had really left its mark on these people!

My teenage appetite urged me to explore all avenues of Epicurean pleasure, but to no avail; most food stores and restaurants were closed the greater part of each day; when they were open, it was for a short time only and then people lined up for several blocks to take their turn in getting their small share of bread or a head of cabbage.

We stood in line twice; once to buy half a dozen small but sweet delicious pastries and once again to get two dozen yellowed and ripened bananas. For many years afterwards, my mother would reminisce and poke fun at me about the time I rode on the rattling and bumpy train to San Sebastián, eating a whole dozen bananas by myself, oblivious to the beautiful Spanish countryside which was bathed in the golden light of the setting sun. Little did I know that this would be the last time in many years that I would see cities illuminated after dark! Crossing the Franco-Spanish border into the war zone the next day would make me well aware that complete blackout precautions at night would be the rule from now on!

Another night in Spain, but this time it was a pleasure. Advance arrangements put us into a cheerful and clean *Pension[1]* in San Sebastián, which is just across the border from France, which had been under German military occupation since the year before.

The next day we arose early and boarded another train, which was to bring me my first experience with typical European "Passport Stampers". The train trip from San Sebastián to Hendaye should have taken less than an hour, but as things were, it took almost three! I had never seen so many different uniforms before; every department had their own distinctive colors and styles with red, green or yellow braid....and their caps with visors, caps without visors, caps with gold braid, caps with silver braid and caps with no braid at all; finally, of course, came the massive gray-green steel helmets of the Germans! First the conductor checked our tickets, then a Spanish border official checked and stamped our passports, then came the French Gendarmes, the French Customs Officers, then the German Military Police and finally two steely-eyed men in civilian clothes who barked questions at each and every one of the passengers in fluent German, Spanish and French. Someone whispered, *"Gestapo......*be careful what you say"! To our relief the men looked at our passports and then moved on to the next rail car, constantly questioning people on the way.

At the Spanish-French border we pulled into a rail siding for another wait, while the train changed engines and crews. The German MP's stayed on board the train while this took place and rode with us as we slowly pulled into the station at Hendaye. I stood near one of these fellows in the aisleway of the rail car; well over six feet tall, tanned of face and muscular, he stood erect in his hob-nailed boots, his

---

[1]European "Bed and Breakfast"

body swaying slightly in rhythm with the rocking motion of the train. The soldier seemed so impressive as he alighted onto the station platform, his submachine gun slung purposefully over his shoulder and his large, shiny crescent-shaped *Feldgendarmerei*[1] shield suspended from its chain upon his chest. The soldier clomped with noisy stride toward the officer waiting at the station doorway, while my first view of a real Swastika flag flying from the station flagpole gave me goosebumps of anticipation....what did this Nazi world have in store for me?

As our group dismounted from the train, shuffling along the station platform with our heavy suitcases, the *Feldgendarm* turned around and shouted to us:

"All you returnees from America assemble inside the station right away; the *Hauptman*[2] wants to talk to you!"

The officer, his visored cap cocked at a jaunty angle and shiny black riding boots pacing back and forth across the wooden station floor, began his little speech:

"In the name of and by order of our *Führer*, Adolph Hitler, I have been assigned to welcome you returnees to the *Vaterland*! We are proud that you have recognized your duty to return from foreign lands to join us in our fight for German freedom and *Lebensraum*[3]! Welcome home and good luck....we are proud that you have listened to the Führer's call."

As I was trying to concentrate on the *Hauptmann*, I heard the clomping of horses' hoofs on the cobblestone street just outside the station; the officer dismissed us and invited us to our first meal inside German Occupied France, courtesy of a military field kitchen.

I had never seen or heard of such a contraption before. This field kitchen was a large and square black firebox, about five feet wide and three feet high, with a tall, smoking flue-pipe and a roaring fire inside; it was mounted on a pair of large wagon wheels. Drawn by two immaculately groomed horses who hauled it wherever the troops went, it held a mammoth, self-contained cooking caldron, probably forty gallons or so in size, in which the mess personnel cooked their single-

---

[1] Military Police
[2] Military rank equivalent to U.S. Captain
[3] Living Space

entree military meals. Our fare today was the typical staple of the German *Wehrmacht*[1] ....thick pea soup with potatoes and large chunks of ham floating throughout. Each of us was given a slice of black bread, a dab of margarine and a large, steaming bowl of pea soup. After the meager diet in Spain, we thought we were in seventh heaven!

As we grouped around the steaming field kitchen, savoring our first good meal in several days, the MP strode up to us and said:

"I have a message and orders for you from the *Hauptmann*; you returnees are free to roam the city of Hendaye until 15:00 o'clock, at which time you will be back at this station. At 15:20 a train is leaving for Paris, via Bordeaux and Tours. The train will depart on time and you are not to be late under any circumstances!"

My first question was: "What time is "15:00 o'clock?" When I asked one of the soldier cooks, he explained to me that throughout all of Europe a twenty four-hour method of time telling was used and 15:00 o'clock was merely "3:00 PM". It would take quite a while for me to get used to adding twelve hours to all afternoon times to make myself understood!

While the ladies went window-shopping, peering into windows that had very little to offer, I went strolling down toward the beach. Hendaye, a beautiful and popular summer ocean resort on the Bay of Biscay, had an impressive waterfront, similar to some of the cities on the New Jersey coast I had visited as a child, except there was no boardwalk. A carefully hand-laid cobblestone street was built right up to the white sand beach. Bordering this street was a tight row of three and four story, brightly stucco-covered resort hotels, with balconies overlooking the Atlantic. One added feature I'd never seen before was the ugly looking barbed wire strung along the beach as far as the eye could see, a constant reminder that I was not in New Jersey.

While watching the pounding and noisy surf, the regimented sound of stomping boots on the cobblestone drew near. As a company of sun-tanned and singing German soldiers came closer, my heart swelled with pride. Boy, these guys are really something, the way they sing and march! As I fell in behind the last row and tried to keep up

---

[1] German Ground Forces

with this smartly marching group, I thought to myself, "Someday soon I'll be marching and singing like this!"

I was marching behind the soldiers, keeping in step with them in my own childish and innocent way....all of a sudden I heard a sharp command by the *Feldwebel*[1] and a hundred men started "goose stepping" in perfect unison. You can't imagine the noise and vibration caused by two hundred hob-nailed boots crashing down on the hard and century-worn cobblestone. The soldiers did about six or seven paces in goose-step, then came to a perfect halt upon another sharp command....what a sight and what discipline!

Later on I found out that goose-stepping just prior to a "Halt" was common procedure for the German military. It is one of the many ways that they kept discipline honed to the finest edge and paved the way for constant "instant obedience" of the troops. It also kept the men in top physical shape and had everybody pre-trained for any parades that might come up, where all participants had to goose-step for several hundred yards while passing the reviewing stand.

The soldiers were dismissed and charged down to the beach, shouting exuberantly, throwing sand at each other and tearing off their hot, woolen uniforms while they ran. When they reached the water's edge, they all plunged headlong into the cold Atlantic surf, splashing and cheering like little kids. Train time was approaching, so I reluctantly turned away and headed toward the railroad station.

As I rounded the last corner leading to the station, I noticed a very peculiar looking truck parked at the curb. It had a huge, round cylinder mounted vertically behind the cab, from which a steady flow of black smoke erupted. As I came closer, I noticed that this contraption was nothing more than a large firebox of some sort. The driver was standing next to the truck, leaning on the front fender; I walked up to him and asked: "What in the world is this big tank for?"

"Young man, this is how we run many of our trucks in Germany. The wood fire generates gases which are piped into the carburetor and propel the truck, just like gasoline fuel would. The trouble is that natural petroleum fuels are in very short supply in

---

[1] Military Rank equivalent to U.S. Technical Sergeant

Europe, so we have to be clever and develop *Ersatz*[1] products and methods. Would you like to go for a ride?"

I accepted the offer eagerly and climbed aboard. We drove around the block and back to the station again; I could hardly believe that the vehicle moved right along, propelled by a shovel-full of wood chips!

I sat for a while on the well-worn wooden bench in the railroad station watching the green-clad German soldiers laughing and joking with each other and flirting with some French girls. These young men were a far cry from the mean looking cartoon characters I had seen in the New York Daily News. Maybe these Nazis weren't such bad guys after all!

We boarded the train which left right on time and started chugging toward Bordeaux, the picturesque French countryside slipping faster and faster by the wayside.

It was hard to believe that there could be such a difference in climates; although we were at a latitude several hundred miles north of New York, whose frigid harbor we had left barely two weeks ago, the warm flow of Gulf Stream air had already coaxed forth the peach and cherry blossoms in the orchards along the railroad tracks.

Unaccustomed sights prevailed all over; horse carts, ox-carts, people-carts and bicycles galore! These were all quite a sight for me, being used to motorized U.S.A. The patchwork-quilt pattern of French farm country passed swiftly by as the train chugged northward toward Bordeaux.

All of a sudden Mutti emotionally called my attention to an object ahead in the roadbed next to the tracks. As we drew closer, I could discern a small mound of earth and cinders marked by a cross of white birch with a gray-green German helmet dangling in the air stream of the train. This was the first soldier's grave I had ever seen, but one of many thousands I was to see in the next four years. Apparently this German lad had been killed while advancing down the railroad tracks and his comrades had buried him right where he had fallen, which was common practice with the German military. I felt sad and reflective as the first cold reality of war dampened my adventurous

---

[1] Substitute

spirit; maybe there was more to this stuff than fancy uniforms and stirring music!

The train sped northwards, stopped at Bordeaux for a short while and then continued on through the night. We dozed and slept fitfully on the hard wooden seats, wishing the journey would soon be over. At daybreak we pulled into the Paris Main Station and were allowed to dismount and stretch our legs. Some German Red Cross ladies gave us each a slice of black bread, some sticky *Ersatz* marmalade and the bitterest *Ersatz* coffee you can imagine.

A young *Unteroffizier*[1] walked up to us and said: "There will be a 24 hour layover for your group in Paris; I will lead you to your hotel shortly. You are permitted to see the sights of this beautiful city all day tomorrow and are required to assemble again right here at 09:00 o'clock the day after tomorrow. You may roam about the city during the day as you wish, but be sure to be back at your hotel by 22:00 o'clock at the latest. There is a strict curfew for all civilians and anyone found on the street after that time will be arrested, regardless of nationality!"

We glanced at each other furtively....Someone whispered, "These militarists surely sound like they mean business, don't they?"

The *Unteroffizier* caught the drift of our murmuring, cast a very stern look our way and said, "Look folks, we're happy that you are returning to Germany, but you might as well get used to the way we do things here. You are no longer in relaxed and easy-going America. We are engaged in an important and victorious war which requires unquestioning obedience by all of us. If you wish to be a part of the new German Reich you must conform like the rest of us do!"

Somewhat subdued, we were directed to join the line of German soldiers queued up at the billeting sergeant's desk. I thought to myself: "No matter which way we turn, there's authority, authority and more authority......can't you do anything on your own over here?" The hotel assigned to us by the billeting *Unteroffizier* was only a few blocks away. What a different world this was; we rode on the creaking cage elevator to the third floor and dragged our luggage into a little room with black paper tacked over all the windows. By now I knew

---

[1] Military rank equivalent to U.S. Sergeant

the reason for this, as I had seen a large poster in the dingy lobby with a picture of a British Blenheim bomber dumping a load of bombs and the emphatic words: *"Blackout violators will be severely punished!"*

In exploring the double room assigned to the four of us, my eyes fell on an appliance I had never seen before. In the middle of the small bathroom there was an oval shaped, white china bowl that looked to me like a toilet without a tank, except there was already a toilet up against the wall.

"Mutti, whatever is that funny looking thing for" I said.

After deliberating a while, she replied evasively, "That is a special bowl to wash your feet in."

Later that evening I just had to try out this strange gadget myself. I took off my shoes and socks, perched on the edge of the bidet and turned on the water. A sudden fountain of spray shot straight up into my face....what strange things these Frenchman have!

The next morning bright and early we embarked on a sightseeing venture through the city of Paris. The Eiffel Tower came first, of course. What a majestic structure! The elevators were out of order, so we had to huff and puff our way up step by step. We only made it to the second level café, as the ladies got tired of climbing.

Seated at a window table we peered at this beautiful city, the red tile roofs of her suburbs stretching to the horizon, as far as the eyes could see. It was here that I got my first exposure to the universal European drink: *Mineral Water!*

Mutti's passable French enabled her to help us choose the refreshment to celebrate our ascent in this famous tower. There were flavors galore: lemon, cherry, strawberry, orange, apple as well as unflavored seltzers from many different cities in France, each claiming it's own special talent of improving digestion, limbering up rheumatism or shrinking swollen ankles. We made our choices and engaged in people-watching for a while.

There were numerous German soldiers in the cafe, laughing and joking with their French girl friends, many of who were well dressed and pretty. One could not help noticing the disdainful looks presented by some of the French men sitting at the next table.

My mother whispered to me "I can't understand how those girls can associate with enemy soldiers so obviously; they should be ashamed of themselves."

Over the years I was to find out time and time again that love and the lust for the good things in life won't be stopped by wars, politics or rules and regulations.

After descending step by step from this dizzying height, we walked under the Arc dé Triumph, took the *Metro* subway to the Monmartre district. It was so strange seeing such a large city with almost no motor traffic. Some German trucks and officers' cars with a sprinkling of rattling and chugging French trucks were the only motorized vehicles to be seen. Pedestrians, bicycles and horse-drawn wagons made up the rest of this bustling city.

Soon it was train time again. We picked up our suitcases, which we had checked with the baggage-master that morning and were directed aboard the train to Saarbrücken. This was the final leg of our journey back to the *Vaterland*.

The trains themselves were quite an experience for me. The only cars which resembled those we were accustomed to stateside were the European Second Class. These were "one room" cars in which there were two rows of bench seats with a center aisle and you could overlook all the passengers in your car. First Class was somewhat like our Pullman cars with separate compartments connected by a side aisle which ran the full length of the car along one side. Both of these were nicely upholstered. Now the Third Class cars were something else; these were designed for short-haul commuters and each small compartment contained a pair of hard wooden bench seats with entrance doors on both sides of the train; a high running-board step was used to climb in and out of each car. At age fourteen it seemed to me like climbing onto a farm wagon.

When a Third Class train pulled into a small rural station it was quite a sight to behold. Even before the shrill squealing of brakes had stopped completely, every single door would swing open as if on cue. Disgorging of passengers was instantaneous with the most comical assortment of people I had ever seen. All the women had monster handbags, shopping nets or suitcases; sometimes all three. There wasn't a man aboard who didn't carry a briefcase of sorts in addition to his other baggage. I found out later that carrying one isn't necessarily a badge of executive office in Europe. Briefcases are the accepted lunch boxes for all classes and can contain anything from daintily wrapped liver paté tidbits to whole loaves of coarse dark pumpernickel. The bread is then dissected chunk by chunk with a large pocketknife and devoured with large mouthfuls of summer sausage, also cut off in large pieces.

There were also many rucksacks, especially for the people who were traveling by bicycle. Those folks, incidentally, had to line up at the baggage car as the baggage man handed down their bicycles, one by one.

Leaving the Main Station in Paris we were soon clattering through the pretty French countryside. A breath of history touched us as we passed through the infamous World War One battleground of Verdun. The weed-covered old escarpments here soon gave way to the cheerful and tended countryside again. Only an occasional freshly mounded soldier's grave reminded us of history repeating itself.

Later that day as we approached the Franco-German border, the compartment was filled with "Oohs" and "Aahs" as we crossed the fabulous Maginot Line and shortly thereafter the German *Westwall*. It was almost comical to see the cannons of these two gigantic and expensive projects pointing uselessly at each other.

As we slowly chugged around a long curve in the railroad tracks, I pointed to numerous parallel rows of cone-shaped concrete posts. These rows wound endlessly through the pretty fields and stretched all the way to the horizon.

"Whatever are those funny looking concrete bumps for?" I asked.

"Haven't you ever heard of Dragon's Teeth?" one of the ladies replied; "They were made by our boys in the *Arbeitsdienst*[1] and they are there to protect our Fatherland from enemy tanks."

"What is the *Arbeitsdienst*?" I asked.

"When our Führer reorganized the *Vaterland* he established this organization soon thereafter. All young men and women are required to serve one full year and live in specially constructed camps

---

[1] Labor Service Corps

spread out all over Germany. The women are assigned to help busy mothers with small children in the nearby villages or help farmers with animal care or field work. The young men are usually involved in heavy construction of our national superhighway called the *Autobahn* with its many bridges or in building military fortifications for our defense."

I was to find out later how useful this National Labor Service was to Adolf Hitler's total war effort. Not only did these young people perform lots and lots of hard labor for the cost of room and board, but also it provided valuable pre-military training, especially for the men. The only difference from the regular *Wehrmacht* being that close-order drill was performed with polished spades rather than rifles.

3

Nightfall was approaching as we crossed the Franco-German border and entered the city of Saarbrücken. As the train screeched to a halt we pulled our suitcases down from the overhead racks and piled out of the compartment onto the station platform.

Here we were, finally, thirty tired repatriates milling about the station in the cold evening drizzle. When we identified ourselves to the stationmaster he said:

"Nobody informed me that you were coming; there is a refugee hostel about 6 blocks down the street. Why don't you see if they can put you up for the night?"

Dragging our luggage we trudged to the hostel; what luck.....they were able to accommodate us. Even though the rooms were damp and cold and the sheets somewhat soiled by our predecessors we were glad to find a place to rest. We had reached the *Vaterland* at long last; what adventures were in store for us here?

Early the next morning, which was Easter Sunday, we set out for the railroad station again. We said good-bye to our travel companions of the last 2 weeks and headed in our respective travel directions. Mutti and I went north through the rolling hills of the Palatinate and down the beautiful Rhine River Valley. What would my *Grossmutter* say, who hadn't seen me since I was three years old? She knew we were returning to Germany but had no idea when. We couldn't use public phones until we crossed the German border and when Mutti dialed her number from the refugee hostel there was no answer. We decided to proceed unannounced.

My grandparents had retired to Bad Godesberg in the early thirties. My grandfather, at that time Chief of Staff of a large hospital in Dortmund, had chosen this quaint town on the Rhine River for its restful but prestigious atmosphere. The prefix "Bad" in German denotes a "bath" or resort of some kind. Bad Godesberg has natural mineral springs, as do many cities in Europe. These springs are tapped and diverted to public bathhouses. Here one can soak away the pains of arthritis, bursitis or rheumatism. These baths are so recognized and popular that the socialized medicine program will pay for scheduled treatments as long as they have been prescribed by your doctor.

Bad Godesberg is in a beautiful setting on the west bank of the Rhine River. Right in the center of town is a steep hill upon which are the crumbling remains of a small medieval castle. The town is across the river from the renowned Seven Hills where the legends of Siegfried and the Dragon and Snow White and the Seven Dwarfs originated. More recently, Neville Chamberlain stayed here at the Hotel Petersberg in 1938, as he met with Adolph Hitler in Bad Godesberg, making one last attempt to keep the world at peace.

Amid peach blossoms in the orchards and throngs of churchgoers we arrived at Bad Godesberg in the early afternoon. After the train braked to a halt, we retrieved our heavy suitcases from the baggage car for the last time. Walking up to the ticket clerk, Mutti asked: "Where is 33 Friedrichstrasse, please?"

"Just follow this street toward the Rhine River for about 5 blocks and you'll come to Friedrichstrasse; then turn to the left and you'll soon come to No.33!"

Again dragging our suitcases, we trudged down a beautiful tree-lined street until we reached our turn. Not far from the corner we came to No. 33; what a magnificent old house it was!

We peered through the tall, wrought iron spiked fence into the colorful beds of spring flowers. In a typical setting for Europe, where all countries are plagued with a shortage of land: the front yard was only about ten feet deep. A carefully groomed gravel walk led to the stone front steps. The house itself was a three story duplex, clad in weathered yellow brick with a gray slate roof. With its heavy stone windowsills, leaded-glass front door and rose bushes twining alongside, the house reeked of century-old tradition.

I twisted the polished brass doorbell crank; no response. I rang again; still nothing. After a third try we finally heard someone coming down the staircase and then a shuffling of feet across the shiny terrazzo floor. The door opened slowly and an elderly Protestant nun appeared in a blue habit and wearing a white lace-trimmed bonnet.

"Whom do you wish to see?" she said.

Mutti replied: "Is *Frau Doktor* Volmar at home?"

"No, *Frau Sanitätsrat* is with her daughter in Duisburg for the Easter holiday. Can I be of service to you? My sister and I are her tenants and live in the mansard."

This was my first, but by no means my last experience with German titles. Except for those inherited by nobility, titles and military rank are hard earned in this country and therefore used without fail when necessary or unnecessary. A wife automatically receives her husband's title or rank and God help the poor soul who doesn't address the major's wife as *Frau Major*!!

In this case my grandfather had earned the title of *Sanitätsrat*, which means "Health Advisor". Even though he had passed away seven years prior, everybody including the neighbors, the butcher and the mailman, addressed my grandmother as *Frau Sanitätsrat*, not *Frau Doktor*, which is a lower rank........ lesson learned!

When we informed the sister who we were, she was delighted and led us into the spacious hallway dragging our bags. Our journey of fifteen adventurous days was over. Tonight we would sleep in soft beds in this quiet old house with not a care in the world.

The nun asked Mutti: "Why don't we telephone your mother-in-law to let her know you've arrived and we'll go upstairs and have some coffee?"

We moved into the living room, with its massive, leather upholstered lounge chairs and sofa. The double-layered, heavy lace drapes let the sunlight filter across the massive, hand-carved walnut credenza, giving the room a secluded and aristocratic air as my mother dialed the phone.

"Hello *Mutter*, this is Trudel, your daughter-in-law. Jochen and I have just arrived from America. The sisters let us in and I'm calling from your living room!"

"You are in MY house? I can't believe it! Oh, I'm so excited; make yourselves at home and I'll be there tomorrow afternoon."

The sister said: "Why don't you put your bags in the guest room and then come on upstairs for coffee; this young man must be starved."

We settled in briefly and then trudged up the wide stairway to the third floor mansard. The two sisters, who were also biological sisters, had already prepared *Kaffee* for us in the true German fashion. Laid out in neatly engineered rows were lunch meats, cheeses and three types of bread, not to mention at least four different cakes with delicious looking toppings. The hospitable setting was completed with the rich aroma of fresh coffee, finely ground in a hand mill using freshly home-roasted coffee beans. I was to find out over the years that, regardless how meager food supplies were to become, you were offered *Kaffee* within the first five minutes of any visit, business, personal or otherwise. *Kaffee* could consist of anything from the aforementioned spread to, in leaner times to come, a stale cracker spread with jam made of saccharine sweetened fruit skins and a cup of *ersatz* coffee brewed from roasted barley.

After enjoying the food and the sociability for a while, we retired back downstairs to explore my grandmother's home. Downstairs was a large hallway, which housed the wide, open staircase. Living room, dining room, salon and kitchen were on the first floor; all with 10 foot ceilings and oversized windows and doors, almost like a castle. The furniture was heavy and antique with cabinets filled with delicate china and glassware. Persian rugs covered most of the floors and oil paintings and family photographs adorned the walls.

The bedrooms were equally ornate, with large hand-carved wardrobes instead of built-in closets. Rarely can you find integral clothes closets in Europe; as a consequence, large but portable wardrobes are part of everyone's furniture inventory there. The bathroom was also a dressing and ironing room about twelve feet by twelve feet instead of the customary five by seven bathroom we have in the U.S.

As we prepared to retire for the night and I pulled back the mammoth fluffy featherbed cover, I asked my mother:

"Why are the pillows so awfully high? I won't be able to sleep tonight. You know how I like to lie flat on my tummy!"

"I had almost forgotten about German beds, *Jochen*. Look here; the mattresses are in three pieces so they can be turned or carried by a woman alone instead of struggling with those monsters we have in America. The upper section has a wedge under it as you can see, for people who like to have their heads elevated. Here, we'll pull this wedge out and you'll be able to sleep flat like you're used to!"

Before I dropped off into a sound and dreamless sleep I mused to myself:

"What a strange country where they have full meals in the middle of the afternoon and where they practically sit up in bed to sleep. What other surprises are there in store for me?"

The next morning I was in for another shock. As I turned on the water to draw a nice hot bath there was a loud *"WOOSH"* above my head which made my heart skip a beat or two. Looking more closely at the porcelain-clad cylinder hanging on the wall above the tub I could see the flickering jets of gas flame inside the instantaneous demand hot water-heater!

After returning from the nearby bakery with a half-dozen crisp and warm freshly baked rolls I sat down to enjoy breakfast. This was my first exposure to the custom of buying fresh food once or twice daily. With very few residential refrigerators, this was a must. The German housewife therefore spent a good part of each day shopping for milk, meat, bread and vegetables on a frequent basis. This became extremely time-consuming in later years of the war when queues as long as two city blocks were commonplace due to food shortages.

I spent the next few hours exploring the house, room by room. Many things were strange to me, such as the *Rolladen*, which are tight-fitting, self-storing window shutters similar to a roll-top desk cover, and can be tilted out on their tracks like an awning to allow for ventilation but still keep the rain from coming in the window. All electrical switches and receptacles were made of porcelain and surface mounted; this is probably because there is very little wood construction in Europe; almost everything is stone or masonry.

That afternoon my grandmother returned; a little chunky but very refined with silken, gray hair and a quick smile appearing frequently behind her pince-nez we soon became good friends. She couldn't believe that her grandson from America could stoke the coal furnace by himself and also be quite handy with a garden rake. This was work generally done by the houseman or the gardener.

Now came the time when my torturous German letter writing and studying paid off; at least I could ask directions and read street signs. I spent the next few days exploring the pretty little town of Bad Godesberg. Being a water lover, I spent many hours on the banks of the Rhine River. The neatly built stone and mortar-clad riverbank tapered into the clean and fast-moving current. Heavily laden barges were towed both upstream and downstream by mammoth paddle-wheel steam tugs, their whistles exchanging signals as the barge trains passed each other in midstream. The remains of the medieval hilltop castle right in the center of town were fascinating; I must have climbed up and down the steep tower stairs a dozen times, my imagination buzzing with images of knights in armor clanking through the courtyard.

The serene and peaceful mood came to an abrupt end each evening at nightfall. My grandmother scurried about the house, closing the shutters where available or carefully inserting form-fitting black cardboard into window openings to keep any glimmer of light from escaping and possibly providing a navigation aid to British bombers.

Shortly after dark each day volunteer air-raid wardens patrolled the streets checking for complete blackout. Occasionally a loud cry of *"Licht Aus[1]"* could be heard requesting that a careless homeowner comply, or else......There were heavy fines for violators of the blackout rules or of the many, many other rules, as I was to find out as time went on.

It was really difficult for me to get around after dark until I developed a keen night vision and acquired the habit of crossing my arms in front of my face to prevent running head on into a tree or telephone pole. The few motor vehicles on the streets had headlight lenses painted black except for a small slit to emit a minimum light

---

[1] Lights Out !

beam. Bicycle headlights and flashlights were screened in the same way, but during an actual air raid alarm no lights whatsoever were permitted.

We had been in the country for less than a week, when I experienced my first air raid warning. A series of shrill siren wails in a monotonous up-scale and down-scale penetrated my cozy bedroom about 3:00 o'clock in the morning.

My grandmother called out loudly "Jochen, hurry and get dressed and into the cellar with you; there's an air raid coming!"

I had never experienced such a feeling of fear, uncertainty and helplessness as we stumbled down the cellar stairs, grabbing a jug of water, some candles and my grandmother's prayer book. We took refuge in a small storeroom next to the coal bin where we found half a dozen chairs, a few blankets and gas masks for my grandmother and her tenant nuns.

"Trudel, you must go to the City Hall tomorrow and get gas masks for you and Jochen. They haven't used any poison gas yet, but one never knows what'll happen in this crazy war."

No more than fifteen minutes had passed when and we heard a faint droning in the distance. As the noise came closer and closer my heart started pounding and a powerless fear replaced whatever bravado I had shown during the day. I wonder how many planes there are? Are they coming or going? Will they drop any bombs on our little city or are they just flying through on the way to Duisburg or Berlin? There weren't many planes in the formation and very soon the engine noise became weaker and weaker and subsided completely. Shortly thereafter the *"All Clear"* was sounded, which was a steady monotone by the same sirens; what a welcome sound!"

The next morning, after a rather fitful sleep punctuated with dreams of droning airplanes and screaming bombs, we went to City Hall for our gas masks and food ration coupons. The City Hall, called *Rathaus,* was situated in the center of town adjacent to a lush and well-groomed park. With flower beds galore the scent of blossoms hung heavily in the air as we walked past the storefronts lined up along the park perimeter. It was still early and the shopkeepers were all busy cranking down decorative canvas awnings or scrubbing and hosing down the sidewalk in front of their stores. Accustomed to the littered streets of New York City, I marveled at the immaculate appearance of everything: sidewalks, streets, buildings, gardens......whatever you looked at appeared to have been freshly scrubbed that day. As I was to find out time and time again later, this neatness and orderliness was to project itself to all phases of life, from a perfect school essay to clean fingernails to a soldier's freshly greased boots as he went into combat.

My first experience with German bureaucracy was typical: in order to get gas masks we had to have Ration Coupons which we couldn't get until we registered at the Housing Office which wouldn't accept our registration until we had Identification Cards which we couldn't get until cleared by the Police Department. After an entire morning of standing in lines and being shuttled from one department to another we finally had our gas masks, together with pamphlets on air raid procedures and fire fighting instructions.

The gas masks were different from the standard military ones I had seen, which were basically a face mask held in place by straps over the back of the head. The *Volksgasmaske* was a complete and tight fitting rubber bonnet covering the entire head. One instantly started sweating profusely while wearing one of these and fogged lenses made mask wearing even more claustrophobic for a 14-year-old. The masks were blue-gray in color and came in sizes for babies, children and adults. It was quite a spooky sight to see a group of people participating in an air raid drill, staring at the air raid warden like so many goggle-eyed monsters grunting in muffled tones under the constricting masks.

Air raid drills were frequent and strict; anyone not appearing or forgetting his or her gas mask was severely reprimanded. Non cooperating folks were classified as "enemies of the *Vaterland*" and were threatened with imprisonment. Just a few days after our arrival I participated in our first air raid drill and instruction session. After scurrying to our respective shelters were recalled by the all clear siren and summoned to assemble at a nearby village square. A young *Flak Unteroffizier*[1] and two helpers had cordoned off a demonstration area on the cobblestone street.

---

[1] Anti-Aircraft Sergeant

"Everybody quiet now, and pay attention!" the *Unteroffizier* shouted.

"This is what a British incendiary bomb looks like" he said, holding up a hexagon shaped metal tube about three feet long.

"Some of them are adjusted to ignite upon impact, some are delayed to penetrate several floors first and some are duds. Therefore you'll never know when they'll start spitting phosphorus all over. If you can, stuff the bomb into a bucket of sand or throw it out the window into the street. If it's already ignited, pour sand on it. In any case, don't get too close as the burning phosphorus will cling to your clothing and skin and you won't be able to get it off. Watch this now!"

The instructor did something to the end of the bomb and it suddenly started spewing bright arcs of flaming, teardrop shaped globules of phosphorus into the air and all over the cobblestone. The crowd shrank away from the hissing spectacle. What else could be added to the terror of a night air raid?

The next day was Sunday and time to go to a German church for the first time. The whole town was quiet and peaceful; not a store was open, not a car, truck or horse and wagon could be seen. Deeply pealing church bells rang steadily every hour on the hour and the whole town was alive with prim and properly dressed people on their way to and from church. My grandmother, a very good Catholic, led us to her favorite church about four blocks from her house.

"If you want to know the truth, Trudel, I don't enjoy church as I used to," she said.

"The Nazis usually have a Gestapo man in the congregation during each and every Mass. If the priest says anything at all that doesn't agree with the government or it's policies, off he goes to a concentration camp. It's just terrible, they're afraid to say what they really believe!"

Mutti interjected, "I know exactly how you feel. As you know, my sister Waltrudis is a teaching nun in Aachen. Those poor ladies are so afraid that the Gestapo will shut down their convent and school, that all the nuns are letting their hair grow out under their habits. They would look quite pitiful walking around town with their usual shorn heads!"

Grossmutter replied, "Yes, I don't know what these Nazis are doing to our country. At first they seemed to be doing the right things but now I'm not so sure that they're aren't just too fanatical."

"Another thing that rubs me the wrong way is that they want you to say *Heil Hitler* all the time instead of *Guten Morgen* or *Grüss Gott*[1]. I don't know what this world is coming to."

As much as I loved and respected my grandmother, her comments went in one of my ears and out the other. I felt that her attitude was quite old fashioned: my father had always said that church and state should be separated and not interfere with each other. Besides that, the sermons were boring and much too long anyway!

---

[1] Greetings to God

4

We had been in Germany about ten days when the telephone rang; it was my father calling from Berlin. He had finally arrived there after a long and frigid trip across Russia aboard the Siberian Express. He informed us that he had some military business to attend to; he would then come to Bad Godesberg in a few days.

I could hardly wait to see him again, as we hadn't been in contact for six long weeks. When he arrived in Godesberg, tall and handsome as ever, all three of us were ready to start a new life. As he was describing his visit to German Army Headquarters in Berlin, Fritz handed me my present: a beautiful, hand-tooled cowboy belt he had purchased at a bus stop somewhere in Nevada. He also gave us a photograph of his repatriate group posing in front of a large Buddha in Tokyo.

I never did figure out if his story of an interview with the German Army in Berlin was the truth or just another tall tale. He claimed that he would be assigned to the *Afrika Korps* because of his knowledge of the English language. He was to begin taking Atabrin (a malaria preventative drug) very shortly in preparation for his African mission.

A few days later, after a visit to an Army office in Cologne, the story changed somewhat. Because of his injured foot and missing left index finger, the Army thought he wouldn't be able to perform in accordance with infantry officer standards; it was suggested that he seek a civilian assignment with the German Government.

As his customary luck would have it, Fritz was assigned to an agricultural planning department in Kaiserslautern after his first interview. Mutti and I would stay at grandmothers until he got settled and found a place for all of us to live.

The next day there was a long family discussion about Jochen's schooling: the participants were Fritz, Onkel Paul, *Grossmutter* and I.

"I think he should go to the *Gymnasium*[1] to keep up the family tradition" my Grandmother said.

"He'll never make it....there will be far too much Latin and Greek language studies to make up" said Paul. "Besides, he already knows English, which will give him at least a little advantage at the *Oberschule*[2]!"

My mother chimed in "Why can't he start by going to the regular *Volkschule*[3] until he catches up on his German studies and then he could transfer to a High School?"

Grandmother was aghast; "No member of my family will ever be seen in a common *Volkschule* as long as I'm around; that will never do! Let's send him to the *Oberschule* and see how he does; he can be tutored for transfer to the *Gymnasium* later on."

I wondered what all the discussion was about. I was just nearing the end of the ninth grade as a straight "A" student in New York City, at that time a very "tough" system. What was everybody so worried about? I was soon to see!

Mutti took me on the five-mile trolley ride to the *Oberschule* in Bonn (which was a subsidiary of the *Gymnasium*) and waited while I was interviewed and tested.

I couldn't believe my ears when the principal said: "I'm sorry, Frau Volmar, but we'll have to place Jochen in the second grade right now (sixth academic year with four years of Grammar School preceding); there are just too many things he doesn't know. Granted he speaks German quite well, but there is so much grammar he has yet to learn; besides, his knowledge of math and history is quite minimal for a

---

[1] High School stressing Greek and Latin Studies
[2] High School with contemporary curriculum
[3] Public School

14 year old boy. If he gets on well, you can always have him tutored for advancement."

Thus the decision was made; I was to attend the *Oberschule Für Jungen,* beginning the following Monday morning. As the name implies, this was an all boys' school; in those days there were no co-ed high schools until university level was attained. Classes were from 8:00 AM to 1:00 or 2:00 PM daily, including Saturdays. Thirteen or fourteen subjects were taught concurrently, all of them mandatory with no electives available and at least three or four hours of homework daily.

There was no dress code *per se,* but all I could see in the school hallways were short pants, knee socks and short haircuts. The principal shook hands with us and said:

"I'll see you next Monday, Jochen. Go to Classroom 2C right away and be prepared to work. I'll tell your teacher, Herr Lederman, to expect you!"

Over the weekend I prepared myself mentally for the new school with mixed emotions. Although I was very experienced in adjusting to new situations, since I had already attended ten different schools in the U.S., this was somewhat different with the language and cultural variances.

I asked my Grandmother "*Grossmutter,* can I get one of those leather book-packs the other boys are all wearing on their backs?"

"My dear Jochen, I'm afraid you don't realize that this war has caused many shortages for us. Leather goods are almost impossible to buy, as the German armed forces need lots of boots, belts, holsters and the like. It's a good thing that you brought those three pair of shoes from America, as we are each allowed only one pair of shoes every two years. You'll have to manage without a book-pack. Your Onkel Paul still has his university briefcase upstairs which you can use for the time being. He won't need it while he's in the Army!"

Fortunately my mother had been forewarned of the critical shortages ahead and had shopped well, budget permitting, before we left New York. A second hand store on Third Avenue had produced two men's suits about three sizes too large for my growing 14-year-old frame. Bloomingdales supplied a heavy, red woolen sweater for $5.00 as well as a green windbreaker two sizes too large at the time!

The sweater still hangs in my closet after 50 years, Russian bullet-hole and all; what an attest to Bloomingdales' quality!

Monday morning came quickly and I boarded the streetcar for the half-hour ride to Bonn. I was dressed in shorts made from cut off American knickers, a Sears Roebuck mail order shirt and Onkel Paul's knee socks. I carried the borrowed large leather briefcase containing several new notebooks, a quill pen with a bottle of ink and a black bread and marmalade sandwich.

Glancing furtively at some of the other boys riding the streetcar, I could hear them snickering at my cut off pants and adult briefcase. Why did I always have to be different? In New York I was "The Nazi"; I suppose here I'll be called "The Cowboy"!

The school was easily found just by following the other boys as they alighted from the streetcar. As I entered Classroom 2C, there were already ten or twelve boys inside. Timidly I introduced myself and was shown a vacant desk in the back row.

Each time a boy entered the room, he made the rounds of all others present, shaking hands with each one.

"*Guten Morgen,* Hans!"

"*Guten Morgen,* Herbert.....*wie geht es Dir*[1] ?"

What a strange custom, but kind of nice!

As I sat at my desk, chatting with my new neighbor, the teacher suddenly strode into the classroom. As if by silent command, all the students jumped up out of their seats and stood at strict attention.

I was caught by surprise and remained in my seat about two seconds too long.

"Who do you think you are by not standing when your teacher enters the room?" Herr Ledermann shouted at me. "In which school did they teach you such poor manners?"

"*Heil Hitler,* class!"

"*Heil Hitler, Herr* Ledermann!"

"Be seated and we'll get down to business. That includes the new boy; introduce yourself and tell us where you're from!"

---

[1] How are you?

"My name is Jochen Volmar and I am from the United States of America", I replied.

Twenty eight pairs of curious eyes stared in my direction.

"Alright, class; you may be seated! Let's get to work now; you can ask him all the questions you want during lunch recess".

Classes didn't go to well the first day. German grammar was almost overwhelming with its precise genders and many, many rules. Math was tolerable since I had excelled in that subject and I was, after all, back in the sixth grade. A welcome relief was the English session where the teacher let me demonstrate the rolling of "r-s" for the class. History was also overpowering, with more dates studied in an hour than I had learned in a month back in the States.

Noon recess was a treat, as the whole class thronged around me with a multitude of questions.

"Have you ever been up in a skyscraper?"

"Have you ever met a gangster?"

"Are there really negroes in every city?"

"Are the cowboys still fighting with the Indians?"

Always looking for a joke to play on people, the last question prompted me to fabricate a very tall tale:

"Well, the cowboys have the red men pretty much under control in America. However, I lived on a farm and still carried a pistol while I rode my horse back and forth to school. Once in a while I could see an Indian warrior peeking out from behind a bush, but I was never attacked. They are afraid to cause too much trouble; had anything happened to me, the farmers would have organized a posse right away and captured them."

I left the boys in their amazed and envious frame of mind until the next day when I admitted to the fib. Would you believe, it took a lot of conversation to convince my classmates that I really had been fooling! The stage had been wonderfully set for me, as some of the most popular books in those days were contained in an adventure series by Karl May who wrote many novels about the American West in a very descriptive and breathtaking style.

Very soon the German literature for teenagers enthralled me. Instead of the comic books I was accustomed to, the bookstores abounded with military adventure booklets, all slanted to the German cause, of course. Titles ranged from "The Anti-Tank Gunners of Abbeville" to "U-Boot Raiders in the North Atlantic" and "The Great Paratroop Jump on Fort Eban Emael". The writing was always upbeat and touted military heroism and chivalry toward the enemy. Very little mention was made of the war's horrors; just good clean adventure and military victory.

I soon became acclimated to the heel-clicking strictness of the school. There was little time to play, though, as I had to study twice as hard as the other boys with so many gaps in my learning. If my history teacher from P.S. 92 in Manhattan could see me now, struggling with lists of reigning years of kings and popes by the dozen!

At this time I suddenly developed an uncomfortable affliction; I started stammering. It was probably a combination of "always being the oddball" and my sub-standard knowledge as a student that brought on this malady, which would suddenly descend upon me when I was required to recite in front of a class or when I was in other "center of attraction" situations. The cruel snickering of classmates compounded my embarrassment so that I became increasingly reluctant to speak in front of a group. At times things went so badly that I was unable to pronounce certain words at all and would substitute a different word in order to continue the conversation.

My *Onkel* Paul, who was on military leave at the time in order to complete his medical studies, offered some valuable advice.

"Jochen", he said, "as you know quite well, I also have trouble with stammering. One of my professors told me to inhale deeply just prior to pronouncing one of my known "stumble words" and then forcefully exhale while blurting out the word. This technique has helped me quite often!"

Sure enough, I tried this little trick and it helped immensely. At least I could force the word out of my mouth and be done with it, even if it sounded a little peculiar. By constant repetition of this technique I eventually rid myself of these embarrassing incidents.

The twice-weekly physical education class was another surprise.....the gym building seemed to me to be equipped better than a circus: trapezes, rings, bars, parallel bars and leather covered horses in all shapes and dimensions. *Jochen*, the clumsy farm boy, didn't do too well in this department. The soccer games frustrated me in the same manner as the practiced classmates ran rings around me in the dewy grass down by the Rhine river promenade. Never making any goals, all I had to show for my efforts were bloody shins and grass-stained clothes!

Herr Siebert, the music teacher, must have experienced the worst frustration of his entire career. The boy from America not only sang terribly off-key, bothering the other students, but he engaged in spells of uncontrolled giggling at one time or another during every music session. One time the poor man had his fill; when I didn't stop snickering, he tried to pull my hair in reprimand. Being newly cut very short to conform to German schoolboy standards, my blond strands kept eluding his grasp. The teacher finally gave up in desperation and slapped me across the skull instead. Shaking his head in frustration he went back to his desk and made a notation in his classbook. It probably read something like: "Behavior unacceptable, singing equally as bad!"

As the weeks went by, I adjusted somewhat to the radical changes in my lifestyle. Even with the heavy homework load, I found time to make friends, to go to the movies, to swim at one of the public bathhouses or to sightsee in the scenic "Seven Hills" across the Rhine from Bad Godesberg.

To complete my integration into the *Vaterland* all that I needed now was to join the Hitler Youth. I asked my new friend Hans Schlossmacher:

"I want to become a member of the *Hitler Jugend* like all the other boys.....how do I go about joining?"

Hans replied, "What's your hurry, Jochen? I've been in so long that the meetings are very boring to me. All we do is march around, sing soldier songs and throw dummy hand grenades. I think I'm going to transfer to the marine division one of these days; at least I'll get to row a boat!"

"Well, I still want to join up now. I want to learn how to march and sing like all of you do. When I hear those big drums booming my heart really starts throbbing."

"You should join in Bad Godesberg, not in Bonn where I am; it would be too far for you to go to weekly meetings. When you see one of the troops drilling some evening, just go up and talk to the troop leader; he'll tell you what to do."

A few days later as I walked by the Public School I heard the loud and rhythmic blend of drums and bugles coming from the playground. There they were, a group of about 30 teen-age boys. Dressed in orange-brown shirts with swastika armbands, black shorts and white knee socks, they marched smartly to the drumbeat.

I sauntered toward them nervously and watched their precision movements, punctuated with the sharp commands of the troop leader. When the boys were released for a break, I approached the leader who looked very mature to me, probably at least 18 years old.

"I want to join your troop, sir!"

"What do you mean "join"? Boys don't just join the *Hitler Jugend*, they transfer in from the *Jungvolk*[1] when they're old enough! What detachment do you belong to?"

"I was never in the *Jungvolk*; I just came over here from America!"

"From America??....you're kidding. How could you ever get across the Atlantic, with the U-Boats and everything? I thought our navy had a total blockade in force and wouldn't let any American ships through at all, even though we're not at war with them yet."

"I came over on a Spanish boat and we weren't stopped by the Germans at all, just by the Tommies."

"Well, we really don't have provisions to take in a new member unless he transfers in from the *Jungvolk* like I told you. If you really want to join, I'll check with my superiors. Come back next Wednesday night and I'll let you know."

When I related this conversation to my grandmother, she said: "Why don't you just forget about the *Hitler Jugend* for the time being if they aren't at all eager to have you. You're so busy anyway with your school work; besides that, some of them are such ruffians!"

"No, *Grossmutter*, I really want to be the same as all the other boys. Besides, it'll be fun camping out overnight and playing war games."

---

[1] Young People (roughly Cub Scout age group)

The following Wednesday I showed up at the playground promptly at 18:00 hours. The troop leader said to me: "We still haven't worked out the official procedure for enrolling you. Why don't you start coming to the meetings and we'll work things out ? Do you have a uniform?"

"No, I don't have a uniform and they won't sell me anything at the clothing store unless I have a *Hitler Jugend* identification card; besides that, they don't have any shirts or shorts....you have to get on a waiting list!"

"Alright, just start reporting every Wednesday evening and I'll hurry things up to get you an official membership card."

What a sight that must have been....the ill-at-ease foreign boy in civilian clothes stumbling along behind the smartly marching Hitler Youths on the parade ground! I went home proudly that night.....finally I was like the rest of my peers (except for the lack of a uniform, of course, and a few dozen other little things I was still to find out about)!

For the next few days I stewed and fretted about not having a uniform like the other boys did. My mother must have become sick and tired of my teasing and said: "Why don't you just wear your old Boy Scout shirt? It's almost the same color and nobody will ever notice the difference."

The next day we went accessory shopping: black neckerchief, epaulets and swastika armband were all we could find. When the store clerk asked for my ID Card, my mother said: "Can't you just overlook the card this one time? By the time we go home to get the card and come back you'll be closed and he needs them tomorrow!"

Reluctantly the lady rang up the sale and we were on our way! This was one of the very few times that I experienced an exception made to the very strict bureaucratic rules that prevailed in Germany.

A pair of black shorts procured from a helpful neighbor, *Onkel Paul's* knee socks and a few hours of *Mutti's* patient sewing to switch Boy Scout insignia to Nazi emblems and I was in business. The next Wednesday I showed up proudly in my new, pieced together uniform. What a disappointment when I stood next to the other boys.....the Boy Scout shirt was olive drab compared to the definite orange tinted brown of the Hitler Youth fabric! Oh well, what else is new.....little Jochen is still the oddball!

A few weeks later my official ID card finally came through. With this card and enough *Reichsmark* saved from my allowance I went to the store to buy my official dagger and a marching compass. The dagger was a far cry from my little utilitarian Boy Scout pocketknife. It looked like a smaller size army bayonet, had about a five-inch blade, broad and shiny, and was sheathed in a black metal scabbard. The checkered handle had a Swastika inset and was inscribed *Blut und Ehre* (Blood and Honor).

This summer of 1941 was probably the most carefree of all those I experienced in Germany. The six-week summer vacation was spent learning the ways of this new country. Sure, there was a war going on, but air raids were minimal compared to the ones to follow, we had no relatives in direct combat and I wasn't yet caught up in the grind of school tutoring and extra assignments to catch up with my age group.

The one and only movie theater in Bad Godesberg had a weekly film change so we all went to the movies once a week. The fare was either a comedy, love story or an occasional war saga of young German sailors on a U-boat fighting the superior British navy. Proverbial discipline prevailed in the movie houses, in that nobody dared enter and look for a seat after the lights went out; you had to wait for the intermission to sit down.

The first feature was always the news, called *Wochenschau*. The dramatic and well produced (and properly infused with *Herr* Goebbels propaganda) show had much front-line action with live sound track taken by some very brave cameramen. I held onto my seat for many a Stuka dive attack and was saddened on several occasions when it was announced that "These were the last scenes filmed by this photographer just prior to his heroic death for the *Vaterland*". These feelings were all amplified with the dramatic clarion blasts that opened and closed the newsreel show.

In reminiscing about the atmosphere in Germany during these times, I can now easily see how all media were controlled and directed by *Herr* Goebbels and his Propaganda Ministry. Newspapers, billboards, motion pictures and newsreels, school books, children's books and adult books.....all were produced under his powerful influence. Cleverly slanted toward the Nazi ideology they were also entwined with the traditional German nationalistic sentiment. I was soon well on my way of being transformed from a naive and idealistic Boy Scout to an ardent Hitler Youth.....brainwashing at its finest! Within six months my American roots faded into the background and my mind and body dutifully followed the *Führer's* leadership!

I visited the outdoor swimming pool almost daily and was exposed to some more different customs. Rather than pay for a locker and changing room privileges, the boys changed clothes right on the pool lawn, using their long-tailed shirts as a screen. My American shirts weren't quite as long, so I experienced considerable embarrassment before and after each swimming session. This was topped by an even worse habit. While walking down the street, any boy or man, as the need arose, would stop at a hedge or stone wall and urinate right in public! It took a long time for me to do that one without blushing!

It must have been my second or third visit to the pool, which was a very nice facility with good depth and a three-meter as well as a five-meter diving board. I became chummy with a young boy about my age and swimming ability and told my grandmother about it when I got home.

First question "What school does he go to?"

"He is finished with *Volkschule* and is an apprentice clerk at the hardware store, *Grossmutter*."

"*Jochen*, you should know better by now. You shouldn't make friends with boys of that social class. Please don't bring him to the house and try to find friends that go to a high school, please!"

I thought to myself, "What strange attitudes these people have.........!"

I never seemed to be on the right track with the friends I made. One of my classmates at the Oberschule lived only a few blocks from my grandmother's house. In a short time I became friends with this red-haired and somber boy named Kurt Fried. We rode the Bonn streetcar together and occasionally combined our efforts in figuring out difficult math assignments. I was aware that the friend's father was

Jewish and that he was confined to an internment camp somewhere.....Kurt didn't talk about it very much.

One day my grandmother said, "Jochen, I was talking with our neighbor *Frau* Brüning yesterday. She had seen your friend walking down the street with his mother last week and recognized her as being the wife of a Jew. Though his mother is an Aryan, your friend is still a Half-Jew. They may be very nice people, but I suggest that you don't become too friendly with him.....it could attract the attention of the Gestapo."

"*Grossmutter*, I don't see why anyone could hold my friendship with Kurt against me. I am certainly loyal to the *Vaterland* and I'm sure that he is also. He wants to join the *Kriegsmarine*[1] as soon as he is old enough!"

"That may be true, Jochen, but I still suggest that you keep your friendship at a minimum. The Gestapo keeps a close watch on active Catholics like me anyway!"

I paid only scant attention to *Grossmutter's* warning, however, and continued to associate with Kurt (maybe not *quite* as frequently as before)!

When I moved away a few months later the problem ceased to exist, but I still wonder how I would have acted had I continued to live in Bad Godesberg.....I'm sorry to say that Nazi ideology and the herd instinct would probably have prevailed!

It was around this time that I realized the ominous extent of the thorough and efficient Nazi political structure. Beginning at the lowest level, each city block had an appointed "Block Leader" who was responsible for maintaining political ideology in his block or large apartment complex. Each group of "Blocks" was then organized into a "District" with its leader and a group of "Districts" formed a "Region" with its leader and so on up the ladder to form "Provinces". All positions were doled out as political plums to loyal Nazi Party members. Their function was to insure Party loyalty throughout their respective areas and to report any treasonous or suspicious activities or conversations. (The Russians had a similar set-up with their Communist political "Commissars"). The end result was that

---

[1] German Navy

everybody was spying on everybody else.....superiors watching their subordinates and vice-versa! A subordinate liked nothing better than to "get something" on his boss and possibly earn a promotion by having the boss sent off to a KZ (concentration camp). Infractions ranged from harboring fugitives to open disloyal conversation or merely listening to foreign radio broadcasts. The fanaticism was so extreme that there were known cases of children reporting their own parents for listening to the BBC!

There was never a scarcity of adventure. At this time the Rhine River still abounded with ship traffic. Large, paddle wheeled towboats pulled an average string of four or five heavily laden barges both upstream and downstream. The upstreamers were the most fun, as the net speed of the barge must have been at least ten or twelve knots, considering boat speed plowing against a five knot current. The object was to enter the water upstream of a barge, swim out to it at just the right angle and grab the top edge of the hull, which was usually only about a foot out of the water. With skillful timing, the speed of barge and river current combined lifted you right onto the deck of the boat, in a prone position, of course. If the captain was kind-hearted, he would let us ride upstream for a half-mile or so, at which time we would dive in and do the same thing over again on another barge. A very tiring pastime, but what a way to stay thin and mean!

I never advanced to the real daring stage of this sport, as did some of the older boys. The paddlewheel towboats had an anchor suspended from the bowsprit, hanging down to about three feet above the water. The brave ones swam right up to the bow of the boat and leaped up out of the water to catch and hold on to the anchor. With some difficulty, they pulled themselves up to stand on the anchor, holding onto the bowsprit or anchor chain. When they had rested a little (or the captain approached to chase them away), they dove back into the water with a wide, sweeping dive to avoid getting involved in the massive side paddlewheel. I never saw a misjudged dive, but what a mess that would have been!

One day we were sitting on the rear veranda enjoying coffee and cake. This was an afternoon ritual for all Germans, even if the coffee was *Ersatz* and the cake made with potato flour and sweetened with saccharin. The dull clomping of horse's hooves on the asphalt announced the arrival of the "fruit and vegetable man". My grandmother walked out to buy her weekly allotment of potatoes, some beans and a small basket of *mirabellen*, a delicious cross between a cherry and a plum. All the fruit seemed much sweeter than the fruits I was accustomed to. I was told it was due to the slower ripening process in all of Europe because of the Gulf Stream's balmy influence on the northern latitudes. While my grandmother was making her selections, the old black horse decided to go to the bathroom right in front of our house. *Grossmutter* wasn't phased at all.

"*Jochen*, hurry and get a shovel; my roses could use some fresh fertilizer!"

Hereafter, whenever I heard the clomp of horses hoofs I ran for the shovel and brought home many a steaming pile of rose food. This, together with my expert lawn mowing and floor waxing soon made me a favorite grandson.

Lawn mowing was no different from the laborious and boring job I had in the United States. Readers born in the power-mower age will have difficulty visualizing a young boy struggling behind a reel mower with cast iron-wheels and no tires. The handle, designed for adult physiques, was always situated somewhere between the breastbone and the Adams apple, making it even harder to push. It seemed that no matter how many times I filled the oil holes with fresh lubricant, the mower just barely moved through the high grass. Conditions improved somewhat when a rubber tired model arrived on the scene, but it was still a hated and easily postponed chore. Luckily *Grossmutter's* lawn was tiny compared to some of the farmhouse lawns where I had lived, but other chores readily took up the extra time.

Shortly after my arrival I displayed a here-to-fore hidden talent for waxing floors. Following my grandmother's patient step by step demonstration, I soon became quite proficient. First, the smooth terrazzo was scrubbed by hand with soap, hot water and a stiff brush, sliding across the large hallway on our knees. After mopping up the dirty suds with a "scrub cloth", a coarsely woven towel-like affair designed to replace the string mops we're accustomed to, we rinsed with clear water and dried it up with a clean scrub cloth. The terrazzo was then allowed to dry thoroughly before the fun began. With a careful, even and circular motion the brown paste wax was applied to the floor.

Not a tiny spot was missed nor did I dare smudge any wax on the molding or woodwork. The heavy coating was permitted to dry for at least an hour or so before the buffing began. A long-handled, heavy, cast iron block with short bristles attached was carefully and endlessly pushed back and forth until an almost mirror finish was achieved. The entrance hallway, kitchen and inside steps all received this bi-weekly treatment. The first few times this job was a challenge and good exercise, thereafter it became an unpleasant chore.

The only job less pleasurable yet was polishing *Grossmutter's* steel cooktop. The flat surfaced gas cooking range was made of shiny steel that was not stainless at all. After every meal by the time the dishes were done, each droplet of spilled liquid or food particle had caused a rusty stain on the stove's shiny surface. The stains were readily removed with steel wool stove polish and plenty of elbow grease. This again became an unwelcome chore and I often wished that my 63 year old Grossmutter had a more steady hand. She was, however, an excellent cook, which somewhat made up for this unpleasant task.

Compared to the hearty farm meals I was accustomed to, the fare in Germany was quite restricted, even though it was early in the war. All items were rationed, especially fats, meats, sugar, milk, eggs and coffee. *Grossmutter* apparently had a fair sized bank account, as she engaged in frequent black market transactions with an elderly farmer who came to visit her on an almost weekly basis. When the doorbell rang, she would quickly usher him and his large leather bag into the kitchen and close the door, as he wanted no witnesses to this punishable act. After his departure, she would proudly show us a chicken, a sausage or a sizable roast she had purchased or sometimes bartered for an expensive Meissen china heirloom.

In later years as German currency lost more and more of its value and material goods were the only safe investment, many a farmer defied imprisonment or death in accumulating inventories of paintings, oriental rugs, grand pianos and expensive silver services. Even though the government controlled crops and livestock quite rigidly, there was still some room for cheating, which most farmers did unabashedly as the war progressed.

My Grandmother had a love affair.....platonic or not, it caused me a lot of jealousy and heartache. Sometime after my Grandfather died, she met a Catholic priest called Professor Mausbach. A very corpulent Alfred Hitchcock look-alike with a booming, pulpit trained voice, this man appeared every Tuesday, quite empty handed, to enjoy my Grandmother's generous hospitality at afternoon coffee time. The pair would sit in the dining room or on the veranda, weather permitting, at a coffee table fit for a king. Numerous kinds of bread, sausages, ham, jams, real butter, pastries and genuine coffee with cream, in large part derived from my mother's and my food Ration Cards. This hurt, especially during the days toward the end of a ration month, when we were a little pinched for food in general. There was always enough to supply this weekly visitor enough to keep his overweight body in perfectly distended shape; I still think this man never realized that there was a war on. My resentment was fueled by the priest's dominating attitude when he occasionally quizzed me on my progress in Latin. When I was a little slow in conjugation of a verb he would say, "Now Jochen, you must spend a little more time studying and not so much time playing with your friends!" Needless to say, whenever I attended Sunday Mass at the church where Professor Mausbach was assigned, I inquired about which Mass he was conducting and avoided that time-slot if possible.

An interesting Rhine pastime was long distance hitching-a-ride on the river barges. The personal river vessel in those days was the two-man kayak. These were quite elaborate crafts, with spray skirts and foot pedal controlled rudders. There was the rigid style like those used in the U.S. and a clever folding model called *"Faltboot"*, which folded up completely into two bags, each about the size of a hefty suitcase. These were intended to be hauled upstream by train, and, when reaching a certain destination, the kayak was easily assembled for the effortless journey downstream. Another facet was finding a kind hearted barge captain who would let the occupants of a couple of kayaks hitch a ride upstream to Karlsruhe, Mühlhausen or all the way to Switzerland and then let the brisk Rhine current take you back home. For a generous tip, the captain would permit erection of pup tents on the cargo hatches to keep out rain and sun, during the slow upstream ride, which could last 3 or 4 days.

Unfortunately I was a little too young to participate in such an adventure. It must have been fun to drift lazily down the colorful Rhine, winding to and fro between medieval castles, quaint riverfront villages and aromatic vineyards.

When Sundays came around all the emphasis on housework, yard work and homework was set aside and the Sunday stroll called "*Spaziergang*" took its place.

The setting of Bad Godesberg offered a myriad of destinations for such a stroll ranging from 2 miles to 10 miles. First you must visualize the configuration of Germany or any country in western Europe. Other than the large and concentrated cities, the whole countryside consists of countless villages and small towns, most of them not more than a few miles apart. In densely populated areas such as the Rhine Valley, they are almost continuous.

A Sunday outing could range from a short stroll along the paved riverfront to an outdoor cafe in the next village to an all day affair across the river into the Seven Hills, from which you might return after dark, dragging your blistered feet across the hometown cobblestones.

The summer passed all too quickly. My father had found an apartment in Kaiserslautern, which was about 100 miles and a four-hour train ride from Bad Godesberg. We were about to move again.

5

In September of 1941 we moved to Kaiserslautern. A small city of around 80,000, it lies nestled in the gently rolling hills of the Palatinate.

The apartment Fritz had located had been built for families of officers stationed at a nearby army post, which was called a *Kaserne*. Nestled into a heavily wooded hillside, the setting made an ideal environment for the American farm boy, who missed the wide-open spaces of his early youth. There were four apartment buildings, each containing four units:....two up and two down and of recent construction. The exterior was textured stucco with red clay tile roofs. Each apartment had four rooms plus kitchen and bath as well as a shared basement with built-in air raid shelter with its steel door-gasket sealed to keep out phosphorous smoke and poison gases.

It was still early in the war and housing was not yet under strict rationing assignment so we had the whole apartment to ourselves. I even had my own private bedroom with enough extra space to accommodate a worktable for study and hobbies.

The surrounding dense pine and oak woods created a wonderful country-like atmosphere. An occasional rabbit or squirrel scampering through the garden my parents had laboriously tilled in the front yard completed the scene. What a nice place to call home; I wondered how long until I would get uprooted again.

Enrollment in the local Oberschule was easy this time, since I had a report card and transfer papers. A city bus took me to within half a mile of our apartment, which was about 3 miles from the center of town.

After registering with the Police Department, the Housing Office, the Ration Office and the Labor Office we were ready to start a new chapter in our lives.

Not wanting to be dependent upon the crowded buses, I asked my father, "*Vati*, can't we buy a bicycle for me? I could get around to much better than on those buses."

"I don't know, Jochen, it will be difficult to find one. There are no new bikes for sale at all; you can't even buy tires. All production is going to the war effort. We'll just have to ask everybody we know to tell us if they hear of any used ones for sale."

A few weeks later the first lead developed. What a disappointment when it turned out to be a ladies bike! We promptly bought it for my mother, with the understanding that I could use it for errands if I exercised extreme care in handling her new treasure.

There was little danger of my wearing out my mother's bike as the colorful string-mesh skirt guard over the rear wheel was not conducive to a young man's image.

The bicycle was the backbone of German transportation at the time. Automobiles, other than for military use, were permitted only to doctors and government officials. Trucks were in the same category and most civilian hauling was done by horse and wagon. A bike was the way to go, but where was I to get one?

Since every bike repair shop had a waiting list for used ones, my situation seemed almost hopeless. Finally one day a classmate, who knew of my predicament said, "Jochen, I heard of a fellow who repairs old bikes and sells them. He lives downstairs in my aunt's apartment building. Here's the address!"

The moment I got off the bus that afternoon, I ran panting up the hill and burst into the kitchen where my mother was peeling potatoes.

"Mutti, I think I found a place to get a bike. Can we go see this man right away?"

"Your father won't be back until tomorrow night; he's in Saargemünd surveying some farms. He can go with you then."

"Please go with me now, Mutti. If we wait, someone else may have bought the last bike remaining!"

"You're really persistent, aren't you? Alright, show me where to go."

Since neither of us had yet mastered the art of "two-on-a-bike," especially since this is quite tricky on a ladies' model, we took the bus into town.

Arriving at the address, and unkempt looking woman holding an obviously retarded four-year-old boy, came to the door.

"What do you want?"

"We came to see if there are any used bikes for sale."

"I think he sold the last one yesterday; let me call him."

Leaning over the stair railing leading to the basement she cried out, "Hermann, do you have any bikes left? Hermaaannnnn, do you hear me?"

Presently a door opened in the dark basement hallway. In the shaft of emitted light I could see the outline of a squat, gnome-like man smoking a smelly pipe.

"I don't have any ready right now, but come down here and we'll talk."

Mutti and I groped our way down the dark stairway and were ushered into a workshop. The walls, ceiling and floor were jammed with used bicycle parts: wheels, fenders, seats, handlebars, old tires.....everything imaginable. In the center of the small room stood a solitary bicycle frame, inverted on the floor with one wheel missing. My longing eyes quickly identified it as a man's bike. Badly in need of some paint and not a fancy model, but it was a bike!

"Lady, I don't got no bikes to sell right now, but this one will be ready in about a week. If you want it, I'll sell it for fifty *"Reichsmark"*, half in advance right now."

This was a lot of money for a used bike, but I gave Mutti a pleading look. She apparently was tired of my persistent begging and dug into her large suitcase-like handbag for the deposit money.

"The bike will be painted and ready by next Friday. Be sure to bring the rest of the money then or he can't take the bike."

It seemed like an eternity to the impatient 14-year-old, but Friday finally came around.

Herman answered the doorbell himself and led me down to the basement again. There is was, in all it's glory. A shiny coat of black lacquer had rejuvenated the sorry looking mess I had seen a week ago. It was a very simple bike with very worn tires. No lights, no chain guard; the only trimmings were a bell and a luggage rack. Nevertheless I was a happy boy and struggled to carry the bike upstairs and onto the street. I paid the man the balance due, hopped on the bike like an expert and was on my way.

What a feeling of independence I had to finally have my own transportation! This bicycle would be my companion and hauling cart for several years, carrying me to and from my varied activities, carrying two of us in emergencies, hauling loads weighing as much as 70 or 80 pounds and even being a launch vehicle for my model gliders when wind conditions were right!

I pedaled home proudly, ringing my ding-dong bell at the slightest provocation. I experienced some difficulty in negotiating the hill leading up to our home, but didn't think too much of it at the time.

As the weeks progressed and I rode the new bike back and forth to school daily, it seemed to pedal harder and harder. One day I traded bikes with Friedrich, one of my new classmates.

After traveling down the street a few hundred meters he exclaimed, "Whatever kind of a bike did you buy? This thing pedals like a tank! You should take the whole bike apart sometime to see what's the matter with it."

With my limited bike-mechanical experience, I was grateful for his help that weekend to borrow some wrenches and take the entire bike apart.

To my chagrin, as we opened up the wheel bearing and pedal bearing assemblies, they were caked with finely ground red powder and displayed evidence of considerable wear. Our conjecture of brick dust was proven correct a few weeks later when someone made a remark about the old man who sold me the bike: "Oh sure, everybody knows that he pulls bikes out of the bombing rubble, straightens them out a little, dabs some paint over the scratches and sells them right away. It's a sellers market, you know!"

A good cleaning and some fresh oil improved my bike's performance a lot, but it always took a little extra effort to get up some of those long hills!

The next phase to learn was tire and tube repair. Both were already on a limited life span when I bought the bike and my heavy use didn't help matters any. It seemed that at least once a week I had to take off a wheel and repair a tube leak. These were routinely handled with small patches and rubber cement; however, a wear hole in a tire was a more serious problem. Until one could beg, borrow or steal a used tire somewhere, we cut a four or five inch section from a completely hopeless tire and applied it over the old, forcing the double layer of tire under the rim. This was a difficult task at best and made for a bumpy ride, but it put our bikes back in operation again.

Most bikes had some sort of lights for night riding, either battery or dynamo operated. Mine had neither and nothing was available in the shops. Therefore my night excursions were very short and had to be undertaken with a flashlight in one hand and a handlebar grip in the other.

Batteries were in short supply, so when I found a candle lantern in a store one day I was elated. With a sliding glass front and shiny reflector, why wouldn't this work on a bike?

I fashioned a makeshift clamp to attach my new light to the handlebars. That night came the trial run. With a spare candle and a box of matches I headed down the hill toward town. It only took a few hundred feet of downhill travel to find out that I couldn't exceed 5 or 6 miles an hour without blowing out my little candle. If I made the lantern leak-proof, I would also cut off the oxygen supply.....so much for that idea!

Soon my whole life seemed to revolve around my bicycle. The rear luggage rack, combined with a *rucksack*, a large, triangular backpack, hauled all the potatoes, fruits and vegetables we could buy. I became adept at riding single-handed while balancing an open pitcher of skimmed milk in the other hand.

During the first week at my new school one of my classmates said, "Jochen, you seem to like airplanes. Why don't you join our detachment of the *Flieger Hitler Jugend*[1]? We have a pretty good bunch of fellows and a nice workshop."

When I showed up at their next meeting, I could hardly believe my eyes. Right downtown just three blocks from our school was a complete aircraft workshop. Large enough to house a full sized glider, there were workbenches all around with complete woodworking and metalworking tools. Shelves of lumber, spare parts, rolls of fabric and spools of wire cable filled in every available corner. There was even a good-sized classroom with blackboards and aviation charts on the walls.

My eyes stared in wonder at the full-sized training glider in the middle of the shop. It almost filled out the spacious room with it's broad and stubby wings, one of which had part of the fabric stripped off, exposing a badly cracked wooden rib. To me, it was a weird looking contraption. It seemed to be all wings and tail. The fuselage was a merely a slender but massive skeletal frame which held wings and tail assembly together. This frame peaked into a tower projecting above the center of the wings. Attached to this tower were numerous stranded wire cables leading to wing tips and tail. These cables held the entire aircraft together. A turnbuckle in each cable permitted taut alignment and fine-tuning similar to sailboat rigging.

There was no cockpit in these gliders; a simple molded plywood seat with the backrest bolted to the tower accommodated the pilot. A joystick and rudder pedals mounted on a wooden stringer were all that separated us from the open sky. A single landing skid and towing ring at the nose of the glider completed the set-up.

When I inquired about the reason for the shop and all the tools, my friend said "When we smash 'em, we have to fix 'em ourselves; it surely makes us think twice before we get reckless!"

I asked the Hitler Youth *Scharführer*[2] who was showing me around: "Where on earth does the instructor sit?"

"He doesn't fly with us at all. It's much better to learn by yourself, as you'll see. We launch you very gently on short hops until you get the hang of it; then we send you higher and higher as you gain

---

[1] Aviation Hitler Youth
[2] Rank equivalent to Platoon Leader

confidence . We don't use two seaters until we get into advanced flying and aerobatics!"

Just the thought of soaring through the air in one of these machines all by myself was enough to help me make up my mind to sign up in this special branch of the Hitler Youth. I expressed my interest and *Scharführer* checked my ID Card, took down my name and told me to report to him at next week's meeting.....on time!

The German youth movement was cleverly organized to interest the young members and at the same time to provide a good training ground for the German armed forces. The branches consisted of the regular Hitler Youth, which provided training in field exercises, map reading, camouflage, night marches and general infantry type functions. The Motorized Section taught the boys all about engine mechanics and vehicle operation, using motorcycles as their prime attraction. The Marine Hitler Youth prepared the boys for sea duty, using large double-ended lifeboats and sleek sailboats for their training vessels. The Mounted Division used the discipline of regimented horsemanship to keep the boys interested.

I was now a member of the Flying Hitler Youth, the training ground for the famous *Luftwaffe*!. My classmate Friedrich said: "Boy, am I glad you joined up; we can have lots of fun together. Did you know, Jochen, that I'm also interested in model airplanes ? Have you ever built any ?"

"Oh yes, I have built several rubber band powered models; I had trouble getting them to fly for any length of time, though."

"Why don't you come over to my house on Saturday; I'll show you the new model I'm working on."

When I came home that evening I reported excitedly to my folks: "Guess what I did this afternoon.....I signed up for the *Flieger Hitler Jugend*; they teach us how to fly gliders and how to navigate and everything else!"

My father replied "Sounds great, but don't get too carried away so that all this extra activity interferes with your homework; you know that you have a lot of catching up to do. I still find it hard to believe that the American schools have such low academic standards that you're three years behind your peers."

Typically my mother said "Why do they let such young boys fly airplanes? What if you get hurt or even killed? Please do be careful, Jochen, you are our only child!"

"Don't worry so much, Mutti; they have helmets for us to wear and the gliders all have seat belts and shoulder harnesses. Nothing is going to happen to me anyway; I promise to be careful."

Saturday was model airplane time. Right after school I followed Friedrich home on my bike. He lived with his mother and little sister in a small, ground floor apartment not far from the boulevard leading to my home. His father was off in the war somewhere; mother and daughter shared one bedroom and my friend had a whole room to himself.

"So this is the American boy you've been telling me about?" his mother said. "He doesn't look like a gangster at all! Come in and have some coffee and cake; then Friedrich can show you his messy room with his models!"

The room wasn't messy at all, just crammed to the hilt with models on the walls, on the dresser and hanging from the ceiling. On one side of the room was a large worktable with a sleek model glider partially completed. Next to it were neatly stacked rows of wooden airplane parts, all arranged by size. Several shelves held stacks of blueprints, cans of glue and more neat stacks of thin plywood. In the corner was a retired wastebasket holding neat bundles of pre-cut wooden stringers of many sizes, each bundle tagged with its metric dimension.

I asked "Friedrich, where are the kits for the two new models you were telling me about?"

"I don't know what you mean by a kit....we just buy the plans and then follow them carefully to build the model!"

He wasn't fooling; there was no such thing as the kits I was accustomed to from F.W. Woolworth, with all the parts supplied pre-cut and step-by-step instructions. All he had was a set of detailed scale drawings with dimensions and a few basic comments, such as "Glue should cure overnight before applying fabric." Everything else was left up to the skill of the model-maker. Wing ribs were carefully traced from the plans on a sheet of special thin plywood, then cut out accurately with a hand coping saw, hand filed and hand-sanded to perfection. When all the parts for a certain section had been fabricated and neatly finished, the plans were laid flat on the work table and all the parts pinned down with straight pins stolen from mother's sewing kit. Then the glue was carefully mixed by measuring the proper amount of powder and adding water. As each part was nested into it's mate, glue was applied, not too little and not too much.

When the bending radius on a stringer was too sharp for dry bending, the wood was soaked in water to give it flexibility; it was then forcibly pinned and let dry overnight.

"Do you want to see how these babies fly?" Friedrich asked.

"What are we waiting for? I've never seen such large model airplanes before."

Taking a sleek white glider with a wingspan of about 5 feet down from the wall, Friedrich quickly removed the one-piece wing assembly.

"What are you taking the plane apart for?"

"Do you see how the wings are clamped to the fuselage with this heavy rubber band? If the glider hits the ground or an object with its wings, they just pop off and the damage is far less than if the wings were stationary. Besides, it's much easier to haul in two sections when you're riding your bike."

"Where are we going to launch the glider?"I asked.

"There are some nice hilly pastures about 5 kilometers North of your house where there's almost always a breeze. It's called *Fröhnerhof* and we're allowed to launch there as long as we don't get in the way of the big gliders."

Friedrich's mother fixed us each a black bread sandwich with homemade blackberry jam and off we rode; my friend carried the massive wings while I tucked the main section of the model glider under my arm. A short stop at the small store produced two bottles of lemon mineral water and we were on our way to the launch site.

I'll never forget that day; what luck.....there was no one else at the field. It was a bright, sunny day with just the right amount of breeze flowing over the gently rolling grassy hillside. Friedrich painstakingly attached the wings, checked the wind direction carefully and then started running, holding the glider just at shoulder height. He gradually increased his running speed until he had taken about 12 or

15 steps.....then he gave the glider one last push and it was on its way, immediately ascending toward the clear blue sky. Perfectly balanced, it swooped and swerved in a downhill direction, occasionally picking up some altitude as it passed into a thermal updraft and then gliding slowly earthward as the warm air column released its grasp. The beautiful performance probably lasted only one and a half or two minutes, but it seemed like a half-hour to me. I was hooked!

6

Winter descended softly on the picturesque German countryside. Nestled in the evergreen covered hills, Kaiserslautern offered the same childhood diversions I was accustomed to in upstate New York. Sledding, ice skating and snowball fights all had their rightful place in my lifestyle. However, a strict regimen of homework and private tutoring took up most of my spare time.

I struggled to keep up with my classmates in a diverse curriculum, which included all the natural sciences simultaneously throughout all the high school years. Compared to the American way of having only one science subject during every high school year, this seemed to be overwhelming. As I found out later, though, this progression of learning all sciences at the same time provided a natural integration of knowledge in all the fields. It did require 3 to 4 hours of homework daily, which cut deeply into my leisure time programs.

Leisure time during this particular winter included weekly sessions at the Hitler Youth aviation center. These studies, however, were far more fun. We learned chart reading and navigation as well as aerodynamics and meteorology. We all paid rapt attention, as each of us had this burning desire to fly, fly, fly! We counted the days remaining until summer, when our turn would come to become airborne.

Sandwiched between class sessions was the shop work. Divided into small groups of three or four boys, we learned every facet of glider repair and construction. There were few power tools; almost everything was done the old-fashioned and painstaking way. One month we would work at wood shaping. First the various hand planes were used; then we learned to choose just the right grade of rasp or file; then came the hand sanding which produced the end result of a finely polished piece of woodwork.

The next month was the time for metalwork, performed in the same time-consuming and meticulous manner. In making a cable bracket, for instance, we started out with hacksaw cutting, careful tracing radii with a scribe and then filing, filing and filing until the shape was perfect enough to please the instructor. We didn't mind the exacting standards, though, as we knew that these machines would be carrying us around in the air someday.

All this preparation culminated into the summer of 1942.....I often referred to it as my "flying summer". Every Saturday after school we congregated at the small glider field called *Fröhnerhof* and toiled with our machines, eagerly awaiting our turn for a short flight. On Sundays there was more of the same. When the weather was bad, we stayed home and worked on our models; in all cases, the word was "fly, fly, fly!"

The memory of my first flight still creates a tingling in my spine. It was an overcast day with very little wind. Our basic training glider was a primary model, the SG-38. We pulled the boxy looking aircraft out of the hangar on its two-wheeled dolly, two boys pulling the dolly and another holding a wing-tip in his gut to guide the machine over the grassy field while six others held on to the fuselage and tail at various points, pushing all the while. Three other Hitler Youths followed, dragging the rubber starting rope through the grass. The instructor followed with his shiny black boots and inevitable clipboard. It wasn't very far to the starting spot, as rank beginners worked on level ground.

The instructor said, "Today we're going to launch some virgins, boys! Volmar, you're next on the list. Put on the crash helmet and climb aboard the machine."

"*Jawohl, Flugleher*[1] I'm ready to go!"

---

[1] Yes Sir, Instructor

My pulse racing, I fumbled with the waist and shoulder harness as my friends prepared for the launch. Two of the boys sat down in the grass at the plane's tail and held onto short attached ropes, their feet firmly planted into the ground. The launching rope was a ¾ inch diameter elastic shock cord with a large ring attached to the center. The ring was snapped into a nose hook on the glider while the boys split into two identical groups. Each group spread out along their part of the shock cord and started walking, taking up slack until this giant slingshot was poised for action.

"Staaart pulling", the instructor bellowed.

With that command, the boys started walking forward at a slight angle away from the aircraft. As the tension on the launching rope increased, so did my pulse rate. Clutching the joystick in my right hand while my left hung onto the hard plywood seat, 15 year old Jochen was ready for his first glider hop---solo from the start!

Upon the instructor's command, the boys quickened their pace and the elastic rope became tauter and tauter. Suddenly a barked command "Los![1]" made the world come alive. The "holders" released their grip on the plane's tail and the cumbersome craft began skidding over the grass. The right wing started dipping toward the ground. I immediately over-corrected by whipping the stick to the left too far and too long. As the left wing dipped precariously, I slammed the stick to the right. By this time the glider lost momentum and slid to a stop.

"Volmar, you dumb donkey! Can't you be a little more delicate with your controls? You're not flying a Heinkel bomber you know!"

Ten seconds of skidding through the grass with your heart beating in your throat doesn't give you much time to make decisions!

Three more ten second launches were mine that day: each one more thrilling than the last. With each flight my mind was a little clearer and my reactions a little faster and more controlled. The fourth launch was like a perfect dream; by extending the "holding time", the teacher increased the elastic tension on the launch rope before commanding "*Los!*"

---

[1] Release

The plane catapulted ahead, with the skid runner bumping through the grass. Suddenly things turned smooth......I was airborne! The glider climbed, probably no more than 2 or 3 feet off the ground. As the left wing started dipping, I expertly made the delicate correction required and the glider leveled off. With no time for a downward glance, my eyes were glued to the horizon, ever alert for the telltale signs of a "stall". All too soon, the heavy craft settled into the grass again. The flight, which probably had lasted a mere 15 seconds, was over and so was my turn....!

"Not bad for a beginner, Volmar. Take the glider back to the other end of the field. Schwarz will be the next virgin to go; let's get a move on, fellows!"

We lifted the glider onto the two-wheeled transport dolly and started the long trek back to the starting point. It was hard work, but the thrill of flying made it all worthwhile. I went home that night proudly showing my parents the first four entries in my personal logbook. The entries showed the date, flight time in seconds, comments and instructors signature. His comments for this date were "learns well".....I had taken the first step of the long and tedious road of becoming a fighter pilot or maybe even an astronaut.

My mood was always positive, upbeat and competitive. All of us were in our glory: improving our flying skills and staying in superb physical and mental condition; we felt that we had the world by the tail and could do no wrong!

The damper came one overcast Sunday afternoon. We were almost ready to pack it in and wrestle the heavy glider back to the hangar. There we would spend another half-hour putting away launch ropes, dollies and other gear after carefully wiping off all mud and grass stains.

The instructor said: "Alright, Hellman, let's give it one more try. If you don't learn to treat that joystick like a fragile raw egg, you're never going to make it into the Luftwaffe, even as a navigator!"

When the broad-winged machine was hurled into the misty sky, it seemed that the student did just the opposite to defy the instructor. As the glider reached its peak altitude of probably fifty feet or so, it kept on slowly climbing instead of settling into the accustomed routine of leveling out and gracefully gliding back to earth.

The instructor bellowed, "Push the stick forward..forward forward.....you dumb asshole; you're going to stall!"

The words went unheard or unheeded. As the plane slowed to a stall, Hellmann lost control and panicked. We could see him violently pushing the joystick forward all the way, but nothing happened. After what seemed an eternity, the machine picked up a little speed and veered off sharply to the right. Now it had been overcorrected and started acting like a dive-bomber. At the last moment the student was able to regain level flight.....just before the plane disappeared into the patch of woods bordering the airfield.

We all made a mad dash for the crash site. Unbelievably our colleague was unscathed. We found him still securely strapped to his seat, sitting in a glider without wings. The plane's fuselage had miraculously slid between the trees as the wings were being sheared off without inflicting even a scratch on the young pilot. Hellmann was grounded for a month; the rest of us all lost a little of our cockiness.....it seems that these machines could be dangerous after all!

As the weeks went by our flights became longer and our skills became more honed. We stopped working on level ground and started moving up the hill for our launches. Flight times increased from a few seconds to 30 or 40; by mid-summer we were approaching full minute flights. With longer flights inevitably came the longer and longer plane retrievals. It required much pulling and shoving over the bumpy grass to get the heavy glider back up the hill for the next launch. Even with the longer flights, each of us managed at least a few flights each weekend. The pages of my logbook began filling up and approached the required flights to qualify us for the coveted "A" badge. This would promote us from the category of a mere beginner to a qualified glider pilot of the lowest rank. The insignia was a single bird with wings spread wide embroidered in silver on a round blue patch.

It was a bright Sunday morning in August; with the entire glider troop assembled before him, the *Gefolgschaftsführer*[1] shouted:

"The following glider students front and center..... Bachmann, Huck, Schwarz, Klein........VOLMAR !"

---

[1] Group Leader

Twelve excited young boys marched to the front of the formation where the leader and the flight instructor were awaiting us. Four of our group of 16 were not summoned; they had, for one reason or another, not qualified. With a short congratulatory speech, we were awarded our "A" patches. A firm handshake by both leaders and the ever-present raised-arm Nazi salute sent us back into the ranks, grinning from ear to ear. When I came home that night after flight instruction I was "hot stuff".... a 15 year old glider pilot!"

The letdown followed two days later when my father sat me down in the living room for a serious talk. He started out:

"Jochen, I'm really proud of you for qualifying as a basic glider pilot. However, I've been meaning to talk with you about this conflict between flying and schoolwork. It seems that all I've been hearing is "Fröhnerhof, Fröhnerhof ...... flying, flying, flying" instead of "Latin, Latin ...... History, History". You're well aware that you are three years behind your age level. I think you should do something about that and study hard for a few years. You can always fly after you've caught up!"

Father's word was law; dejected and downhearted, I transferred from the Flying Hitler Youth to a small equestrian troop, which only met once a week and didn't have all the ground school and shop work.

Again I experienced the shortage of materials.....since riding boots were available only to the military, I had to make do with my father's American-made high top boots, These monstrosities were laced all the way from instep to top and served the purpose.....they also made me stand out from my peers in my customary manner!

The horsemanship turned out to be lots of fun and quite a challenge. I had ridden quite a bit on the farm in New York and thought I was quite good. What a shock when I displayed my casual western style to the burly and loud-voiced riding instructor! In a sawdust arena with mirrored walls all around, I took my first lesson in Prussian military horsemanship.

"Volmar, arch that back...... Volmar, loosen those wrists...... Volmar, do you think you're in a rocking chair? ...... You're supposed to be working WITH the horse, not AGAINST the poor animal!"

As time went on I managed to change my style and became quite proficient at disciplined riding, including standing upright on the saddle, riding slalom courses and jumping barriers.

The camaraderie of this small group was savored by each of us. There were only ten Hitler Youths and the instructor, a retired artillery *Feldwebel*. This man was like a chameleon: a sarcastic taskmaster in the arena changing to a humorous good friend after the horses were curried and put away.

There was a clubroom in the stable area where I had my first exposure to beer consumption in volume. As was the traditional custom with German cavalrymen, after the day's ride the troop would congregate in the club bar and drink out of a giant community glass boot, about three feet high. The boot was passed around the table and you had to drink as long a draught as you could without breathing while the toe of the glass boot pointed skyward. The object was NOT to be drinking when the beer level dropped to the point where a whole toe-full of liquid was suddenly released, gushing foamy beer all over the drinker's face and shirt.

Even though the beer was wartime low-alcohol grade, it made us giddy and giggly after several "boots-full" and quite often our bicycles seemed to weave a little on the way home.

As my studies improved, my parents relaxed somewhat regarding my leisure time. Since my father was an avid hunter, I had little difficulty in gaining permission to join a shooting club. Most of the members were off to war, so I soon became the "teacher's pet" of *Herr* Sieffert, the gray-haired and jovial senior instructor.

Dressed in the well known green woolen hunter-garb called *Loden*, this kindly but exacting gentlemen would constantly coax, nag and flatter me into improving my scores.

In typical German fashion, very little ammunition was expended. Serious routines of breath control, aiming practice and dry firing preceded each shooting session. My interest was held by his constant honing and refinement with a loving touch. This fine man was so thrilled to have found a dedicated student that he sold me his favorite target rifle for a token price. This was an exact replica in shape and weight of the official German military 8 millimeter 98K Mauser, except that it was in .22 caliber and a single shot. The one condition that *Herr* Seuffert insisted upon was that the gun receive a monthly application of pure shellac, lovingly hand-rubbed into the walnut stock and forearm until dry. I dutifully accepted the condition and proudly used the rifle in many matches with superior results.

When autumn of 1942 arrived, to my great relief and my parents' great pleasure, I was advanced a year ahead of my class at the Oberschule. Now I was only a year or two behind my age group; still the oldest in the class, but not such a drastic difference.

By this time the war began to show its more serious side. The British night raids became more frequent and more deadly. Our city was spared any direct raids up to this point, but it seemed that each and every night the piercing wail of the air raid sirens rudely awakened us and sent us scurrying to the nearby underground shelter which had been blasted into the rocky hillside. More than once I refused to get up and *Mutti* would tearfully beg me:

"Jochen, please get up.....there's an air raid warning! I can hear their engines already."

"Please let me sleep just a little bit longer; I'm so tired. They're probably just flying through to Mannheim again."

After much begging and crying, my mother would finally succeed in getting me out of bed. Hastily throwing on a few clothes and carrying the rest, I would follow her outside into the pitch-dark street. For normal nighttime use we were allowed to have small flashlights with lenses masked to reveal only a narrow sliver of light. However, during an air raid alarm even their use was strictly forbidden. Very often we would hear the excited barking of an air raid warden:

"*Licht Aus*[1] .....Do you want the Tommies to drop a thousand pounder on us just because of your stupidity?"

With the ominous droning of countless aircraft engines getting louder by the minute, we would stumble and grope our way to the shelter, which was about 500 yards from our apartment. As we entered the dimly lit cavern, the stifling odor of mildew and perspiration wafted into our faces. Shuffling our way past crying infants, whining children and complaining adults we would search for a space on one of

---

[1] Lights Out!

the damp wooden benches. The next two hours would be spent in constant fear of a bomb hit. We all knew only too well that even this cave dug into the hillside would be no match for good-sized British bomb.

When the "All Clear" was finally sounded, we wearily returned home and crawled into bed. Often there were subsequent alarms toward early morning but we usually ignored them in our tired stupor. Even my worrisome mother realized that these alarms were usually triggered by aircraft returning from raids with no bombs left to dispense.

During the winter of 1942 the German war machine began to show signs of faltering; Field Marshall Rommel was pushed back at El Alamein and the Russians had encircled the German Sixth Army at Stalingrad. Almost everyone we knew had at least one close relative killed or missing in action. Our food rations became slimmer and slimmer each month; a quarter pound of margarine per week was quite minimum for an active and growing boy, especially when the bread ration was around 6 ounces per day.

One morning just before class my friend Friedrich came up to me and said excitedly:

"An English bomber crashed into the woods last night just east of the city. Let's go look at it this afternoon after school."

"Sure, I want to look at the wreckage, but what if we get into trouble? You know it's against the law to mess around with downed aircraft!"

"I know all about that, but let's try anyway; if there's a guard at the site, we'll just tell him we're hunting for blueberries and head for home."

We could hardly wait until the school day was over; at the sound of the last bell we dashed out of the classroom and pedaled home furiously on our trusty bikes. After a quick sandwich of rye bread and synthetic jelly I hopped on my bike again to arrive at our pre-arranged meeting place at the edge of the woods. We padlocked our bikes to a tree and proceeded to make our way up the first hill. Just beyond the crest the devastation began. The twin engine Blenheim had apparently glided to a crash landing, decapitating countless trees and cutting a sweeping swath through the dense pine forest. Working our way through a maze of broken-off treetops, we soon came upon scattered pieces of torn and twisted aluminum aircraft parts. Some were completely blackened by fire, others were still covered with the mottled pattern of green and black camouflage paint. There was not a guard in sight, so we continued on. We then came upon the mangled fuselage with wing tips clipped just before it came to rest. The right engine was missing, simply torn out of its mountings. We found it sometime later, a hundred feet or so beyond and stuck into a small embankment.

Like vultures we climbed into the twisted cockpit which was covered with pieces of shattered Plexiglas.

"Look here, Jochen, there's the compass."

"That's the bombsight over there; what a complicated looking contraption!"

"There's blood all over this panel; someone must have been hit!"

In spite of our youthful bravado, I felt a little queasy and sad. For a moment the personal side of war showed it's face; who was this young man, wounded in the remote night sky far from his home? Did he survive the bailout ? Where was he now.........?

My thoughts came back to earth with my friend's remark: "Wow, just look at all this machine gun ammunition it must be at least 12 or 13 millimeter. We don't have anything this big!"

"Look, every seventh round is a tracer; let's try to ignite one!"

Using our youthful ingenuity, we painstakingly removed a tracer bullet from its casing and carefully scraped the tracer magnesium with a pocketknife. When a small heap of shavings had accumulated on the rear end of the projectile, we stuck it into the ground and lit the magnesium with a match. A bright and hissing flare-up ensued....what a boyish thrill! A good thing we didn't try this with an explosive shell!

It was also a good thing that nobody caught us climbing around the wreckage as there were strict rules prohibiting such activities!

My school tutoring continued, but at a slightly slower pace. I didn't need to skip a grade any more, just keep up with the class.

One of my tutors was a pitiful fellow; in his late thirties, he was afflicted with cerebral palsy and therefore was confined to a wheel chair. Completely immobile from the waist down, he had to stay in his parents' second floor apartment. When an air raid alarm sounded, his parent's would lay him on a piece of carpet and gently carry and slide him down two flights of stairs to the basement air raid shelter.

Another tutor I had for a short time was a university physics professor serving in the army and stationed near my home. Looking back, I now marvel at the fact that he was teaching me fundamentals of atomic energy in 1942, long before the American public had ever heard of the "Manhattan Project."

7

Time and time again, World War II reared its morbid head to remind us of the cold realties of a great conflict. One evening just before Christmas 1942 we heard the sudden anguished and uncontrolled wailing of our neighbor lady in the apartment next door. We knew without asking what her problem was; her only son had been struck down by a Russian bullet. Details confided to us the next morning revealed that he had been killed on his very first day at the wintry front.

It was less than a week later that another neighbor and good friend of Mutti's called her, sobbing over the telephone: "Ernst has been killed.....Oh my God.....Ernst has been killed!"

Several weeks went by when this poor lady just started to get over the original shock of her husband's death and regain her composure. One day a cruel and thoughtlessly sent package arrived for her in the mail. She opened the carefully wrapped carton and found her husband's leather officer's coat, pistol, holster and belt carefully rolled inside together with a compassionate note from his battalion commander. Upon opening the parcel she immediately viewed the ghastly sight of dried bloodstains spread over the back of the coat. With typical German frugality, his comrades didn't want to waste the expensive and hard to replace coat and shipped it to the widow. They were so engrossed in the cold business of warfare and saving their own hides that they couldn't take the time to scrub off the blood and brain tissue. The battle-hardened comrades apparently never realized that this ghastly sight subsequently would throw the widow into a renewed state of shock and sadness. The letter gave more details of the *Hauptmann's* misfortune. He had been riding through a small village in his command car, directing the organized retreat of his company. Without warning, a Russian partisan's bullet smashed into his skull from the rear, bringing instant death. The partisan was caught immediately and executed on the spot, but what good did that do? The Russian philosophy of expendable human resources immediately put a new partisan in his place!

We always thought that the training and discipline of the German soldier was exemplary until soldiers returning from the Russian front told some incredible stories of the *Ivan's* incredible prowess and self-control which even surpassed the renowned Teutonic military discipline....example: a major Russian counterattack against a well-entrenched German position: The first assault wave of Russian foot soldiers were heavily fortified with Vodka and bellowing their customary attack cry of "Uuuurrrraaaay" while pushing forward in suicidal ferocity. The men of this first wave were armed to the teeth, many with automatic weapons such as the well-known "burp gun" style sub-machine gun of 7.65 caliber holding 72 rounds in a circular drum magazine. As deadly German fire decimated the ranks of the first wave, these weapons were picked up by soldiers of the second and third waves, who were completely unarmed until they could salvage a weapon from one their fallen comrades. This scenario repeated itself until all of the Russians had been annihilated or taken prisoner.

Other stories and eye-witness accounts about the dedication and ferocity of the Russian soldier and partisan abounded such as the amazing story of white clad soldiers lying motionless in the deep snow in front of a German position for 8 or 10 hours after a failed attack, feigning death and waiting for the Germans to let their guard down, permitting the Russians to launch a surprise assault.

It became common practice for Russian infantrymen or partisans to hide in a covered and well-camouflaged foxhole, intentionally waiting to be over-run by the rapidly advancing German tanks and infantry. They would often remain in hiding for several days at a time, never leaving the foxhole for any purpose. Training included the extreme discipline of keeping all empty food cans and wrappers within the foxhole and even burying all excrements inside the hole to prevent detection by the watchful Germans. When all was quiet, sometime during a succeeding night, the partisans would then come out of hiding and wreak havoc among the sleeping and unsuspecting Germans.

As the fighting grew in intensity and bitterness the atrocities also increased, each act followed by a revengeful counter-measure against the perpetrators. When partisans killed some German soldiers it was understood that resident villagers would be executed in reprisal. The partisans would then return, capture a few Germans and run them through a buzz saw lengthwise. When the Germans returned to the village and discovered their mutilated comrades, they thought nothing of shooting or hanging more Russians, whether they be civilians or partisans in disguise didn't really matter. Not long thereafter a German hospital train was stopped while enroute to the rear echelon. When the overdue train was finally discovered by motorized patrol every man aboard was frozen to death, encased in a layer of ice. The Russians had stopped the train, shot all able-bodied Germans and sprayed water on the wounded, insuring inevitable death at the below-zero temperature.

With the German war machine in full production and all able bodied (as well as some not so) men drafted into the armed forces, an acute labor shortage prevailed throughout the country. This affected the farmers especially, since they depended heavily upon manual labor, particularly at harvest time. When my father offered to find me a summer job on a small farm as an *Ernte-Helfer*[1], I jumped at the opportunity.....maybe my voracious teen-age appetite would be satisfied for once. By this time strict food rationing had reduced the individual daily allotment to around 1500 calories, resulting in considerable belt-tightening for all of us.

The influence of the medieval feudal system can still be seen today when looking at German farms. The farmers all live in their villages instead of in the center of their one-piece farmland property as they do in the U.S. During the Middle Ages the villages afforded

---

[1] Harvest helper

protection against enemy raiding parties and also allowed for shared water supplies in the form of community wells or fountains in the village square. The fields remained as narrow strips scattered throughout the countryside, a carryover from the small parcels tended by serfs and passed down from generation to generation. A small-scale farmer could conceivably own 15 or 20 small fields, all strewn about. The parcels range from 5 or 6 acres to as many as 50 or so, all butted closely to their neighboring parcels so as not to waste any productive farmland.

My father didn't waste any time; that Friday evening when he came home from work he announced:

"Jochen, I've already found a helper's job for you. You can go to work for a client of mine who is a very good Mennonite farmer."

"Let's not wait any longer; I could use some good farm food!"

The next morning a two hour train ride brought us to the small town of Weierhof, quaintly nestled in the gentle rolling hills in the northern part of the Palatinate. We ambled along the bumpy cobblestone main street to the farmer's neat stucco home situated at the edge of the village. The farmer greeted us with a cheerful and hearty "*Grüss* Gott, Herr Volmar!"

"*Grüss Gott*, Herr Neff" my father replied. This is my citified son I have been telling you about. His name is Jochen; please feed him well, but make him earn his keep."

"Don't you worry, Herr Volmar; Jochen looks like a strong young man. I think it'll be a fair exchange: some substantial meals in exchange for a few weeks of his energy around here. We're very short-handed......the only farm hands I have are my wife and daughter and two French P.O.W.-s."

Frau Neff showed me to my room, accessed by a narrow and very steep stairway above the kitchen. The small bedroom was sparsely furnished but spotlessly clean and comfortable. The bed was covered with a huge and fluffy eiderdown featherbed. As it turned out, the unaccustomed hard work of farming by hand took its daily toll on my body so that it didn't matter how or where it took its needed rest. I could have slept on a hard wooden floor and not known the difference.

After a short while of exchanging pleasantries with the farm couple, my father departed.

"I'll see you in three weeks, Jochen. Let's see if you can keep up with these strong farmers!"

The first obstacle I had to overcome was the language problem. I had been taught and was accustomed to so-called "High German". The Neffs spoke in one of the countless low German dialects, which are so regionalized that traveling only 50 miles or so can produce words or pronunciations that are almost unintelligible. For example *Pferd* means horse in the Rhineland whereas its equivalent in the Palatinate is *Gaul*.

The farmer took me on an inspection tour of his establishment. House and barns were all attached and shared common structural walls, the entire complex forming a cobblestone-paved courtyard. There were no tractors and all machinery was horse-drawn. Hand tools abounded, such as scythes, sickles and large wooden rakes.

There were no screens on the residence and flies prevailed in the farmyard. Special dome-shaped screen covers protected the food items standing on the table, such as butter and cheese. The horses were constantly switching their tails in futile defense against the pesky and persistent critters. Just as futile were the spiral and adhesive-coated flycatchers hanging in the barn. For every dozen insects caught, another dozen immediately appeared to replace the prisoners.

After a hearty meal of black bread sandwiches and unlimited amounts of butter, lunchmeats and cheeses, Herr Neff sent me to bed; "Life on our farm begins at five thirty, Jochen; you had better get lots of sleep!"

I climbed up to my room and was soon asleep. The man wasn't kidding.....promptly at 5:30 the next morning Frau Neff hollered up my stairway: "Let's go, Jochen, it's time for the city boy to have a good breakfast!"

It was difficult for me to comprehend that such food supplies still existed in this fourth year of total war. As I was to find out on my first day, five meals would be served to this hungry teenager. The first breakfast was promptly at 6:00 and consisted of fresh hard rolls, assorted lunchmeats and cheeses as well as many boiled eggs as my hungry frame desired. After the cows were milked the men took care of heavy barnyard chores like shoveling hay or manure. Time permitting, we would undertake the first trip to the fields, either cutting grain or loading hay cut a few days before. During this time the women were busily feeding the chickens, ducks and geese and preparing the second breakfast. Around 10:00 AM we were served a hot meal of soup or stew with plenty of freshly baked *Fruchtkuchen*, a delicious open-faced yeast cake covered with fresh peaches, plums or *mirabellen*. Sometimes boiled potatoes were the main staple, served with sour milk or cottage cheese. Now it was off to the fields again while the women did the housework. They gathered up the featherbeds they had hung out of the windows earlier for their daily airing, made the beds and even swept up the courtyard in their spare time. Promptly at noon the women showed up where we were working. They were loaded down with large lunch baskets and their hand implements for the day: scythes, sickles, rakes and hoes. After a substantial lunch of black bread sandwiches and a full liter of wine per person we began the backbreaking fieldwork again. Not being accustomed to alcohol except for an occasional glass at holidays, it took me a while each day to clear my foggy brain after each lunchtime libation.

Now it was time for the women to join us in the fieldwork. Even though we had mechanized horse-drawn harvester binders, there was much hand work to be done. Not an inch of space had been left unseeded between the fields in order to fully utilize all the tillable ground. Because of this a machinery path had to be cut around each field by hand. Since binder-twine was at a premium and used only on the machine, I soon learned the art of tying a shock of grain with a twisted rope made of stalks. The shocks were then stacked in piles of 5 or 6 ever so carefully, with the last shock lying flat on top to afford some rain protection.

It was here that I found out why European farmwomen all looked alike: weather-beaten faces, gnarled fingers and stooped postures were omni-present and once a woman was middle-aged, I couldn't tell if she was 40 or 60! They toiled from dawn till after dusk at tasks far too demanding for a woman and had to do all the housework, cooking and mending to boot!

At 3:00 PM (15:00 German time) the ladies trudged back to the farmhouse to pick up afternoon *Kaffee;* they brought the loaded baskets back to the field again. This time it was more cake accompanied by real coffee and rich cream. Most farmers had become clever traders, exchanging much sought-after potatoes, fruit and poultry for valuable black market items like coffee, chocolate or tangible porcelain china, silverware or other collectors' items.

The women stayed a few more hours and were then sent back to prepare the evening meal: dark bread, butter, sausages and cheeses completed our day. My last chore consisted of escorting the two French prisoners back to their lightly guarded camp about two miles away. There was really no need to escort them and I was not armed as they had no desire to escape. For them the war was over and besides, where else could they get such good food? The only reason we escorted them was government decree!

The horrors and depravations of war faded into the background and I felt like I was living in a dream world. I had never had such good and plentiful food ever since I arrived in Germany. There were no air raid shelters in this little village and, with the exception of occasional bomber formations passing far overhead, we were far removed from the constant fear experienced in the cities.

One morning on the way to the fields I came upon a strange and unfamiliar sight. Scattered at random throughout the wheat stubble were countless twisted strips of aluminum foil. We gazed in wonderment at the glistening strips as the wind made them flutter ominously.

"What are these strange things doing here? They must have been dropped from the air during the night!" I said.

Herr Neff replied: "We'd better not touch them; they could be poisonous!"

Carefully avoiding the strips, we continued walking toward our field for the day. As we came upon a neighbor in the process of replacing the sickle bar on his binder, *Herr* Neff asked him: "Herbert, did you see those funny looking metal strips back there? What do you think they're for?"

"What those Tommies won't think of next....my son told me about those foil strips last week when he was home on a weekend pass from the *Luftwaffe*. Our night fighters have really been knocking down a lot of British planes at night by using ground control radar. The enemy has apparently invented a way to confuse the radar operators with this metal foil and they drop the stuff all over the place."

"Is it alright to touch the stuff? It won't explode or burn or poison us?"

"No, it won't hurt you; it's just plain old aluminum. In fact, my son told me that the *Hitler Jugend* is collecting the stuff in the cities, putting it in bundles and turning it in for metal reclamation."

My cheeks became plump and my muscles brawny as my three-week task came close to an end. One afternoon *Herr* Neff said: "Jochen, your father said that you are a crack shot with a rifle and want to become a hunter someday; is that right?"

"Yes sir, *Herr* Neff, I belong to a marksman's club in Kaiserslautern and practice every week. I also hunted in America and brought home several rabbits and squirrels. Why do you ask?"

"I noticed some fresh wild boar tracks at the base of the hill this morning right near the mirabellen orchard. The pigs are having a field day gorging themselves on the fallen fruit and pretty soon they'll be coming over into my potato field. Do you have the guts to shoot one of them for me?"

"Sure, Ill try it; what kind of a gun can I borrow?"

"I don't have a rifle.....you'll have to use my 12-gauge shotgun with slugs. If you're brave and patient you can pick a spot right beyond the stone fence. You should get a good shot at one just at dusk. Want to give it a try?"

"Yes, I'd like to kill a boar; my dad would surely be proud of me! What'll I do if I get one?"

"Make sure he's dead and then gut him right away. When you're done, come to the farmhouse to get me. We'll then take a horse and wagon to pick up the carcass!"

What a challenge for a 16 year old who had never before killed anything larger than a rabbit!

Wolfing down quick supper of smoked ham, boiled potatoes and sour milk I carefully took *Herr* Neff's double-barreled twelve gauge shotgun down from its rack, pocketed the five slug shells which my mentor handed me and headed off toward the orchard.

It was almost two miles to the base of the hill where the orchard began but it was a pleasant walk in the evening sunset. As I took my first stand under a large oak tree my nerves calmed down a little and I settled in for the wait.

Before long a large bunny came hopping along, stopping occasionally to munch a bright green cloverleaf or two. He had just disappeared into the hedgerow that bordered the drainage creek when a pursuing red fox appeared. The fox stealthily loped a few yards, settled into a tense crouching position and then sneaked forward again after a few seconds. He was so intent on his prey that he passed within 5 yards of me. I sat motionless, heart pounding, shotgun at ready, but exercising the strict hunter's discipline my father had taught me. I can still hear him saying "When you're hunting big game, don't get tempted to mess up your entire hunt by shooting at little animals--you can shoot them another time!"

The same rule applied here; even though I had never bagged a fox, I was hunting for boar for the first time in my life and didn't want to settle for lesser game. The fox never knew how lucky he was as he sneaked into the hedgerow and disappeared in hot pursuit of his supper.

I settled down once more and again intently scanned the orchard right to left and then left to right, carefully holding my head almost motionless and letting the eyes sweep back and forth--the technique learned from my father while chipmunk hunting in New York State.

As the red sun slid closer and closer to the wooded horizon and the fruit tree shadows grew longer and longer. As a slight chill crept into the air I wondered how much shooting light remained. The words of the framed prayer above my father's easy chair flashed briefly before my eyes *"Dear God, please let me shoot clean and kill clean.....but if I can't kill clean, please, Lord, let me miss clean!"*

As the shadows under the mirabellen trees changed from light gray to dark gray I began to worry. What if one of those big boars was already feeding and I couldn't see him? Maybe I should get a little closer! No, my movements might just frighten away a nice boar just approaching the orchard from uphill......but what if it gets too dark to shoot and I haven't seen one yet?

As I was debating what to do or not to do, the images of bushes, stumps and rocks in the old orchard became fuzzier and fuzzier.....almost too dark to shoot.....it's now or never!

Stealthily I sneaked toward the stone fence that bordered the orchard, carefully placing one foot in front of the other in soft, Indian style steps. I had just stepped over the piled-up stones when I heard a loud crashing in the brush ahead of me. In the semi-darkness a large black animal came crunching toward me with lightning speed. Forgetting all the rules of marksmanship, sportsmanship and shooting light, I whipped the shotgun to my cheek, took a quick and sloppy bead on the oncoming monster and pulled the trigger. The boar, by this time only about 20 yards away, reared slightly but kept coming in my direction, finally veered just enough to avoid running into me and disappeared into the bushes, snorting loudly all the way.

When my heart stopped pounding I assessed the situation. If I had hit the boar, I should go look for him now and finish him off. If I wasted all that time in getting *Herr* Neff to help me it would be pitch dark and impossible to find him. However, if I went into the orchard alone I might stumble upon the wounded animal and be attacked....I had heard many stories about sharp boar tusks ripping open a dog's belly or a tree-climbing hunter's leg! Sensibly I cocked my ear and listened intently for about 10 minutes as the final curtain of blackness settled over the orchard.....end of hunt for the day!

Returning to the farmhouse with my report, I hung my head a little when *Herr* Neff gently chided me for shooting with insufficient light. He ended the conversation with "This will be a good lesson for next time.....remember, a good hunter has to exhibit the utmost discipline to retain his standing as true sportsman!"

Early the next morning the farmer and I went to the orchard but found no blood or other trace of the charging boar; it just wasn't his time.....nor mine!.

Two days later it was time to say good-bye. The main purpose of my three-week career as a farm hand, which was to fill my hungry stomach, had been well achieved. Eggs, meat, butter, unlimited bread and potatoes were all like a dream come true. At the time our official rations were not very sufficient for a growing and active teenager! My temporary gluttonous lifestyle would not be without consequences, though. In addition to all the rich staple foods I also gorged myself on the delicious French fruit *mirabelle*. Shortly before my term as a hired hand ended, I noticed some small, ugly looking open sores on both of my legs. By the time I got home the infection spread, covering about 80% of my legs below the knees and including my ankles. The doctor's diagnosis was "too much rich food and fruit acids in your blood".....nothing could be done except to wear bandages to absorb the high volume of pus that drained out constantly.....Oh well, it was still worth it to have a full stomach for 3 weeks!

During these times of ever-diminishing food supplies it became more and more important for all of us to find "something extra" to eat. Memories of the runaway inflation after World War I promoted bartering which prevailed as the only safe way of trade. Mutti, who worked as a bank teller during that period, described the instability of the times: "We used to get paid twice a day; at lunch time and just before we went home. The value of the Reichsmark sometimes fell 50% in one day, so we hurriedly made purchases during our lunch break as the cost of an item could double by quitting time. I remember once buying a pair of shoes for 27 million Reichsmark."

The farmers and food vendors really made out well in these times. Oil paintings, exquisite porcelain figurines, Persian rugs and grand pianos changed hands regularly and the happy city dwellers went home with bushels of potatoes, bags of flour and even a smoked ham or two. Scrimping, saving and hoarding became daily habits.....nobody knew how much worse things would get.

My father once made a deal for 50 pounds of dried peas, which I was sent to pick up about 60 miles away. It took me a whole day traveling by rail and changing trains 3 times each way! By the time I got home I was exhausted but happy.....now we would have many servings of substantial and filling split pea soup!

Another time I went to pick up a large basket of mirabellen on my bike, which I transported by train part of the way. This trip took about 16 hours and ended up with my bike luggage carrier bent badly out of shape as the fruit was so heavy. Again, the trip was well worthwhile, as Mutti processed the fruit immediately and put up many jars of delicious mirabellen jam to make our dry dark bread more palatable.

We left no stone unturned when there was even the remotest possibility of procuring some extra food. One day word spread about town like wildfire.....there was a bumper crop of wild blueberries ripening in the forest near Neustadt. It was quickly decided that I should go on a "blueberry excursion" and try my luck. Early the next morning I departed for the rail station on my bike, armed with a tin can and a large basket. As I arrived at the train to put my bicycle on the baggage car I was not alone. Scores of people converged upon the train with their buckets and baskets and with the same idea in mind: stocking up on some free berries! After the 30-kilometer trip we all grabbed our bikes and followed the crowd to a hilly wooded area about 6 kilometers west of Neustadt. Pushing our bikes up the last steep hill, we came upon hundreds of like-minded people laboriously moving from bush to bush, greedily stripping the blueberries into containers. Unfortunately, by the time I had reached the area it was late forenoon and the pickings were already mighty slim, working against hundreds of competitors, some of who had been picking berries since daybreak. My entire take was less than five pounds for a whole day expedition, but it was still an enjoyable supplement to our meager and bland diet at the time.

A growling stomach can prompt a hungry teenager to do some strange things. One day, walking home from glider flying, I pulled up a large sugar beet from a farmer's field, cut off the stalk and scraped off the dirt with my dagger and devoured the entire funny-tasting beet.....better than nothing!

These were indeed hard times, but we still managed to enjoy life and have a little fun. It seems that hardships can be tolerated more easily if all your friends are in the same boat.....we all had ill-fitting and worn shoes, patched bicycle tires, socks that were darned dozens of times and constantly growling stomachs! When we saw a queue of people, we would join the line without hesitation as we knew that there would be something valuable for sale.....a portion of fish paste not covered by ration coupons, maybe some flashlight batteries or some darning thread; it was always a nice surprise for us and for our mothers as we brought the booty home.

The Hitler Youth had always emphasized pre-military training as an important part of their program. As the war became more serious and the need for replacement troops increased, the infantry-type exercises took place more often and became very realistic.

Here is an example of our "War Games" that took place Several times during the summer of 1943. During the summer vacation, a Hitler Youth *Unterbann*[1] consisting of three or four

Gefolgschaften[2] of 13 to 15 year old Hitler Youths were assembled in the town square. We all had our packs, blankets, mess kits and canteens and were ready for a weekend of fun and competition.

We marched through town in perfect cadence, with drums rolling and trumpets blaring. Every 3 or 4 kilometers the leaders gave us a short break. We flopped into the roadside grass, gulped down some water and took a short breather. Soon our leader bellowed: "FAAAALL IN, you slowpokes.....let's get moving!"

We struggled to our feet, groaning in protest but eager to comply and not let the other troops get too far ahead of us.

By late afternoon we reached the little village which the leaders had pointed out to us on the map. Nestled in a valley divided by a small winding stream, the hamlet was a typical farm community. The small village square, featuring the ever-present fountain and ringed by a bakery, a butcher shop and a *Gaststube*, became the center of activities. The leaders set up a temporary command post on one of the massive stone benches bordering the fountain and the fun began.

First of all we needed accommodations. The *Unterbannführer* sent three of his *Gefolgschaft* leaders scurrying from to the nearest farmhouses asking permission for us to be quartered in the barns for the night. Nobody refused and soon we had all dropped our packs in our assigned barns and scurried back to the square. Carrying only canteens, knives and compasses we assembled for the briefing. First we were split in half and identifying armbands were issued: blue was for the home team and red was for the enemy. The reds were sent out immediately to plan their attack on the village while we with the blue armbands were left to plan our defense

After the enemy had disappeared from view we took our positions in an orchard to the East of the village. Our leader

---

[1] Organization comprised of around 600 Hitler Youths

[2] Group of about 150 youths

methodically placed us along the orchard perimeter; some of the youths scrunched down behind the ancient and overgrown stone wall whereas the others were placed in the tall grass which was growing around the fruit trees. We carefully applied camouflage to each other. The stone wall fellows stuck branches from the bushes and weeds growing out of the wall into their hats and uniform epaulets while those hiding in the grass applied vegetation to match their surroundings.

Now the waiting game began: Low pitched remarks were bandied about the orchard..... "What direction would they come from? Would they send scouts or would the whole gang descend upon us all at once? Who would spot whom first?"

The *Scharführer* broke in from his position with an angry and rasping whisper:

"Alright, you guys, PIPE DOWN! What do you think this is, a little girl's tea party? They probably don't expect us to be right in this orchard, so let's shut up and surprise them!"

Surely enough, in a short time we saw the first "Red", sneaking in a semi-crouch along the drainage ditch alongside of the orchard. Hardly daring to breathe, we waited motionless until he had passed. Pretty soon, two more Hitler Youths came following. They had almost passed the orchard when one of the partners let out a muffled cough. The rearmost enemy blurted out the challenge "Who goes there?" When no immediate reply came forth, he quickly removed a dummy "Potato-masher" type hand grenade from his belt and hurled it over the stone all into the orchard.

"Time out" shouted the referee. "Everybody gather 'round for critique. I'm giving the Blues three points for good concealment but two demerits for that damn cough. The Reds get one point for that grenade throwing; you were right on target and would have eliminated five or six men under real combat conditions."

"You scouts are now neutralized; we'll wait for your comrades to show up and see if they also miss this orchard position."

With this type of action the afternoon moved rapidly on. During the numerous critique pauses we kept absorbing hints and techniques on handling real life infantry combat situations.

After a practice session of hand grenade throwing in the orchard and a camouflage lecture conducted by one of their leaders, we marched back toward the village. At the last curve in the road we came upon a rippling stream flowing though the forest. Without hesitation the *Scharführer* bellowed:

"Alright you guys, time out for a swim! Be sure you line up your clothes piles in perfect rows; any piles that are out of line will be thrown into the water before you know it!"

In very short order we undressed and stacked our uniforms, underwear and shoes and socks as we'd been directed and plunged into the cool water, naked as jaybirds. What a refreshing break this was after a day playing infantrymen in the hot sun! The whistle blew and the fun was over; since we had no towels with us, we struggled into our uniforms and assembled as ordered. In perfect step we crossed the little bridge leading to the village and broke into a favorite marching song *Erika*.

During our war games in the orchard a field kitchen and attending Hitler Youths had pulled into the village square. We marched into the square and were dismissed to get our mess kits from our respective haylofts. Scrambling back to the steaming field kitchen it was "first come, first served". A delicious lentil soup awaited us; very little meat, but as much soup and dark bread as we could put away.

We couldn't believe it, but the leaders gave us a break after supper.

"Boys, you're free to roam around the village for the next hour. We'll assemble here in the square at 20:00 sharp for the briefing for the night orientation march. Don't pester the farm girls too much and get back here on time."

There wasn't much to see in the small village and we weren't hungry enough yet to pay the bakery a visit. There were only a few girls to our large number of boys, so they really enjoyed our stares and humorous catcalls. It was all in fun and ended as we heard the assembly whistles blowing at the fountain.

We split into four large groups, each having a leader and a topo-map. Each group was assigned a target destination in a different direction, the object of the exercise being to find our way in complete darkness by map and compass. We took turns taking the lead position of our column, plotting our course to the target and taking frequent compass bearings on close-by waypoints as we progressed toward our objective. Only the column leaders were allowed to have flashlights; everyone else followed blindly, often holding on to the belt of the boy in front of you. When my turn came to hold the compass and lead the group my first attempt was a dismal failure. We were right in the bowels of the dark forest and the luminous dial of the marching compass was barely visible. As I looked down upon the swinging needle and then raised my head slightly to take aim on a landmark the entire compass faded into an indistinguishable blur.

"Look here, Volmar.....let me show you how this is done" said the *Scharführer*, taking the compass out of my hand.

"Don't try to look down upon the compass, but raise the instrument almost to eye level and then hunch over the compass like this! Now you can see the needle as well as the objective at the same time."

Surely enough, when I followed his advice things fell into shape easily and I was able to direct our movement to a tree about 100 meters ahead. Over hill and dale we worked our way following a straight compass reading. Fording a stream and sloshing through a small swamp we finally reached our destination, a road intersection about 3 kilometers from the village. Apparently our leaders were happy as they let us march home by way of the road, our wet shoes squishing on the asphalt but our voices belting out the last song of the day.

Arriving at our assigned barn, we stripped off our shoes and socks, hung them neatly on the loft beams and crawled into the warm hay. Sleep came immediately after a day filled with physical challenges and feelings of tasks well done!

It seemed that at this time in my life physical fitness and conditioning were primary goals. No sooner had we returned from the "War Games" late on a Sunday night then I arose early the next morning to perform my daily early ritual. We lived at the edge of a hilly pinewoods which opened up into a spacious meadow about 500 yards from our quadplex. Each morning I would put on my black running shorts and "training shoes", a soft running shoe with absolutely no support, resembling a dance slipper. Grabbing my dummy grenade (*every* young boy owned one) I burst out of the house and up the hill at top speed. Rather than move forward in a straight line, however, I would zigzag around the pine trees and clumps of bushes on my way up the hill. Every once in a while I would suddenly choose a bush target. imagining that it was an enemy machine gun nest, hurl the grenade and dive for cover. After 15 or 20 minutes of this I had worked up a good sweat as well as a coating of sand and pine needles clinging to my body.

After a quick shower and a breakfast of rye bread with *ersatz* jelly and a cup of *ersatz* coffee I was on my way, pedaling my trusty bike with patched tires and tubes. I would either head for one of the local swimming holes or to the gun club or to the glider field.....it was always go-go-go! Boredom was an unknown word in my vocabulary.

It was during this summer of 1943 that I was "discovered" by a leader of a Hitler Youth .22 Caliber Rifle Sharpshooter Team. After he had watched me shoot quite well in one of the local matches he approached me and said:

"So your name is Volmar, eh? How come I've never seen you shoot before? You're not bad. Where did you learn to shoot?"

"Yes sir, *Scharführer*, I learned to shoot as a small boy in America; then I joined the *Kaiserslautern Schützenverein* when I moved here. I just love to shoot!"

The *Scharführer* then said: "How would you like to join the *Gau Saarpfalz*[1] Sharpshooter Team? We practice at least once a week and have a lot of fun. Besides that, all of us are pretty good and have a chance at the German National Championships in Innsbruck this Fall. How about it, Volmar?"

Excited and thrilled with a puffed-up ego, I hurried home to ask my parents' permission.

After pushing my battered bike the last 200 yards up the hill to our building, I panted to my mother who met me at the door: "Mutti, I have a wonderful opportunity: they have asked me to join the *Gau Saarpfalz* Rifle Team. Is it OK with you?"

---

[1] Political region of Saar Palatinate

Mutti replied: "Jochen, you keep coming up with more and more things to do; don't you ever want to slow down? On second thought, when I was young I was always active in many things--maybe you come by it honestly. Since your school grades have been pretty good lately I don't see why we shouldn't let you join the team. Your father won't be home until the week-end but I'm sure he'll say yes, since you're following in his footsteps as a marksman."

Delighted with this new challenge, I immediately pedaled to tell my gun club instructor *Herr Sieffert* the good news. He was very proud of me and wished me the best of luck.

For the rest of this summer, I didn't miss a single practice session, either at the club or at the Hitler Youth firing range. I ended up consistently shooting a score of 190 to 194 out of a possible 200. Our invitation to the National Competition was assured and all of us on the team could hardly wait to go to Innsbruck in the Fall.

8

It was October 1943.....I had finally skipped a grade in High School, after two and a half years of tutoring and cramming. The subject matter I had to catch up on almost overwhelmed me..... architectural concepts of Eastern European churches in the sixteenth century, the life history of Johann Sebastian Bach, translation into German of the Latin *"Marcus Aurelius"* and, would you believe, the fundamentals of atomic energy and nuclear fission !

At this time I was sixteen years old and in the sixth grade (equivalent to the tenth grade or sophomore year in a U.S. High School). One day at the end of our last class, we were each given a sealed, official-looking envelope to take home to our parents. Anxiously I pedaled home at top speed on my battered bike. When my mother opened the letter, she turned as white as a sheet !.

"What does it say, *Mutti*?"

She said: "There is an important meeting at the school this Friday, and all parents are required to attend. It's a little vague, but it has something to do with the students' contribution to the war effort. What are we going to do now? You're much to young to be going into the Army or anything like that; I'd be worried sick about you !"

"Don't worry, *Mutti*, they probably want us to clean up air-raid rubble during our lunch hour or after school, or maybe they want us to collect some of that tinfoil the American bombers have been dropping all over.....that'll be fun !"

When Friday came around, the school gymnasium was packed with parents and students of the upper three classes. Without much ado, the school principal introduced a young officer who wore a blue uniform with the unmistakable collar insignia of silver wings on crimson background denoting the *Flak* or anti-aircraft branch of the German *Luftwaffe*.

"Parents and students" he began, "my name is *Leutnant*[1] Scheller and I have come here today to bestow a great honor upon you boys. Since the *Luftwaffe* Flak divisions are spread out halfway around the world from France to Italy to the Balkans, along the entire Russian front all the way to Scandinavia as well as all over the *Vaterland* for the defense of our home cities, we are quite understaffed. Our great *Führer* has just instituted a new program which will allow certain high school boys and girls to participate in this important struggle and therefore will enable our regular *Flak* personnel to be moved up to the front lines, where they are sorely needed."

"You will all report to the Kaiserslautern train station at 7:00 o'clock next Wednesday, October 6th; all you will need is a small bag with underwear, socks and your toilet articles. We will take care of everything else!"

Many of the mothers started sobbing; the few fathers who were present shook their heads in disbelief :

"What is this world coming to, when they start taking fifteen year old kids to fight a war?"

To us, of course, this meant another exciting adventure; to be away from home together with all your classmates and to be able to wear a special uniform, no less, and to be called *Luftwaffenhelfer*[2] .....WOW !

It seemed like an eternity, but Wednesday finally arrived. The *Flak Leutnant* was waiting for us at the railroad station. A light fog was drifting across the tracks, making the officer look like an arising ghost in his blue-gray leather greatcoat with its huge collar turned up to ward off the early morning chill. Most of us arrived quite early and formed class clusters, just as we used to in the schoolyard. There were

---

[1] Lieutenant
[2] Air Force Helper

76 of us milling nervously around on the platform, awaiting our destiny.

Suddenly a shrill whistle blast pierced the air surrounding the misty rail-yard.....

"Everybody assemble in front of me in three columns; face the train tracks, shut up and hurry up !"

The *Leutnant* then barked: "Alright, boys, you are henceforth considered to be men. You are under my military command and will be treated as soldiers, even though you haven't been officially sworn in yet. I require unconditional obedience and will punish the slightest infraction with an appropriate penalty.....All Abooooard !"

We quickly piled into the two reserved rail cars on the Ludwigshafen-Mannheim Express and off we went. The train chugged along for the hour and a half trip to Ludwigshafen with no problem; all of us were singing and laughing with gusto. To get across the Rhine River, however, was a different story. During an air raid the night before, the tracks leading to the river bridge had been completely torn up, their twisted remnants pointing skyward as if in defiance of their attackers. Bomb craters, piles of dusty rubble and a score of overturned railroad cars completed the devastation. Repair crews of German workers, Polish slave laborers and Russian P.O.W.-s were all over the place, digging, shoveling debris and repairing the rail beds and tracks. The Feldwebel in charge estimated that it would take at least six hours before a train could pass over the bridge. The *Leutnant* made a quick decision :

"Alright men, we'll start you out just like real soldiers; we'll march the rest of the way on foot !"

What a motley crew we were; some of us had rucksacks, some had suitcases and a few had only string wrapped cardboard boxes with personal items. We were directed to the main street leading toward the Rhine and were on our way! Seventy six boys (not really men), some short, some tall; some strong and athletic, some not so strong and more of the bookworm type, but all of us were in the same boat: we were on our way to do our part in defending the *Vaterland*. We didn't know where or when, but we were all in good spirits and eager to do our part.

We had all seen quite a bit of bomb damage in our hometown of Kaiserslautern, but what we marched through on this day was awesome. Ludwigshafen was a fair-sized city, especially since it was the headquarters of the famous *I.G.Farben* Company, one of the largest chemical firms in the world. The destruction was commensurate; we trudged on and on, past endless blocks of total ruin. Some of the damage was old with weeds sprouting out of the rubble heaps and some was so new that the stench of burned human flesh still permeated the air. Finally we reached the shrapnel-scarred bridge across the Rhine.

"We've made it half way, fellows; let's take a five minute break."

We broke ranks, dropped our bags and boxes and flopped down in the rubble beside the bridge approach.

We had just gotten comfortable when, all of a sudden, the afternoon peacefulness was interrupted by the eerie wail of dozens of air raid sirens. The large siren on the bridge tower next to us seemed to emit an especially ear-splitting shriek.

Even though we had grown quite accustomed to daily air raid sirens in our hometown, each time one of them started it's pulsating screech, my heart skipped a beat or two. What tragedy would this air raid bring ?

The *Leutnant* led us hurriedly off the bridge approach and down to the Rhine River bank. Here he soon found a sign *Luftschutzkeller*[1] above the basement entrance to a large river front café. We scrambled down the natural stone stairway and nobody tarried, as the ominous droning of hundreds of American aircraft engines had already filled the air.

We had barely settled down in the basement, most of us leaning back against the dank, moisture-laden stone walls, when the whole building started quaking with each loud bang.

"Don't worry, men; it's only our own *Flak* shooting at the enemy. You'll soon learn to tell the difference between bomb blasts and cannon fire !"

---

[1] Air Raid Shelter

After about forty-five minutes of these deafening anti-aircraft salvos, the firing finally subsided. Shortly thereafter there followed the relieving monotone of the "All Clear" siren.

"Everybody back outside, on the double!" the *Leutnant* shouted.

Up the stairs and up the hill we clambered through smoke and acrid cordite smell, back to the bridge again.

"Let's get a move on; we have almost an hour to make up!"barked the *Leutnant*.

This march across the Rhine River bridge marked the beginning of a new era in my life. At sixteen I was just transitioning into carefree and enterprising adolescence when we were all abruptly thrust into immediate adulthood. We were still kids but suddenly had the responsibilities, fears and challenges of grown-ups.

As we clomped over the cobblestone street leading eastward from the bridge toward downtown Mannheim we could see and smell the after-effects of the air raid. Black smoke plumes were billowing skyward from several locations. Fire-trucks with bells clanging and ambulances with their "Eeega---eeeega" horns kept crossing our path. The sick-sweet smell of burning flesh wafted through our ranks as we approached one of the smoking buildings and we could see rescue crews clawing at the tangled rubble in search of survivors.

Skirting around overturned vehicles and severed overhead power lines, which were dangling dangerously from splintered poles, we worked our way through the downtown area of Mannheim. After a while the suburbs appeared; some sections were in perfect order with row upon row of single family homes with their small gardens. Other sections were just decimated by continuous carpet-bombing where we would walk for blocks and blocks of solid rubble with not a single house left intact.

At last we were at our destination, the *Flak-Kaserne*[1] at Mannheim-Käfertal. This monstrous facility consisted of dozens and dozens of single story and multi-level buildings and housed the regional anti-aircraft operational command, training and maintenance facilities as well as medical and dental departments.

---

[1] Military compound assigned to Anti-Aircraft Forces

The main gate was guarded by a sentry clad in *Luftwaffe* blue-gray who smartly presented arms as the *Leutnant* led us into the compound. As soon as we passed, the sentry retired into his diagonally striped guard hut.

By this time we were pretty weary and were happy when we stopped in front of a two-story building marked with a new sign *Ausbildungsbatterie*[1].

As we approached the building we could see a muscular and fit-looking *Feldwebel* scurrying toward us. The *Leutnant* bellowed: "Everybody halt.....put down your baggage and pay attention."

"Boys, I want you to meet *Feldwebel* Beckerman. I am entrusting all of you in his care and for the next two weeks he'll be your teacher, your father and mother and, if you pay attention, he might even become your friend!"

The *Feldwebel* took over and in short order had given us room assignments and led us to the mess hall for a bread and lunchmeat supper. Nobody felt like doing anything thereafter since we were all dog-tired. Long before the "Lights Out" whistle sounded all of us had crawled onto our straw mattresses, covered up with clean gray Luftwaffe blankets and were off to sleep.

The next morning all hell broke loose. We were rousted out to the sound of blasting whistles and screeching noncoms at 06:45.

As customary while being introduced to the German military, a certain amount of hazing and exaggerated dressing-down was the order of the day. Not only of this day, but of 14 full days crammed with accelerated and strenuous basic training. One of the *Unteroffiziere*[2] made the remark that it was intended to give us a normal eight-week basic training session in only two weeks. Within a few days we found out that they weren't fooling.....we were kept hopping from dawn to dusk and even after dark. They needed us badly to staff a newly organized battery and were going to transform 76 snot-nosed students into acceptable *Flak* soldiers at any cost.

The fiasco began at reveille: "Alright, you spoiled, lazy high school students.....get your butts out of the sack and get your faces

---

[1] Training Battery
[2] Rank equivalent to U.S. Sergeant

washed! You have exactly 15 minutes to get washed and dressed, to make up your bunks and assemble in front of the barracks."

We were accustomed to an occaisonal dressing-down by some of our sharp-tongued Hitler Youth leaders, but we were to find out that none of them could hold a candle to these *Flak* basic training specialists.

Constant name-calling, ridiculing and goading became the order of the day. We were never allowed to walk, but were commanded to trot in double time from one location to the next.

The first stop was the mess hall. The food turned out to be very substantial and far more plentiful than we had enjoyed at home. Dark bread in unlimited quantities, margarine for every slice, good quality jams and smoked lunchmeat were always on the table. The noon meal always included hot soup or stew or a hearty combination of meat, potatoes and gravy.

After breakfast we were broken down into groups of ten and sent through a whole day's sequence of induction. Medical exam, inoculations, outfitting which consisted of a specially designed *Luftwaffenhelfer* uniform. The color and texture of the woolen garments were identical to the regular *Flak* garb, but cut and insignia were radically different and included a swastika armband to identify us as "non-soldiers".

Along with our new heavy woolen uniforms, we were issued the traditional long underwear worn by all German military personnel during all seasons. This not only kept us warm but also afforded some protection against the abrasive action of the coarse woolen fabric of the outer garments.

On one of my shuttles between offices and supply rooms I stopped at the Battery Headquarters with a request. I was referred to one of the noncoms and asked him: *"Herr Unteroffizier,* I'm a member of the *Gau Saarpfalz* Rifle Team and we're scheduled to go to Innsbruck for the National matches next week. Whom do I see to get a few days' leave so I can participate?"

"Young man, I can tell you right now that your chances are practically nil of leaving this place for ANYTHING! This is a special accelerated training program for *Luftwaffenhelfer* and you can't afford to miss even a single day. I'll ask the *Leutnant* later, but don't get your hopes up. If there's any hope at all I'll get back to you; if you don't hear from me by tonight you might as well kiss Innsbruck good-bye."

With shoes too large, a helmet too small and disappointment in my heart, I ended up in my room to put my gear away. The rooms housed eight men and contained 4 bunk beds, four double lockers and a large table for eating and studying.

A major change for us was in footwear. The German military shoe was either a heavy jackboot or a heavy, laced work shoe. In our case we were fitted with work shoes and short puttees to protect our trousers. The shoes had substantial soles, steel heel and toe plates and the entire soles were covered with large-headed steel hobnails. We didn't mind the loud clacking caused by the hobnails (it surely made our presence obvious wherever we went) but we had to get used to their slipperiness, especially on concrete or terrazzo floors. During the first few days it seemed that every few minutes we would see a classmate trotting smartly down the hallway and all of a sudden slip, lose his balance and go gyrating down the hall like a drunken ice-skater until he regained his balance.

On our third day at the *Kaserne* I became a perfect example of a clumsy recruit getting used to the military. My gums had developed a painful infection, which became more and more aggravated, especially with all the extra physical activity on the parade ground. I signed up for sick call and was directed to the Dental Dispensary. Arriving at the spotlessly polished waiting room, I clicked my heels together and drew up my right arm with a snappy prescribed Nazi salute.....would you believe, the waxed floor and my eager emphasis was too much for my sense of balance and my hobnailed shoes just slid out from under me. Red-faced and embarrassed I took a seat amid the amused snickering of a half-dozen or so regular *Flak* soldiers.

My embarrassment soon gave way to extreme agony, as my turn came and the dentist stuffed silver nitrate swabs between my infected teeth----Owwwwwww!

One morning at the end of our Aircraft Identification class my friend Friedhard asked the *Unteroffizier* instructor: *"Herr Unteroffizier,* when do we start learning how the *flak* cannons operate?"

He replied: "There will be no gunnery training at all while you're here at *Käfertal*. This is strictly basic training; you'll be taught how to operate the guns when you get to your assigned batteries. Besides, we wouldn't know which cannons to train you on until we know where they're going to send you. We don't have assignments yet and don't know if you'll be on 20 or 37 millimeter or even on 88-s or 105-s. You probably won't be on searchlights or listening apparatus as those will be staffed mostly by your colleagues from the girls' high schools."

It seemed that each time we went to our rooms for a few minutes to put something away or just to sit down for a moment, a shrill whistle would blow in the hallway followed by a bellowed command such as :

"Everybody get out on the parade ground for close order drill.....on the double!" or "Everybody grab your helmets and gas masks.....Air Raid in progress!" We were certainly not bored and were kept running, working and singing all day long.

Membership in the Hitler Youth had brought with it a certain amount of drilling and marching but *nothing* had prepared us for the ordeals on the *Flak* parade ground! At least three times daily we were herded at double-time onto the damp October grass and underwent constant running, marching, changing direction, slamming ourselves into the grass on frequent "Take Coverrrrr!" commands, all of these tortures interspersed with constant abuse.

Remarks such as "Get a move on, you Heini! Do you think the Tommies move that slowly?" or "What kind of an *About Face* do you think that was, you rampaging whiskbroom?" were all part of the curriculum. A twist of humor was always present when considering the form of address used by the noncoms. In the German language there are two basic forms of address in the verbal as well as the written. Family and close friends are addressed with "*Du*" meaning "you". All others are referred to very formally with "*Sie*" which would be translated as "thou".

You can imagine a remark like: "Volmar, thou art the biggest asshole ever.....can't thou get that gas mask on a little quicker? The Tommies won't be nearly as patient as I am!"

In spite of the constant dressing-down and the "never satisfied-with-anything" attitude of the instructors, nobody seemed to mind. The *Unteroffiziere* were old hands at this and cleverly imparted a sense of humor and a spirit of challenge into the program that kept our morale and fighting spirit in tip-top shape in spite of sore muscles and blisters on our feet.

In addition to the popular and well-practiced soldiers' marching songs we already knew from the Hitler Youth, we learned a brand new ditty, which had just been composed by some clever *Flak* musician.

The German military, like all militaries, I suppose, had a penchant for naming all campaigns, projects, programs and the like with code names. Since this habit is universal the world over, it must have its purpose in helping all the participants sort out their thoughts, supplies, bullets and people!. In any case, a new night fighting program against the ever-increasing numbers of British night bombers had been organized. It was dubbed *"Die Wilde Sau"*[1] and consisted of using free-lance night fighters working in conjunction with the usual anti-aircraft coverage of major targets. These pilots operated without the assistance of ground controllers and would hover above a city lit up by searchlights and burning buildings to identify the bomber silhouettes and then attack from above.

The words to the new song went something like this, although much of the feeling and rhyme is lost in translation.

The *Flakhelfer* of The Wild Boar
The heavens are just filled with boars,
And the weather is nice and blue for shooting -
Yes, the Tommy will pay dearly
'Cause alert is the Wild Boar.
As the language of our cannons
Is not friendly but brutal.
We'll pull them out of the sky
'Cause alert is the Wild Boar.
And when you hear booming and banging
You'll know exactly that

---

[1] The Wild Boar

It's the Flak-helpers
of the Wild Boar!

With high spirits and full stomachs we sped through our basic training. In addition to the physical aspects, we received a good sampling of German military thoroughness. Twice daily we attended classroom lectures in Luftwaffe organization, anti-aircraft ballistics and fusing procedures as well as aircraft recognition and basic night-fighter tactics of the *Wild Boar* system.

On the first day each of us was given our own personal aircraft recognition booklet. The *Feldwebel* who conducted the class announced:

"Pay attention, *Luftwaffenhelfer*! These booklets are probably the most important part of your training as Flak personnel. Split-second and proper identification of an aircraft can often mean the difference between life and death for you or for one of our brave pilots. I want you to carry these booklets in your breast pockets at all times. Whenever you have a few minutes to spare, take out the book and practice, practice and practice again. We have a contest at the end of your stay here to see who's the best."

The books had a double page devoted to each aircraft in use at the time: German, Italian, British, American, and Russian. The left page displayed a photograph as well as a detailed description including power plants, crew, armament, bomb capacity and variations of models. The right page had three silhouettes--top view, side view and front view.

In conjunction with these booklets the instructors had a projector capable of displaying either the silhouette page or, as we became more proficient, they would show just a front view or side view to test our sharpness and speed. On the last day at *Mannheim-Käfertal* we were given the ultimate test. The *Feldwebel* flashed a sequence of aircraft on the screen, each plane being visible for only a few seconds. We had to remain silent and write our answers down on a test sheet. When our grades were determined we had all passed but some were shown that a little more study was in order. Those of us with backgrounds in the *Flieger*[1] Hitler Youth did pretty well, as we brought considerable prior knowledge of aircraft with us.

During our stay at *Käfertal* our sessions were interrupted a number of times by daytime air raids. This meant quitting our present activity immediately and stumbling downstairs into a basement shelter. After a half-hour or so the *Flak* detonations would cease and the "All Clear" sirens would summon us back upstairs.

One such raid occurred on October 14th, 1943 and I remember well the *Unteroffozier* reporting: "They went to Schweinfurt again today.....there's been a hell of an air battle going on. Those Flying Fortresses up there must be on their way home!"

Incidents such as these air raids may have interrupted our training but in no way did they sidetrack our trainers from their objective, which was to indoctrinate us with German military protocol. Our first Saturday morning was the best example yet. Right after breakfast the *Unteroffizier* in charge of our section announced:

"This morning we're going to show you guys how a soldier keeps his quarters clean. Remember yesterday when there was all this snickering on the parade ground and I said that you'd pay dearly tomorrow? Well, tomorrow has come!"

"We're going to show you how to do a nice cleaning job on your rooms.....doors, windows, lockers, floors and all. The only difference is that we can't find the floor brushes today so you'll have to use toothbrushes that we saved from the last gang of recruits that was here."

He wasn't kidding; after we did the regular cleaning and dusting they actually made us brush the whole damn floor of our room with toothbrushes!

The climax of the cleaning session was the inspection conducted by the *Leutnant*; when he entered our room, we snapped to erect attention and had the privilege of watching him as he deliberately and carefully slid his white-gloved fingers across locker doors, window sills and even bed frames, Unbelievably we passed with flying colors and were allowed to roam about the *Kaserne* for a few hours without any assignments.....what a treat!

---

[1] Aviation Hitler Youth

Time flew by with all the activity that went on and before we realized it, our two weeks were up. Our group of 76 was assembled together with several other groups that had trained at the same time. With helmets on straight and backs erect we listened to the Major in charge of the school give us a pep talk sending us off into a world of danger and uncertainty. Emotionally, we repeated the major's words of commitment to *Führer and Vaterland*. The sun was hot, collars tight and emotions high so that five of our comrades collapsed during the swearing-in ceremony. Was this a sign of things to come?

Back to our rooms we went to pack our new gear into our new rucksacks. We couldn't believe our eyes and ears as the *Feldwebel* and his assistants wandered from room to room to shake hands and wish us all well. What chameleons.....these guys just spent 14 days tormenting us and now they're our friends.... an example of military bonding, I guess!

9

The return trip was a treat compared to our arrival. The tracks had all been restored into working order and the trains were operating more or less normally. Clutching four-day passes in our hands and strutting smartly in our new blue-gray uniforms, we split up at the Kaiserslautern railroad station. Dragging my new rucksack aboard the local bus I was surprised but happy to see one of my teammates from the rifle team.

"Hello, Helmut; I'm glad to see you. How did you guys make out in Innsbruck?"

"You won't believe this, Jochen, but we came in second for our category. Your substitute shot a 184 in the finals. With your habit of scoring in the 190-s all the time, I'm sure we would have made first place, since the winners beat us by only 5 points. Can you imagine that, we almost made national champions!"

"Damn, if those stupid *Flak* people had only let me go.....oh well, I guess it wasn't meant to be!"

I left the bus with my bulky rucksack and clomped up the hill to our house. What a treat it would be to have four whole days to myself with no whistles and shouting governing every move I made!

This episode in my life with the *Flak* was to be a very memorable one. Besides leaving home and its comforts at the early age of 16, the transition from carefree teenager to a responsible adult soldier was abrupt and emotionally very taxing. The whole experience was amplified since Germany's position in her worldwide struggle was becoming quite tenuous.

During my two year stay in the *Vaterland,* Hitler's forces had attacked the Russian Bear, reached the outskirts of Moscow and then had been pushed halfway back to Germany's borders again. The suicidal siege and German surrender at Stalingrad emphasized the deteriorating situation. The same happened in Africa.....after almost reaching Alexandria, British counter-attacks and the American Operation *Torch* had succeeded in driving the *Afrika Korps* all the way to the Italian mainland.

With German troops in such a spread-out combat area, it was no wonder that almost everyone we knew or talked with had lost one or more family members somewhere on land, sea or in the air. In spite of the admitted setbacks all over, morale was still quite good at this time. The general attitude was still "We'll win this battle against overwhelming odds after all!"

There were, however, some moments of doubt and temporary morale deterioration. The British night raids were becoming more frequent and the American daylight flights showed increased numbers of B-17-s and B-24-s. Stories of horrible civilian casualty counts in Cologne, Hamburg and Berlin upset us all. Fortunately, up to this time, there had been no serious raids directed at Kaiserslautern. Almost nightly the sirens alerted us to take cover while hundreds of droned overhead, on the way to Mannheim or Ludwigshafen. Each time, when the "All Clear" sounded, we thanked our lucky stars that we were spared once again.

In this atmosphere we proceeded to report for active duty as *Luftwaffenhelfer* on October 21st after four days of doing nothing except strutting around town in our new uniforms.

What luck, our first battery assignment was right in Kaiserslautern, We reported bright and early to *Hauptman* Hartman, who was awaiting our arrival at the *Pfaff* sewing machine works on the West end of town.

"Welcome to the *Flak* world, boys! I am *Hauptman* Hartman, commander of a battery of 37-millimeter anti-aircraft guns. The battery consists of 4 platoons, each having three guns. Our job is to protect the *Pfaff* factory as well as the *Reichsbahnausbesserungswerk*[1] against low-flying enemy aircraft. We are assigning six *Luftwaffenhelfer* to each gun. There will be a regular *Flakgefreiter*[2] in command of each gun and you will have *Unteroffiziere* in charge of the platoons. Each platoon will also have a specially trained range-finder operator. Your training on the guns begins tomorrow after you're settled in your new barracks. Next week your schoolteachers will resume classes for you each morning; that will leave the afternoons for gun drill and evenings for homework. Good Luck!"

It was only about two kilometers from the factory to our railroad workshop. This was a large, fenced-in compound housing numerous gigantic buildings, large enough to accommodate steam locomotives. Right near the main gate we marched by a unique air-raid shelter, the likes of which none of us had seen before. Poured out of massive reinforced concrete, it was shaped like an upside down bomb with its point directed skywards to divert any direct hits. The entrance was protected by concrete bulkheads and consisted of two sets of rubber-gasketed steel doors. From there on the stairs lead up to the multiple leveled rooms inside. As we found out later we never got to use this nice shelter as we were always ready at the guns during all air raids. The shelter was occupied by the German and slave labor workers of the repair shop.

We passed the gigantic turntable designed to turn the locomotives around when necessary. More shops, a classroom building and even a swimming pool.....would we still be around next summer to dive in?

At last we could see our new home; adjacent to three newly excavated gun positions was a brand new single story wooden barracks. Next door was a freshly painted 12 hole outhouse. Since there was no plumbing here, we had to use the washrooms and shower in one of the shop buildings.

Immediately behind our barracks was a barbed-wire fence separating us from the slave labor barracks, housing a large number of Russian men and women, who had been conscripted to work in the repair shop rebuilding and reconditioning rail cars and engines that had

---

[1] Government Railroad Reconditioning Works
[2] Flak Corporal

broken down from normal wear and tear. At this point as the Allied air raids were increasing in intensity and frequency, there was more and more equipment damage from bomb shrapnel hits and overturning caused by bomb concussion blasts. As time went on, much more damage was caused by the deadly 50 caliber machine guns that spouted destruction from the P-47s, P-38s and P-51s which were streaking back and forth over the German countryside.

The poor slave laborers lived in a crowded barracks similar to ours but much more tightly packed. They always looked dirty and unkempt in their quilted clothing. The food they received was not much different than ours except they may have received a little less meat and more cabbage. In those days the primary military noon meal was generally a stew consisting of a little meat, some potatoes and lots of cabbage or turnips.....not very tasty but it satisfied the pangs of hunger for a little while, anyway.

Arriving at the new barracks, we were called to attention by our new platoon leader, who announced:

"My name is *Unteroffizier* Petzold. Welcome to the Fourth Platoon of the 7th Light *Flak* Battery! I've been instructed to train you fellows as soon as possible on these 37-millimeter guns. They're captured Russian weapons but they're quite serviceable and will bring down an enemy plane *if you learn to operate them correctly!*"

"Starting Monday, you'll be attending regular high school classes in the Main Building. Your teachers will be going to a lot of trouble pedaling from your old school in the city all the way out here on their bicycles. This is their way of contributing to the war effort, so take their program seriously!"

"Every day after the noon meal, we'll be having gun drill, weapons cleaning and other little military tasks, like brushing up on your aircraft identification. You'll also be assigned to a guard duty schedule. One man stands at the observation binocular and the other stays in the orderly room to answer the telephone and sound the alarm when given from headquarters. Because you're so young and need your beauty sleep, the regular *flak* non-coms will take the graveyard watches from 2:00 AM to 6:00 AM. Unless, of course, there's a full alarm. In that case all of us stand at the guns until the "All Clear" is sounded!"

We were then divided into three groups, one for each of the sand-colored guns, which had already been placed in their pits, their menacing muzzles pointed skyward.

Sometime during the preceding week, our *flak* men had borrowed some of the slave laborers and had dug an excavation for each gun about five feet deep. The positions were then reinforced with old railroad ties to prevent the sand from caving in and to offer additional protection from bomb fragments or machine gun bullets.

There were two small dugouts connected to the main gun pit; one of which housed the steel cases of shiny and menacing 37-millimeter shells. The other dugout was somewhat larger and had a built-in bench along one wall. This was our primitive air raid shelter designed to afford a little protection for the gun crew against bomb blasts and falling shrapnel.

My assigned duty was that of loading gunner and I was to practice slamming in a clip of five 37-millimeter shells in a split second while already reaching for the next clip handed off to me by a comrade. At last we were in business.....as soon as we learned how to shoot these cannons, let the Tommy and Ami beware!

Our daily routine as *flak* helpers began bright and early at 6:00 A.M., regardless of how much sleep we were able to catch the night before. At first it was an interesting new challenge but after a few weeks boredom set in and we started complaining. Up at six, wash up and brush your teeth in the factory wash room (a few of us occasionally had to shave off some peach fuzz), make the bunks, sweep the room and off to the mess hall. Breakfast consisted of dark bread, *ersatz* jelly and *ersatz* coffee made from some sort of scorched grain (probably roasted floor sweepings from a bakery). Then came high school classes conducted by our regular teachers who had to interrupt their sessions at the downtown *Oberschule* and pedal their bikes three miles to our gun positions. I clearly remember our history teacher gamely puffing through the repair shop main gate in his *lederhosen*. The poor man was in his late sixties and had been called out of retirement due to the acute teacher shortage.

The shop itself was a grimy place with coal dust and diesel fuel permeating the air as well as everything of substance in the plant. The classroom seats and tables looked dingy and felt greasy to the touch with their dull coat of grime. The washroom fixtures, originally snowy white porcelain, looked gray and dirty after many years of exposure to their filthy environment.

However, there were brighter aspects to our location. In accordance with the Nazi philosophy of "taking care of the working man" a large swimming pool had been installed on the factory grounds, together with a one-meter and a three-meter diving board. During the summer months we spent most of our free time at this pool. Contests in diving, endurance and underwater swimming were everyday challenges. With the German military's penchant for training all of its troops how to swim, the flak non-coms even drilled us in water survival while wearing uniforms and boots.

As the year 1943 came to an end and winter progressed, the air attacks increased in frequency, intensity and in numbers of aircraft participating. A typical night in our lives of this time period would go something like this: It wasn't unusual for us to be called to the guns around 10:00 P.M. for an hour or so as the British Lancasters and Halifaxes thundered overhead toward their targets in Frankfurt or Kassel. After about an hour the "All Clear" sounded, allowing us to return to our barracks and hit the sack. Invariably, we had just warmed up in our straw filled bunks when the sirens wailed again, announcing the return flight of the invaders. We dragged ourselves back out to the frost-covered guns again to witness the Tommies overhead, engines throbbing in the cold winter sky. When we finally heard the last "All Clear" siren of the night, we trudged through the snow to our barracks-cold, weary and hungry. Each room had its own small cast-iron stove as a source of heat and limited cooking and coffee-making. Quickly one of us fanned the dormant fire while others cut some dark bread and placed the slices flat on the stovetop. Very soon the bread began to smoke; this was the signal for each of us to devour our allotted slice of hot toast. Even without a spread, the bread was savored by all of us as a welcome treat marking the end of an active night. No matter how little sleep we got, the reveille whistles blew promptly at 6:00 and our daytime lives went on.....wash your face, brush your teeth, make your bed, go to class, nod off to sleep in class, clean the guns, etc., etc.

Christmas in the *Flak* proved to be just as festive as usual. In spite of the ever-worsening food shortage, our mothers all managed, by hook or by crook, to supply each one of us with home made cookies, cakes and candy. Yes, the cookies were limited in numbers, the cakes all contained heavy doses of ground-up potato and the candy was usually a concoction made of dried cereals laced with a little cocoa and sweetened with saccharine; it didn't matter to us......it was *Christmas* and we were all alive to celebrate! Small live trees appeared in every room of the barracks, decorated with ornaments and candles pilfered from family supplies.

Unteroffizier Petzold divided us into three groups: one allowed to spend Christmas Eve at home with a 1:00 A.M. curfew, the second group went home Christmas morning for half a day and the remainder was allowed to be home that evening.

Since riding our bikes was quite difficult in the December ice and snow, we were constantly exploring new ways to get home in a hurry to take advantage of short passes. A few days before Christmas my friend Fritz Klein took me aside and said:

"Look, Jochen, as our homes are close to each other and we're both on leave Christmas Eve, let me tell you about a new trick I learned last week. A buddy of mine showed me this and it really works, plus it's a free and fast ride home! When we get out of this place Friday evening it'll be almost dark by the time we get to the bus stop down the street. The bus will pull up, pick up passengers and when it starts rolling we'll get a running start, grab onto the spare tire and jump up on the rear bumper for a free ride. It's a little scary at first, but once you get used to it, it's a breeze. I've done it twice already and haven't been caught yet. Of course you have to jump off just before every stop and jump on again when the bus starts rolling, but with a little practice you'll have no trouble."

"Sounds good, Fritz, but what happens if driver catches us?"

"I don't know, but he'll probably just give us a chewing out and let us go; everybody feels sorry for us young boys having to do a soldier's job, anyway!"

Christmas Eve came together with a few inches of new white snow. The stowaway idea worked quite well except for being completely covered with white powder churned up by the massive bus tires and *Mutti's* hand-wringing when I told her how I managed to get home so soon!

During my entire 12-month career in the flak, we only had a few brief close-range sightings of enemy aircraft. One of these remains indelible in my mind and it seems as if it took place just a week ago. During this cold winter of 1943-1944 we were out at the guns one morning around 2:00 A.M., scarves wrapped around our faces and steamy breath glistening in the bright moonlight. The sky was crystal clear and the full moon lit up the factory roofs and surrounding wooded landscape almost as if in broad daylight. Suddenly the dull rumbling sound of low flying aircraft engines called us to attention. All eyes focusing to the East were treated to the silhouette of a sleek DeHavilland Mosquito skimming at top speed just over the treetops. As fast as she had appeared, the plane vanished from our sight, leaving behind an eerie silence. We didn't realize it at the time, but that airplane was probably returning from an OSS drop of some sort deep into German territory. The Mosquito was a poor radar target anyway with her plywood construction and, combined with her high speed at treetop level made for a low risk return to England. The unannounced and fleeting appearance was naturally too brief for us to take any sort of aim at the speeding plane, let alone to get off any shots.

As the air raids, both night and daytime, intensified, our stamina and interest in school waned considerably. It was quite common for several of us to nod off during class, especially when boring subjects like calculus were covered. The teachers would chew us out as they normally would but one could detect compassion and understanding in their tone of voice.

One day my friend Friedhard said: "Guess what, Jochen, I met one of the Flight Instructors in town over the week-end. There's a "B" Badge soaring camp in the Lahr Valley in March; why don't you see if you can get time off to go?"

"Man, it would sure be nice to catch up with you guys since I quit gliding when I had all that studying to do last year. I'll ask *Unteroffizier* Petzold what the chances are to get a leave for flight training purposes."

Our *Unteroffizier* had a small office next to the orderly room. After lunch the next day, I knocked briskly on the door and was greeted with a gruff *"Herein!"*[1]

As I stepped into the room and raised my arm straight in a snappy salute, I was greeted with:

"What is it you want, Volmar? You'd better make it quick; I was just about to blow the whistle for gun drill!"

"Herr Unteroffizier, I may have a chance to attend a one week glider camp next month. I want to be a fighter pilot and they won't even consider taking us unless we have substantial glider training. Do you think I could get a week's leave for this purpose?"

"I'm not sure, Volmar; it sounds like a good reason to me, but I don't know if there are provisions for such cases. I'll ask the *Hauptman* and let you know."

Two days later, as we were in our gun pit cleaning and oiling the gun, Petzold walked our way and said:

"You fellows seem to be doing a good job. Be sure you don't miss even the tiniest area with those oil rags. These cold February nights produce a heavy layer of hoarfrost which turns to water the minute the sun has been out a little while. Incidentally, Volmar, the *Hauptman* says he can issue you leave papers for your glider school as long as it's for the cause of the *Reich*. Bring me a completed request form with purpose and dates shown and I'll send it over to battery headquarters."

Delighted with my good prospects, I wangled a three-hour pass and took the bus into town. At our old *Flieger* Hitler Youth Headquarters I approached the *Scharführer*.

"I understand there's a "B" Badge camp coming up in March; is there still room for me, *Scharführer?*"

"Well, what do you know.....I thought you had quit the flying game on us. I haven't seen you in over a year. What have you been doing?"

"I really hated to quit after getting my "A" badge, but my Dad told me I had to in order to catch up on school work. You'll remember that I came from America in 1941 and they put me back three years.

---

[1] Come in

Last year I had a bunch of tutoring and really cracked the books and they let me complete two school years in one. Man, am I glad that's over! Now I can go back to flying again."

"Well, Volmar, you're in luck. There's still room in the "B" camp at Lahr Dinglingen in the Black Forest. I'll fill out a request form so that you can apply for a leave."

Snapping a smart Nazi salute, I turned briskly on my hob-nailed heels and marched toward the bus stop, grinning all the way.

A few weeks later my leave was approved and I began planning my return to glider flying. Would I still remember how to keep those wings level? What would the instructors be like? What kind of chow would they have? We had always heard that flight schools always offered above average rations to the students; time would tell!

The typical early spring arrived with the sun climbing higher over the horizon each day and its pleasant warmth even penetrating and thawing out our gun pits.

With the increased intensity of air raids, both night and day, traveling became hit and miss as far as arrival times went. For the trip of around 95 miles it took an entire day, as the schedule was interrupted at midday in Karlsruhe by a formation of Liberators heading inland with their cargo of destruction. By the time the "All Clear" was sounded, the only train available for me to ride on was a "local" which stopped at every little hamlet along the way. I finally arrived at the school at 10:00 PM after trudging over 3 miles from the rail station. The *Unteroffizier* who came to the barracks door in reply to my knock said:

"You must be Volmar.... where in the hell have you been? We were wondering why you didn't show at 17:00 like the orders specified. How come you're so late?"

"Sorry, *Herr Unteroffizier*, my train was held up in Karlsruhe by an air raid. After the raid there were no express trains coming this way so I had to take a *Bummelzug*[1] the rest of the way."

"Alright then, find an empty bunk in the second big room over there and I'll see you in the morning. Reveille will be at 6:00!"

---

[1] Slang for slow local train

Awakening to the blast of whistles the next morning, I quickly oriented myself. We were the only occupants of an *Arbeitsdienst Lager*, which was not in use at the time. We marched about a half mile into the village of Hugsweier and received a pleasant surprise. Since the labor camp and its mess hall weren't in operation, the Luftwaffe had contracted with the local hotel-restaurant *Zur Krone* to feed the 24 hungry flight students. What a treat it was to enjoy delicious meals prepared professionally by the owner's wife! During our ten day stay we feasted upon such things as white bread and fresh eggs for breakfast, lentil soup teeming with chunks of real sausage and even an occasional piece of cheesecake, an item unheard of in our *Flak* kitchen.

There were two flight instructors, both were *Unteroffiziere* as well as seasoned combat pilots on temporary assignment to conduct this glider school. The practice field was set up close to the camp on a gradually sloping hill about a mile long. It didn't take very much of the brisk spring wind to keep us aloft while we glided all the way from the top of the hill to the very bottom.

The gliders were the same SG-38 model we were accustomed to; however, one of them had a semblance of a nacelle built around the pilot seat to afford some protection from the air stream of flight and to give slight aerodynamic improvement to the 8:1 glide ratio of these primary gliders. It even had a short Plexiglas windshield!

Flight training started at 7:30 every morning. After hauling the two gliders laboriously to the top of the hill, the first two students were selected to start. In spite of our previously earned "A" badges, we were really nothing more than rank beginners in this flying game. The seasoned instructors patiently reviewed the basic theories with us before sending us off down the hill.

The first student, helmet and goggles in place, climbed aboard the bulky craft, buckled his safety belt and was ready to go. First a gentle launch with only four boys at each end of the bungee "slingshot". When proper tension was attained the instructor bellowed "Looossssss" and the glider went careening downhill a short distance and then gracefully took to the air. The first launch of the day was always a thrill, especially since most of us hadn't flown for several months or even a year or so.

The first flights lasted about half a minute each. All of us would then jog downhill to load the gliders on the two wheel dollies with tow bars and laboriously push, pull and drag the ships back up the hill for the next launch.

After a morning's hard work the one-hour lunch break was most welcome. We lounged around, lying in the new spring grass and discussed our future plans and ambitions.

My new upper-bunkmate Karl asked me: "What are you going to do next, Jochen? I've signed up for the Luftwaffe flight-training program to take effect when I become 18."

"One of my classmates and I plan to sign up as officer candidates and simultaneous flight training. In fact, we're waiting for our orders to take the flight physical very soon. In the meantime, I'm going to attend every glider school I can; they say it's really helpful for your powered flight training."

The first few days went smoothly along with everyone getting one or two flights a day. Classroom sessions were sprinkled in between flight sessions and covered aerodynamics, meteorology as well as aircraft inspection and maintenance. I was soon in the swing of things again and my flying skills improved with each launch. The final goal was to fly a one-minute flight down the hill which was to include two perfectly executed "S" curves while doing so. It may not seem like a very long flight, but for 16-year-old kids flying solo it's quite an accomplishment!

Our morale was superb. On this launching hill we learned a new twist to bungee launching. As the instructor directed us to increase the bungee tension by running forward, we started chanting "Tzicke, tzahcke, hoy, hoy, hoy" over and over again, in time with our ever-increasing pace. As the bungee cord tightened and the glider suddenly popped into the air, we bellowed a loud and final "Hoy" as a farewell salute.

The instructors were very strict and particular of our performance but also displayed camaraderie, which we hadn't experienced before. It must be a characteristic of combat veterans: nerves like cold steel but yet compassionate and friendly, as they may depend upon their comrades to protect their lives someday.

One day in the middle of the afternoon, we watched as a typical spring thunderstorm appeared on the horizon.

"Hurry up and get these ships under cover, boys....we're done for the day. This baby's really going to blow!"

As we approached the hangar with the ships swaying in the already accelerating wind, one of the instructors said:

"Hey guys, let's stop for a minute; I want to show you something! Do you see the shape of that approaching cloud the way it's hugging the ground while in forward motion? Well, that's the typical appearance of the leading edge of a cold front. A couple of years ago I was flying at the Wasserkuppe when one of these fronts came along. I had them launch me right quick so that I could catch the rising warm air just ahead of the front. It was a little scary, but I managed to fly over 70 kilometers before I threw in the towel and landed at an airfield. The secret is to stay ahead of the front, flying back and forth to stay in the rising air and not let the front overtake you. It would be disastrous to get tangled up in the fast moving thunderstorm. You all know from your meteorology classes what velocities are attained inside a thunderstorm cloud!"

One by one, we passed the requirements for our "B" badges. On the last day, when everyone had completed their flights, we knocked off early, cleaned the gliders spotlessly, coiled the bungees and hung up all the gear. We were done!

Marching smartly and belting out a *Luftwaffe* song, we arrived at the *Krone* for our last evening meal. Exclamations of "Wow!" and "Oh boy!" were heard as the innkeeper's wife strode up to our table with a mammoth tray containing eight steins of foaming *Kriegsbier*[1]

"I know you guys aren't normally allowed to drink alcohol, but this is a special occasion; your "B" badge is the second big step toward becoming full fledged pilots. I want you to always remember this day. A beer or two won't hurt you, especially this *Kriegsbier*; it's about as weak as rainwater!"

A few beers, a few songs and our last really good meal for a while; we were now proud "B" badge pilots and in seventh heaven, feeling that there was no obstacle in life that we couldn't conquer!

---

[1] War beer, much weaker than the usual potent German beer

The next morning after hearty good-byes exchanged with fellow students and instructors, we proudly marched to the railroad station, singing all the way. After a pleasant ride home through the blossom filled countryside, I checked in at our *Flak* position and returned to the routine grind of guarding a factory with our popgun size cannons. What was coming next?

The dull routine of schoolwork and the endless waiting at the guns was soon livened up for me. One Sunday in May as I went home for a visit and some of Mutti's lovingly prepared cake, I found a letter waiting for me. It was from the General Command of the *Luftwaffe* and directed me to report to the Physical and Psychological Testing Center for Officer Candidates at Bad Blankenburg on May 30, 1944.

The next morning, somewhat bashful as usual, I knocked on the platoon leader's door and said: *"Herr Unteroffizier*, I hate to keep asking, but I need another leave, this time only for three days! The purpose is to take my Luftwaffe officer candidate physical. Can you arrange this for me please?"

"Volmar, you're spending more time away from the guns than you are staying here doing your share of the duties. I guess it's all right, though, since you'll soon be a full-fledged soldier. Why do all you students think you have to become officers? I had to earn my rank through years of service; you'll be a smart aleck *Leutnant* just by going to high school and taking some special officers training.....oh well, I guess the *Luftwaffe* needs officers too."

A week later I was on my way, marching orders in hand. The train ride, for once uninterrupted by air raids, took me eastwards and practically all the way across Germany. Chugging into the main station of the devastated city of Kassel, the train creaked and groaned as the cars made their way over the often repaired and still misaligned tracks. Piles of rubble and scorched roof timbers were everywhere and I was glad when we had passed through the city and the train picked up momentum. I thought to myself:

"I hope that Kaiserslautern never gets hit like this; they must have had a bunch of fatalities with all these raids!"
As the train clipped along, the scene gradually gave way to the beautiful foothills of the Harz mountains. Gently rolling farmland with countless small villages nestled between the bright green fields of

spring. It was late afternoon when we pulled into the station of Bad Blankenburg. A quick inquiry of the stationmaster as to location of the *Luftwaffe* testing center and I was on my way, marching briskly uphill on the cobblestone paved streets. Suddenly I spied an attractive blond girl about my age, walking resolutely but gracefully in my direction. Giving her a second look (probably more like a stare) I thought I detected a slight smile......I mused to myself:

"Now's your chance, Jochen! This is what you've been waiting for, and she smiled at me, so she surely won't ignore me if I speak to her."

Mustering all my courage, heart pounding, I crossed over to her side of the street.

"Hello, *Fräulein*[1], are you from this pretty town of Blankenburg?"

"Yes I am, *Luftwaffenhelfer*. Where are you from and what brings you here?"

"I'm from Kaiserslautern. I'm going to take my physical up at the *Luftwaffe* center. I sure like your pretty town. Yes, Bad Blankenburg is really a nice town! In fact, I don't think I've ever seen a better looking town!"

Tongue-tied from there on, I couldn't think of another thing to say.

"Well, I have to be on my way" she said, flashing a set of gleaming white teeth. So much for my first real attempt at picking up a pretty girl!

After stewing about my bashful and stupid behavior for a half mile or so, the girl was soon forgotten when I entered the *Luftwaffe* facility. The usual paperwork began when I entered the office and saluted. I was signed in, given a bed assignment for the night and issued a meal coupon. Meeting and chatting with fellow applicants made the evening pass quickly and I was soon fast asleep, in spite of worry about passing all the upcoming tests, both physical, mental and psychological.

The next morning after breakfast the procedures began. There were probably 30 applicants that day and one could tell these folks

---

[1] Form of address meaning "Miss"

were accustomed to the efficient handling of their daily charges. Everything went like clockwork; while one small group was being weighed another was in X-ray and a third bunch went to the centrifuge area to be tested for motion tolerance. The vision test was the most exhaustive I'd ever seen. They even locked us in a completely darkened room for more than half an hour to test our night vision capabilities. The array of medical tests took us well into the afternoon when the mental and psychological procedures began. With all of us sitting at tables in a regular classroom, dé-já vu thoughts swept over me..... "This is no different than school!"

The psychological part was unlike anything I had ever experienced. Sitting alone in front of an *Oberstabsarzt[1]* I was guided through a series of questions relating to my childhood, attitude toward my parents, achievements in school and glider flying experiences. When the subject of females came up, I blushed and told the psychiatrist about my bungled efforts of the previous day.

He chuckled and said:

"Volmar, I think you'll do alright; there's always another time, you know!"

This was the last procedure of the day and the doctor made notes in my folder and sent me on my way. In the anteroom, a female *Luftwaffe* clerk handed me my passbook, now containing the bold notation and ever-present rubber stamp proclaiming *"Bearer is a Fully Certified Officer Candidate Qualified for Flying and Para-troop Duty"*. I had completed another important step in my aviation career!

The return trip to Kaiserslautern was uneventful, except for a one hour delay due to an air raid alarm enroute. The train screeched to a halt during the night, somewhere out in the country in the midst of freshly planted fields. We dismounted to listen and watch as a formation of British bombers droned overhead, their engines out of sync as was customary, to increase the psychological terror-effect on the populace. The planes droned on and soon the nerve-racking engine noise subsided. As we listened to the monotone wailing "All Clear" emitted from sirens in a distant village, the steam engine slowly gained momentum and we were once more on our way.

---

[1] Rank of Major with medical specialty

Returning to my assignment at the repair plant, I resigned myself to a renewed routine of boredom in the classroom and at the guns. Little did any of us know that our world was soon to undergo some drastic changes!

10

Dawn presented itself with a gloomy overcast and gray sky on the 6th of June, 1944........ it looked as if another boring day was ahead of us. We were sitting around the table in the center of our bunkroom sipping the last dregs of our *ersatz* coffee to wash down the ever-shrinking portions of rye bread. Suddenly the shrill and penetrating sound of military whistles sounded throughout the hall of our barracks.

"*Alarrrrrmm. alarrrrrmm!!!!*.....Man your guns immediately! Let's get those babies uncovered and ready to fire right away. There's been an invasion in France! Be on the lookout for paratroopers and balloons!"

Grabbing gas masks and helmets, we rushed into our gun pits and prepared for the worst. Silence prevailed while we took turns manning the tripod mounted giant binoculars, scanning the western sky for any signs of aircraft.

As the morning progressed we were periodically updated by *Unteroffizier* Petzold. Reports kept us up on developments, such as:

"The allies have landed a huge invasion force on the beaches of Normandy. A general named Eisenhower is in command. Allied losses are heavy and our troops are tenaciously holding onto the fortifications of our *Atlantikwall*.[1]"

---

[1] Atlantic Wall-pertaining to all German fortifications on the west coast of Europe

Taking turns as gun "lookouts", we conscientiously scanned the skies to the West, expecting aerial activity to start any minute. Hour by hour slipped by, but nothing happened. Late in the afternoon we were finally allowed to stand down and return to the barracks.

Petzold addressed us again, "It looks as if all the activity is at the *Atlantikwall* right now, but nobody knows for sure what to expect. For the time being, all leaves are canceled and there will be no school for you fellows. I'll let you know as soon as I hear about any new developments from Battery Headquarters. In the meantime, be ready for quick alerts and let's all listen to the radio and follow the action."

Hearing the "no school" announcement, we all broke into a cheer as we headed for our rooms to tune in the radios.

Roommate Fritz remarked: "I wonder who this fellow Eisenhower is; sounds like he's of German origin."

Somebody replied: "He must have something on the ball as he's the general who led the landing in Morocco. We had better watch out; these Americans have untold supplies of men and material. My brother-in-law was in the Afrika Corps and told me that they send tons and tons of shells and bombs before they attack and it's really hell to be against such a force."

For the first few days, the newscasts kept stating that the allies were being held back in fierce fighting near the beaches, one could soon tell that the landing had been successful and a firm foothold had been established. Soon remarks of "strategic withdrawals" were heard and we could foresee trouble ahead.

After a week, our routine returned to normal and school activities were resumed. There was a gradual change in conditions, however. Before the invasion, we occasionally would see a few American fighter-bombers on low-level attacks. From now on, week by week, there were more and more of these guys flying missions into the German heartland. Addition of belly tanks for extra fuel extended their range considerably and gave these devils even more time to make our lives miserable. They were nicknamed "*Jabos*", from Jagd-Bomber (fighter-bombers) and eventually made daytime travel in western Germany a high-risk affair, whether by rail, air or highway.

Even though we never had a direct attack on our position and never had any low level flights close enough to fire on them with our limited range 37 millimeter guns, the fighters eventually made daytime travel by rail or by motor vehicle quite hazardous. Train trips normally taking two hours might take as long as four or five hours with emergency stops along the way as the train crew waited for the sky to clear.

The most common plane used was the P-47 Thunderbolt with an occasional flight of P-51 Mustangs thrown in. These guys were not only well trained, but also had a lot of daredevil in them. Example: A few miles from Kaiserslautern there were railroad tracks laid in a deep gorge, cut into a hill which contained a tunnel to accommodate the tracks. One day, two P-47-s came skimming down the tracks, flew into the gorge and pulled up sharply just before the tunnel entrance, each aircraft releasing a 500 pound bomb. Both of the bombs were catapulted several hundred feet along the tracks into the tunnel. Luckily they were both duds and were later removed by a demolition crew, but *what an example of flying skill and daring!*

Not all the *Jabo* activities were completely honorable, though. An incident comes to mind wherein some young ice skaters were given the scare of their lives when an American fighter raked the group with 50 calibers as they were peacefully skating on a pond near Kaiserslautern.....*c'est la guerre*!

The time soon came during the summer of 1944 when we couldn't look outside at any time of day without seeing or hearing at least half a dozen of these fighter-bombers cruising around looking for targets. Together with the ever-increasing formations of high-level bombers, our lives became more and more interrupted and endangered.

The pilots were really quite expert at their trade. When stalking a train, the first plane would peel out of the formation and concentrate his fire on the locomotive. With the engine disabled and grinding to a stop, steam pouring out of countless holes in the boiler, the train was now an easy target for the other fighters. One by one, they would swoop down in single file, their 50 calibers raking the remaining length of the train.

Under these conditions it didn't take long for our repair shop to overflow with damaged locomotives and rail cars. We inspected the new arrivals on an almost daily basis and were astounded at the penetrating power of the American .50 caliber machine gun ammunition. Even some of the solid steel sectors of the steam engine driving wheels were riddled with holes all the way through the massive metal.

On June 13th we heard the radio broadcasting one of Adolph Hitler's many emotional speeches; this one had an especially vindictive tone and went something like this:

"My German countrymen, today we are introducing the first of a series of brand-new weapons. They will be called "V" weapons, representing our *"Vergeltung"*[1]. At this very moment a revolutionary flying bomb called the V-1 has been launched with London as its target. Hundreds more will follow and serve to bring our English enemies to their knees!"

The next week's newsreel showed a launching of a V-1 and its ominous chattering as it disappeared into the sky over the English Channel. Would these new weapons change the course of the war, which hadn't been going our way at all?

It was soon time for me to attend another soaring camp; there was no argument in giving me a leave this time. With the increased aerial activity and the odds leaning more and more in favor of the allies, we all knew that the Luftwaffe would be in great need of replacement pilots.

A few days later my friend Friedhard and I took a bus to the rail station and we were soon on the way to another adventure. Hoisting our blue rucksacks into the overhead baggage rack, we settled down for the train ride to Alsace Loraine where the glider school was located.

"This course should really be quite a thrill, don't you think, Jochen? We'll finally be advancing from the clumsy old *SG-38* to something with a little more class" Friedhard commented.

"You're so right, my friend. I think we'll be flying the Grunau Baby at Sennheim. That's really a neat ship and has a glide ratio of around 17:1; we'll finally be able to stay in the air a while" I replied.

Arriving at the small town later that day we were directed to the airfield by the stationmaster. Trudging down the country road a

---

[1] Reprisal

mile or so we soon heard an unaccustomed sound. Listening carefully, we could soon discern the putt-putt growl of a diesel engine that suddenly accelerated to a high-speed chatter. At the same time a snow-white glider shot upward into the blue sky at a steep angle. It traveled in a gentle arc and when it reached its apex, the glider suddenly veered to one side and flew smoothly out of our view. Now we could see a small parachute at the end of a cable slowly descending to the ground.

"Wow, look at that baby go!" Friedhard said. "We are going to have a *prima*[1] good time."

"You're right; I can hardly wait to fly like that. I wonder if it'll be a little scary compared to the bungee launches we're accustomed to?"

As we arrived at the airfield we were checked in by the Hitler Youth on duty and directed to the adjacent sleeping quarters.

"What in the world are these?" I remarked as we entered the main bunkroom.

I was referring to the three-decker bunks that were literally jammed into the moderately sized room. We had always been accustomed to double bunks and had never seen the likes of these triple contraptions, let alone climb up into the bed on top, which seemed to be practically touching the ceiling.

Most of the bunks were already taken by new students who had arrived ahead of us, so I ended up with the first-hand experience of sleeping in the upper bunk. It's a good thing I've always had a strong bladder! Having to descend out of the top bunk half asleep and in total darkness would have been quite an experience!

At 6:00 A.M. the next morning a whistle blast began our day. There were no washrooms at the airport so we had to march into the village for our meals and facilities. After hurried face washing and a quick breakfast at the local *Gasthaus*[2] we marched singing back to the glider school ready to start our first long day at winch launching.

There were 24 of us, eagerly gathering around the shiny white two-place sailplane parked in front of the hangar. The instructor introduced himself:

---

[1] Super or prime
[2] Small hotel

"Students, my name is Eberhardt. You are going to spend ten days with us and I hope you will all be proudly wearing your "C" badges when you leave here. You'll find that winch launching is quite different from bungee starts and these gliders are a hell of a lot more sensitive than the SG-38 crates you're accustomed to. I want you all to pay close attention to everything my assistant and I are going to show you. A mistake at this advanced stage of the game can cost you broken bones or even your life! This glider is called the *Kranich*[1] and is ideal for training. For the first time in your flying careers, you will be riding with an instructor. This way we can hit you over the head every time you make a mistake! Now let's get on with it; everyone pay close attention while I inspect the aircraft and explain its features and instrumentation to you as I go along."

Eberhardt carefully examined the glider, inside and out and commented on each working part. Terms such as "spoilers" and "variometer" were new to us, so he went into great detail regarding their operation and theories thereof. An explanation of parachute use followed:

"I'm sure you all realize that we would never get our chutes open at the low altitudes we'll be flying here. The best you'll ever do in my school will be around 400 meters, as I won't let you take the time trying to find thermals. I want all 24 of you to leave here wearing your "C" badges, so we don't have any time to spare. You'll have a chance to play with thermals in your next school. However, from now on you'll be wearing a parachute at all times to get used to their feel. Don't try to bail out a low altitudes; you'll stand a better chance of staying with the glider and possibly doing something to correct your problem."

"You fellows will not believe the difference", Eberhardt continued, "in performance and handling of the *Kranich* compared to those boxy SG-38-s you're accustomed to. For example, the SG has a glide ratio of 8:1 and the *Kranich* is specified at 21:1, meaning that you will travel a distance of 21 meters for every meter of altitude! You will also notice a highly increased control sensitivity, so learn to handle the stick and rudder as if they were raw eggs."

---

[1] Crane

"Now let's get moving and get this baby into the air! The eight boys on my right, load this glider on the dolly and start moving over to the take-off area. The next four will take this yellow canvas landing cross and lay it down in the middle of the landing area. You'll be able to recognize last week's spot from the skid marks in the grass. The rest of you follow my helper to the winch. He'll show you how to carefully uncoil 1000 meters of the wire cable and drag it to the glider for hookup; then we'll be ready for the first start."

"The first student to fly with me will be Ackerman, as I'm taking you in alphabetical order until I get to know your abilities."

Ackerman, the guinea pig, strapped on his chute and climbed into the front cockpit. Eberhardt took his place in the rear seat and they both buckled their safety belts. The instructor closed the canopy and signaled that he was ready for takeoff. With one student holding the wing to keep the glider level, hand signals were given and we soon could hear the putt-putt of the winch as it started gobbling up the cable. In no time at all, the glider bounced down the runway and picked up speed. For a moment the right wing dipped as the student failed to exercise timely correction. The glider leveled off, gained more momentum and suddenly was airborne. The glistening white ship looked so majestic as it pointed its nose higher and higher into the sky. We could imagine Eberhardt coaching the student along:

"Better pull that stick deep into your belly, just like this, Ackerman, or we won't have enough altitude to fly a good field pattern!"

When the *Kranich* reached the top of the arc, it slowly leveled off and suddenly, with a short jerk, it was in free flight on its own. Flying a perfectly rectangular pattern around the glider field, the plane cleared the adjacent power lines and glided to a soft landing within a few feet of the landing cross. A crew had already started to retrieve the winch cable; the rest of us ran toward the aircraft in double time, lifted the ship on the two-wheeled dolly and started dragging it toward the takeoff area.

Thus was our routine from early morning until sundown: Drag the cable, launch the glider, drag the glider and drag the cable again.....walk a little, run a little, juggle the glider on the dolly and off the dolly again. A constant flow of organized activity coupled with the thrill of an occasional flight made the time pass quickly!

In the afternoon of the second day my turn in the *Kranich* finally came. With chute strapped, belts secured and canopy latched I gave the "Ready" signal. We always had a fair amount of adrenaline produced heart throbs on takeoff, but this was something else! The excitement of climbing into the sky at a steep angle with no earth in sight was exhilarating!.

"Remember those raw eggs, Volmar! Don't be so extreme in your corrections. Try to anticipate the glider's reaction a little sooner and you can get by with much finer movements, *verstehst Du*[1]*?*"

After a somewhat rough landing, Eberhardt took me up again. This time my control movements were much more delicate and he mumbled his approval. I made the necessary four 90-degree turns with fair precision and touched down quite a bit beyond the landing marker.

"Not bad, Volmar! You were a little late in getting your spoilers out; that's why you landed long. Next time put them out as you're crossing the power wires and play with them as needed to put you down right on the cross."

Toiling in the hot sun from 6:00 AM until 8:00 PM we had little time to get bored. Our spirits were high and enthusiasm was constant.

On the third morning as we marched from the village to the field, we could see the trees swaying in the wind, leaves upturned, giving them a whitish sheen. We pulled out the single seater and began our morning equipment check. Eberhardt scrutinized us with furrowed brow and said:

"It's pretty windy this morning, probably 15 or even 20 knots. Let me see whom we'll launch first. Volmar, you're pretty good..... want to try it alone today?"

"Yes, *Herr Fluglehrer*, I think I'm ready!"

The glider was a battered Grunau Baby, the most widely used glider in Germany at the time. It was nicely enclosed except for an open cockpit and even had a windscreen. Adjusting my parachute harness, I climbed into the glider, buckled up my seat belt and snapped

---

[1] Do you understand?

my goggles in place. The cable man approached the front of the glider and shouted:

"Ready for hook-up?"

"*Jawohl*[1] ready for hook-up!"

Engaging the release mechanism to secure the cable tow hook was my final chore before signaling for the take- off. As my wing runner picked up the right wing tip to prepare me for launching and to signal the winch operator that we were ready, my heart skipped a beat or two. I heard and felt a strange creaking noise as the gusty wind swirled around the wings of the sailplane. As the ship started sliding down the grass runway, all my thoughts concentrated on keeping the wings level and the aircraft on a straight heading. Suddenly we had acquired enough speed to fly and I gently pulled the stick backwards. Everything happened as planned and we rapidly gained momentum and altitude as well. I had lost all sight of anything on earth or even of the horizon and was on my way into the heavens.

Suddenly my world came apart at the seams; a torrent of sawdust and wood chips started streaming at my face from the inside of the front of the aircraft. The particles banged into my goggle lenses and some found their way into my mouth. I managed to hold the glider at the prescribed attitude, in spite of the gusty wind and my somewhat unnerved state of mind. The sawdust kept coming in erratic bursts as it was forced from its hiding places by the strong airstream entering the glider from the hole in the nose where the tow-hook mechanism was installed. Was I ever grateful when the sailplane reached the top of the launching arc and I was able to pull the release lever!

Still nervous, but settling down a little after recognizing the cause of my problem, I made a sharp turn to the right to begin my landing pattern. I quickly remembered that this sailplane had just returned from the repair shop after being involved in a crash; contrary to their normally meticulous habits, the mechanics had failed to clean out the sawdust and other debris remaining on the floor of the cockpit.

As I made my turn, the glider was suddenly seized by the strong headwind and I could see the earth slipping by at a tremendous

---

[1] Standardized reply meaning "Yes Sir"

clip. Now I became unnerved again; would I make it over the wires if I followed a normal, squared off landing pattern?

Without a moment's hesitation, I made another right turn, which was the beginning of my "great circle route" taking me back toward the landing area. With this abbreviation of flight, I had altitude to spare when I crossed over the wires at top speed, in a big hurry to get back on the ground. With this speed and completely forgetting that this sailplane had spoilers I approached the landing cross and banged the glider into the turf. The glider bounced up, I overcorrected and the glider hit again, and bounced upward another time. I landed this ship a total of four times on my first solo flight in a Grunau Baby..... what a performance!

As I sheepishly walked over to the instructor, he shouted, "Volmar, what kind of a circus show did you just put on? Did you go completely crazy up there? Didn't you remember a damn thing I told you about using those spoilers? You let a little wind completely unnerve you, that's all! I want you to review every minute of this flight for the rest of the week while your friends are earning their badges. When everybody is done, I just may give you another chance!"

Disappointed in my performance and worried about not getting a chance to redeem myself, I jogged, tugged and sweated as ground crew for the next few days. One by one, the other students made flight after flight, honing their skills for their badge flights. Soon all had earned their badges and the school was almost over. Finally, on the last day, Eberhardt beckoned to me and said:

"Well Volmar, I hope you've reviewed all of the mistakes you made on your "great circle flight" the other day. I'm giving you a chance to make good; get into that Grunau right now before I change my mind!"

I hurried to the glider waiting on the flight line, climbed in and was soon on my way skywards. When the glider attained the proper altitude, I confidently pulled the release lever and was on my way! Soon I made a smooth right turn, straight flight, right turn again, more straight flight down the entire length of the airfield, another turn with straight flight to my final turn.....all executed smoothly and accurately!

Clearing the wires with no problem, I slowly pulled out my spoilers and touched down properly close to the landing cross. Just before touchdown, I turned my head to the left where Eberhardt had positioned himself and quickly flashed him a confident grin as I sped past him.

With the remark, "Keep your damn eyes straight ahead when you're landing, Volmar! Let's not get overconfident now", the instructor let me make three more flights. They were all well executed and completed my requirements for the "C" badge.

After rolling up the winch cable and cleaning up the gliders, the instructor assembled us in front of the hangar. He said:

"You fellows are a pretty sharp group and you all earned your "C" badges in record time. I've already called ahead to the school at Saargemünd and made arrangements for the entire group to report there tomorrow morning. You will learn aero-tow methods there and will be able to earn your L-1 Glider Licenses. Heil Hitler and Good Luck!"

On our way to the train station Friedhard said:

"Do you know what Eberhardt wrote in his report? I happened to look over his shoulder while he was writing evaluations and he was working on yours as I was waiting. He wrote: *Flies well, but somewhat cocky!*"

The train ride to Saargemünd, normally a one-hour run, lasted more than two hours due to *Jabo* interruptions. Luckily our train wasn't attacked; we just stopped to cut off visible steam while the planes swooped by on the way to another target. Spared once more!

Departing from the train station with our rucksacks shouldered, we made our way to the glider field, which was about a twenty-minute walk from the town. After signing in and unpacking our essentials, we went on a tour of the facilities. A large hangar housed perhaps half a dozen sailplanes and two powerful looking bi-planes for towing purposes. A Hitler Youth in coveralls was working on one of the gliders with a paint sprayer. I asked him:

"Why are you messing up that sharp looking glider with green spray paint?"

He replied, "When you're soaring around up there tomorrow and a couple of *Ami* fighters come nosing around, you'll be damn glad for this camouflage. They shot down one of our gliders last week and the student wasn't able to bail out; what a mess that was, as the glider burned up on the way down. These green blotches really make us more difficult to spot, especially if the enemy is above you and you tend to blend in with the color of the vegetation.

Satisfied, we continued our tour. The sailplanes were just like those we had flown before; a *Kranich* and three *Grunau Babies* stood ready for our new group of flight students to give them a workout the next morning. However, over on one side of the main hangar was a glider we didn't recognize. As several of us clustered around the sleek looking craft emitting "Oooohs" and "Aaaahs", the spray painter walked over to our group and remarked:

"I'll bet you guys have never seen one of these babies before, have you? This is called a *Habicht*[1] and it was the first truly aerobatic sailplane in the world. Its glide ratio is the same as the *Kranich* but you should read the other statistics. During the original flight tests, they clocked speeds of 420 km per hour[2] during a diving flight. You should see them do loops and rolls with that ship; it's simply incredible! The craft was gull-winged with an open cockpit and sported tapered blue sunburst striping on the wings."

Friedhard exclaimed: "Wouldn't you want to fly one of those someday. Jochen? I can't imagine a greater thrill, can you?"

"I agree with you, Friedhard; I hope your dream comes true. Maybe they have an advanced school for aerobatics here that we could attend someday."

"Well, first things first; the very next step for us is to qualify for the L-1 Glider License and then get in some hours of practice."

The next morning an *Unteroffizier* named Hirsch assembled us in front of the hangar. He started out, "Boys, you are about to attend a crash course for your glider license. You've been sent to me because your past instructors think you've got what it takes. You'll have six days in which to qualify, so I want all of you to pay attention, follow my rules to the letter and show me the best of your flying abilities. We'll give you two or three flights in the two-seater to familiarize you with aero-towing and then you'll be on your own. Since there are 31 of you, your solo flights will be limited to 40 minutes so everybody gets enough flights and lots of practice being towed."

---

[1] Hawk
[2] 260 mph

Hirsch continued: "The first thing you'll notice is the increased sensitivity of the controls while on tow. Fly accordingly, try to anticipate the glider's movements and don't overcorrect! Should you hear the alarm sirens blowing in Saargemünd, don't panic but make every effort to get out of the sky as quickly as possible. They shot down one of our students last week so we want to take all the precautions we possibly can. Now, let's start flying!"

Other than being towed by a powered airplane, the routine was just like that of our prior classes: launch, land, retrieve.....launch, land and retrieve! These were exhausting but exhilarating days and we had no trouble at all falling asleep each night.

My first aero-tow with an instructor was an exciting experience. Since the tow pilot was also an instructor, all efforts were very coordinated. The powerful biplane towed us off the ground in a very short time and began a gradual but steady ascent. I soon learned to refine my control movements by anticipating the gliders actions, but it was still a tough chore to stay behind the tow ship at the correct level so as not to be blown about by the prop wash. When the towplane had reached the desired level of 1000 meters, the pilot waggled the wings in a very obvious fashion to indicate that it was time for the glider to release.

On the first two days of the course I made one dual flight each day with *Unteroffizier* Hirsch. Both flights were a thrill and I soon developed a feel for following the biplane. Each flight was climaxed with an introduction to thermalling in the beautiful summer skies of Alsace Lorraine. What fun it to lose altitude and then promptly regain it in the steady updraft of a thermal.

On the second flight a few minutes after our release, Hirsch said, "Alright, Volmar, you're getting the hang of it pretty well. Why don't you finish this flight all by yourself and just pretend that I'm not here. I won't touch any of the controls unless you really do something foolish; are you game?"

"*Jawohl, Herr Fluglehrer*, I think I can handle it. Do you want me to fly straight home or can I try to thermal a little?"

"Yes, you can thermal if you want; just don't get too far away from the field."

With great pride I took complete command of the aircraft and performed maneuvers of my own choosing. I did right turns, left turns, 360° circles, more turns and more circles until I suddenly felt the updraft of a thermal. Flying in ever steepening circles I flew just as the book said and started gaining altitude. As abruptly as it had started the air current let me go and I returned to level flight. Losing altitude again, I soon dropped to 300 meters and entered the landing pattern. I landed close to the landing cross with a slight grin on my face. The instructor said: "Alright, Volmar, you're ready to do it on your own in the *Grunau*. Tomorrow will be your day."

The next day dawned bright and sunny; we were having a lucky week as far as the weather was concerned. We launched several of my friends for their solo flights behind a powered aircraft and the excitement grew with every launch. Soon my name was called and I climbed into the Grunau Baby. The tow began and I started bobbing around a little, not accustomed to the lighter-weight single seater. After a few over-corrections I smoothed out my flying and we made a nice ascent to 1000 meters. Glancing at the altimeter I could hardly wait until release time. Finally I saw the biplane begin its rhythmic wing-rocking motion. I pulled the release lever with a sharp jerk and I was free! The feeling of joy and exhilaration of such a moment is almost impossible to describe with words. The towplane left the scene in a steep dive to the left and its loud engine noise faded rapidly. I was now alone with only the sound of air rushing across my windscreen and along the glider surfaces to keep me company!

After a twenty-minute flight during which I alternately did curves and circles and enjoyed the view of the pretty farm countryside below, I landed with my heart still racing in an adrenaline rush. This had to be the biggest thrill of a young boy's lifetime. Only sixteen and a full-fledged glider pilot.....WOW!

Two more days and two more flights brought me to the climax of my flying career. I had taken a flight during the forenoon, after which we were interrupted by an air-raid alarm in nearby Saargemünd. When the sirens wailed the "All Clear" we resumed operations. *Unteroffizier* Hirsch summoned me to the start area and said: "Volmar, this will be your last flight coming up. If you do as well as you have so far, I'll certify you for your L-1 License. Go on up there and give us a good show. Don't forget what I told you fellows yesterday; every thermal ends up in a cumulus cloud and some of those cumulus can get pretty wild. Whatever you do, don't get sucked up by one of those monsters as you'll get eaten alive. The sky has been quite active in the past few days; I think we're in for a thunderstorm soon, so watch out where you're flying!

"*Jawohl, Herr Fluglehrer*, I'll be careful! I don't think it would be much fun to fly in a cloud and not be able to see anything."

The launch and tow went well and I soon reached the 1000-meter goal and released. Relishing the pleasure of my last flight, I again kept looking at the earth, identifying the town of Saargemünd, the river flowing nearby and the lush fields of June sprawling across the countryside, interrupted by variegated patches of dark green woods. As I went through my routine of turns and circles, I descended slowly. Playing with a few short-lived thermals, I was somewhat disappointed that my last flight would be so brief. I was headed toward the glider field and had dropped to about 400 meters when I suddenly felt a rush of air. The *Grunau* swished upwards as I put her into a tight turn and began corkscrewing the glider upwards.

Higher and higher I went at an ever-increasing tempo. I gave out a loud "Hooray" and kept up with the steeply banked circles. Glancing at the variometer I could see a steady climb at 7 to 8 meters per second.....certainly the best I'd ever experienced! Soon my wristwatch showed that more than a half an hour had passed and I was still going up. The higher I went the higher the variometer readings became; when my altimeter showed 1200 meters I thought: "I must be getting close to cloud level!" At this time I was abruptly swept up by a terrific increase in air motion. My variometer needle pegged out at 15 meters per second equaling about 29 knots of upward motion! The "Hoorays" changed to "Oh-Ohs" as I encountered the first thin wisps of the cloud. "I'd better get out of this thermal fast before I get sucked into this cloud" I thought to myself.

Changing quickly to level flight, I tried to get out of the thermal to no avail; the vario kept a steady reading of 15 meters. What should I do now? Remembering prior instructions, I pulled at the spoiler lever and pointed the glider's nose earthwards. Picking up momentum, I gradually succeeded in exiting the area of tremendous lift and started losing altitude. "Whew, that was a close one" I thought, "but what an experience! The thrill of such an elevator ride is something I'll remember the rest of my life!"

My return to the field was without further incident and I landed after 46 minutes. Slightly perturbed at my overtime, Unteroffizier Hirsch broke into a broad grin when I told him of my terrific soaring experience. What a way to end a perfect soaring course!

My paternal *Grossmutter* Elizabeth Volmar, the family matriarch who bore seven children. She lost a son in World War I.

Grossvater, Sanitaetsrat Dr. Heinrich Volmar, the unquestioned head of the family.

My father *Fritz* in 1915 as the youngest sub-lieutenant in the Kaiser's Army.

My mother, *Mutti*, was a translator for the U.S. Army of Occupation after World War I.

My maternal *Grossmutter* Gertrude Kron bore seven children; one son was killed in World War I and another fell on the Russian Front during World War II.

Jochen, the farm baby, in Mayen, Germany, 1927. My parents had great difficulty making a living on this small farm in the Eifel Mountains and emigrated to the United States when I was three.

Tante Grete and *Onkel* Paul: she sent me a Nazi picture book and he later became my mentor.

Joe, the little immigrant, June 1930.

My first airplane ride (with a barnstormer) near Poughkeepsie, New York in 1934.

**On my favorite pony *Patsy*.......
November 1939.**

**Joe the farm boy.....
western New York
State around 1936.**

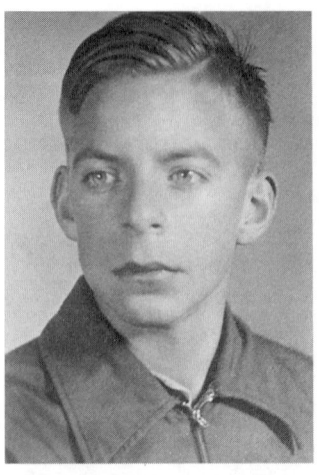

Now *Jochen* again in Germany, April 1941. As a ninth grade student in the U.S., I was placed in the sixth grade after testing for the *Oberschule*.

Onkel Paul, shown here as a Medical Officer, was my brother-like mentor for the rest of his life. I wore his hand-me-down clothes and used his briefcase as a bookbag.

My group preparing an SG-38 for launch. Glider training began early in our lives; I was 15 when this photo was taken.
(Photo: F. Huck Collection)

This primary glider was used to train students as young as fourteen and was launched by a bungee cord used like a giant slingshot. *(Photo-Oldtimer Segelflugclub)*

With his eyes fixed upon the horizon, the young pilot is awaiting the launch command with determination and apprehension. *(Photo-Ullstein Bilderdienst)*

Author shown with a SG-38 glider which was was modified with a nacelle to improve aerodynamics. It also provided a psychological advantage over the scary open model!

Toiling from dawn until sunset, we all managed to earn our "C" badges in one week. Author shown at glider school in Sennheim, Alsace-Lorraine *(now Cernay, France)*.

This coveted "C" Badge was awarded for completion of the first three stages of glider training.

As a *Luftwaffenhelfer*, I attended High School classes in the morning, engaged in gun-drill in the afternoon and stood guard against Allied bombers at night.

A group of *Luftwaffenhelfer* on a quiet day; the clown in the center went to a *Straflager* for falling asleep on guard duty. Author is the second from lower right.
(Photo: F. Huck Collection)

Classmate Friedhard Huck at super binoculars used to count enemy bombers.
(Photo : F. Huck Collection)

Our gun crew ready for action; author is the loading gunner standing.
(Photo: F. Huck Collection)

The author during the nerve-racking times of 1944. We had school in the morning, gun drill in the afternoon and watched allied bombers during most of the night.

Our group in a rare moment of relaxation and singing….author (center rear) had to mouth the words as he was (*and still is*) always "off key". Classmate Friedrich Schwarz front row, second from right.

A melancholy bunch during the Christmas Holidays – 1944. (Classmate Fritz Klein in back row smoking his pipe, author lower right). *(Photo: F. Klein Collection)*

Instruction flights in a two-seater were a rare luxury; this picture was taken after my first winch launch in a *Kranich*.

Reflecting upon my first solo flight in a *Grunau Baby II*, June 1944.

A view of the typical glider student crew, manhandling a *Grunau Baby* back to the launch site for the next training flight. *(Photo: Archiv Peter F. Selinger)*

Considered to be sleek and well-performing at the time, this *Grunau Baby* is taking off for another exciting flight. *(Photo: Archiv Peter F. Selinger)*

Apparently cold temperatures didn't dampen the enthusiasm of these Luftwaffe glider students ready to take off in their *Kranich* for some dual instruction.
(Photo: Archiv Peter F. Selinger)

Another *Kranich* winging its way over Germany's snow-covered landscape.
(Photo: Archiv Peter F. Selinger)

The aerobatic sailplane *Habicht* was cut down from a wingspan of 45 ft. to 20 ft. in order to mimic the flight characteristics of the Me-163 rocket fighter. *(Photo-Archiv Peter F Selinger)*.

A rifle with prismatic gunsight or sometimes a machine pistol was installed in the glider to train pilots in firing accuracy during diving attacks. *(Photo-Archiv-Peter F. Selinger)*.

The Me-163 *Komet* was a revolutionary rocket-propelled fighter, capable of 600 mph speed and could climb to 40,000 feet in three minutes. *(Photo-Eddie Creek Collection).*

Despite specially designed coveralls, the Me-163 pilot faced almost certain death should the *T-Stoff* rocket fuel leak into the cockpit area. *(Photo-Ron Downey Archives).*
I have often thanked my lucky stars that the war ended before I got this far!

The unique Me-163 took off with a removable undercarriage, which was discarded shortly after the launch. This procedure caused numerous accidents when performed prematurely, as the dolly bounced upwards, striking the rocket fighter and often causing crash landings. *Photo: Archiv M. Griehl, via Franz Selinger)*

Another shortcoming of the *Komet* was that it carried fuel for only 8 minutes, after which the pilot was forced to glide home becoming easy prey for enemy fighters waiting in the wings. *(Photo: Archiv M. Griehl via Franz Selinger)*

I traveled this 1900 mile route by train, boat, hitch-hiking and walking, starting on January 1st at Kaiserslautern and returning there on
June 10th, 1945.

This is what the city of Cologne still looked like in 1948, three years after the war ended!

Two survivors, *Mutti* and *Jochen*, about to embark on their return to the U.S. in 1951.

11

July 20, 1944..... a date I'll always remember! In retrospect, it was on this day that the first small chink was driven into my unquestioning Nazi ideology.

It was just after our noonday meal of black bread, pea soup with a microscopic portion of sausage and ersatz coffee that our *Unteroffizier* and platoon leader called us to an unscheduled and unexpected *Appell*[1]

Between piercing whistle blasts he bellowed "everybody *RAUS....RAUS*[2] and stand at attention. *Hauptman* Hartman is on the way over here for an inspection and wants to see everybody.....I mean EVERYBODY!"

We scurried out of our barracks and fell into line. "What's the *Hauptman* coming over here for?.....He hasn't bothered us in weeks." "Who knows, maybe just another pep-talk. Or maybe they're going to transfer us. The *Amis* have really been knocking the hell out of Mannheim lately....maybe they need us there!"

All conjectures were proven to be incorrect. With a drawn and serious face, the *Hauptman* had us stand at ease.

---

[1] Roll-call formation
[2] Outside, outside

"*Luftwaffenhelfer*, I have a very serious announcement to make. Yesterday a despicable and mutinous officer of the *Wehrmacht* attempted to assassinate our *Führer* at his Headquarters in East Prussia. Luckily Hitler was only slightly wounded and the traitor and his associates have been caught and executed. I will remind all of you that it is your absolute duty to report any of your comrades, superiors or subordinates who display even the slightest trace of disloyal or suspicious behavior! It has been decreed that from now on all military personnel in all branches of Deutschland's services will no longer use the regular military salute but will display the Nazi straight arm salute instead, just as the SS men have always done. This will be the symbol of emphasizing our continuing loyalty to the *Führer*!"

Our battery commander seemed sincere during the entire announcement, except when he talked of discontinuing the traditional military salute. Then he appeared to smirk a little, but no one was sure. Not until many years later did we find out that many hundreds of traditional German officers would have cheerfully announced Adolph Hitler's demise. In retrospect, *Hauptman* Hartman was very possibly gritting his teeth and wishing that Hitler had been killed, but was afraid of displaying his true thoughts.

At this time my feelings were still governed by youthful idealism, mis-information and innocence. I was dumbfounded that anybody would have enough treason in their soul to try to kill our *Führer*. I do remember, however, how the regular *Flak* personnel were all irked at having to give up the regular salute in favor of the Nazi straight-arm. The Luftwaffe was a military organization, steeped in German tradition, and should not be tainted with political propaganda symbols! That part made no difference to us, as we had always used the straight-arm salute as we weren't full fledged soldiers, only Hitler Youth auxiliaries.

Business went on as usual except for more frequent and larger flights of B-17's and B-24's overhead. We felt charmed, as none of them paid the slightest attention to Kaiserlautern and the 76 brave *Luftwaffenhelfer* guarding this city with their puny 37 millimeter anti-aircraft guns!

Our rangefinder operator was an older (20 or 21) likable pack of bones named *Werner* from the Wuppertal area, where one of my aunts lived at the time. It was his function to measure the distances of enemy aircraft and shout them loudly so they could be heard by the fire control gunners of our three guns. Since our range was a maximum of 10,000 feet with rapid trajectory deterioration, this distance measuring was crucial to our computations. All other functions were assigned to us *Luftwaffenhelfer*. Because of our youth (and probably because we fell asleep at the drop of a hat) the early morning guard duty assignments between 2:00 AM and 6:00 AM were handled by the regular Flak soldiers. An incident occurred not long after the attempt on Hitler's life, that added just a little more to my slowly developing doubts about the validity of Nazi doctrine. As time and the war progressed, I noticed more and more subtle conflicts between the true Nazis, such as Hitler Youth Leaders, SS leaders as well as their men and the genuine and traditional German officers and soldiers. The conflicts were subtle indeed, as there was always the prevalent fear of being reported as disloyal or politically undesirable and sent off to a KZ.

Early one foggy morning, after an all night alert, poor Werner fell asleep at his guard post. Discovered by the *Unteroffizier* who was relieving him, he was immediately placed under arrest and hustled off to battery headquarters. I couldn't believe that the platoon leader had turned the poor fellow in. With longer and longer nightly raids, we were all tired and took every opportunity we could for catnaps. Besides, we were deep inside Germany.....who would be sneaking up on a battery of captured Russian 37-mm guns manned by a few green *Luftwaffenhelfer*?

Regardless, our friend Werner was sent away to a *Straflager*[1] somewhere in Germany for 60 days. He was fortunate, as he could have been sent to a combat *Strafkompanie*[2] at the Russian front, with almost no hope of survival.

Two months passed quickly for us, but I am sure not for him. One Sunday morning Werner suddenly re-appeared. As he stepped into our barracks room, we hardly recognized him. Already a slender man before he was sentenced, he had been transformed into gaunt pack of bones with sunburned and parched skin stretched over

---

[1]Penal camp for military personnel
[2] Penal combat company

protruding cheekbones, resembling a starved cadaver. His hollow looking eyes no longer showed the sparkle of the wonderful sense of humor we had been accustomed to. With hardly a "hello" to any of us, Werner strode over to our food locker, tore open the door and grabbed a loaf of our military dark bread. With no knife immediately at hand, the man tore the loaf apart with his bare hands and began devouring the bread like a hungry animal. After letting him satisfy his immediate craving for food, we gave him a cup of coffee and gathered around him for a report.

"Fellows" he began, "don't ever do anything bad enough to get sent to one of those *Straflager*.....you won't believe some of the things that I'm going to tell you. It's beyond belief that fellow Germans could treat their countrymen in such a cruel and sadistic manner!"

Werner continued: "We had work details and close-order drill without stopping from six in the morning until eleven every night until we were ready to drop. The second day I was there, I picked up two green apples near our worksite to eat later at our barracks. The bastards searched me and found them.....! Three days in a lousy solitary cell with only moldy bread and a little water!"

He went on: "I wasn't out of that cell for more than a week and they threw me in again; they were looking for excuses so that they could break my spirit. This time, a fly landed on my nose while I was standing at attention during the noonday *Appell*. I tried very hard, but I after a while I couldn't control myself and twitched my nose to get rid of the fly. Naturally the *Feldwebel* saw it and screamed "throw that idiot in the hole again and teach him some discipline!"

The story went on and on while we sat around Werner wide-eyed in disbelief.

I thought to myself: "How can German people treat one of their own in such a cruel fashion? Granted he fell asleep at his post, but is that serious enough to warrant such cruelty? I wonder what they do to thieves and deserters.....probably shoot them on the spot without even a trial!"

My political speculations were soon overshadowed by more pressing and exiting daily events. As the summer progressed, so did the Allied air offensive against German cities. The *Tommies* came by night and the *Amis* made their overwhelming attacks during daylight.

One morning I was on duty at our oversized and high-powered tripod mounted binoculars. I counted assorted B-17-s and B-24-s passing directly overhead, droning steadily eastward, their engines purposely out of synchronization to accentuate their demoralizing effect on us.

I remember counting on and on and finally giving up at a tally of over 800 planes, with still more coming. What an eerie sight to see the tight formations droning on at 30,000 feet, their icy vapor trails tracing like ghostly chalkmarks across the clear blue sky. The whole scenario was very impersonal.....those *Schweinhunde*[1] on the way over to drop tons of bombs on one of our beautiful cities while we're helplessly looking on with our underpowered Flak guns.

I thought to myself: "Why don't you fly a little lower, so we can get a crack at you?"

Time and time again our luck held as the planes passed on to other targets; it just wasn't our turn yet. When the "All Clear" sirens sounded, we packed away our ammunition and gas masks, covered the gun sight and marched over to the dining hall for our trigonometry lesson, which would commence as soon as our gray-haired math teacher arrived on his bicycle.

The war came a little closer one overcast day in August. We couldn't see what was going on, but the sound effects made up for it! As a bomber formation was passing directly over Kaiserslautern above the clouds, we suddenly heard the beginning of a fierce aerial battle. Above the steady droning of the bombers we heard the higher pitched whining of one fighter after another closing in for the kill. The staccato of rapid machine gun fire and the slower and measured cannon rounds dominated the skies for several minutes when suddenly a B-24 Liberator pierced the cloud layer headed straight earthward at top speed, cruising like a dive bomber but spewing an ominous trail of black smoke. It never recovered from its deadly dive nor did any parachutes open up; a dull explosion followed by a mammoth orange fireball ended that episode.

A cheer erupted from our group of hyped-up boys, "Hurrah, chalk up another one for the fighter pilots of the Luftwaffe!"

---

[1] Profane slang meaning "Pig-dog"

A little later, right after a short session of concentrated gunfire, a B-17 also dived down through the cloud layer, but at a slightly shallower angle than the Liberator's diving crash. The bomber had lost one of its wings and was screaming earthwards in a deadly spiral dive.

Suddenly three white parachutes blossomed near the plane and floated gently downward. Just at that moment I was overcome with the most unreal feeling, as the missing wing appeared out of the clouds, spinning slowly earthward like a falling maple seed. A sudden realization that there were human beings aboard the stricken craft made us all hold back our boisterous cheers....this was the cold reality of war!

Later that day, after the "All Clear" was sounded, several of us took passes and went to visit the downed Fortress. It had crashed just outside the city, losing its tail turret some distance away. As we approached the wreck, a carefully covered body was laid out about 50 feet from the fuselage. A woeful feeling suddenly overcame me and was accentuated when I approached the wreck and saw blood-spattered personal items scattered around. A pair of broken Air Force glasses and a red-stained fur boot brought me close to a vomit....! I thought to myself: "My God, these are real people....maybe I even went to school or to Boy Scouts with one of them!"

On August 14, 1944 luck finally ran out for the city of Kaiserslautern. A giant formation of bombers approached our city from the West, flying directly over our position. This time things weren't the same. I gasped as a streaming white smoke flare was released by one of the lead planes right after they passed over us. An indescribable sound, part whistle and part screeching, developed into a crescendo as hundreds of bombs were dropped in a blanket pattern enveloping the heart of Kaiserslautern. A second wave dropped another pattern several minutes later into a housing development just to the East of the first craters. To our relief, the flight soon departed and no additional aircraft could be seen. A short time later the "All Clear" was given. Clouds of smoke and dust drifted over our position and soon the sickeningly sweet smell of burning flesh found its way to us. Within half an hour my mother showed up outside our gun emplacement on her bicycle, out of breath and her eyes filled with anxiety.

"What on earth are you doing here?" I said angrily. "It's crazy to be out right after an air raid. The *Amis* might drop some more bombs on their way back and you'll be caught right out in the open!"

"I just had to see if you were alright. They dropped bombs all over town, you know, and I thought your position might have also been hit. You're my only child and I would never forgive myself if you were lying here with fatal wounds and I wouldn't have come to see you for the last time."

"Mutti, I know how you feel, but you can't risk your own life on such a speculation. Please go to the shelter now as they're blowing the alarm again; when it's over, please go home and don't come out here again. Nothing will happen to me....you'll see."

I was greatly relieved when my mother pushed her bike over to the shelter and disappeared inside. When the alarm was over, I could see her emerging from the giant shelter, a pitiful soul remounting her bicycle to return through the smoldering ruins back to her home.

My next visit home took me past the cemetery at the base of this hill on the way to our house. The place was bustling with activity; there was a stack of wooden caskets stacked by the office awaiting burial and the crematorium smokestack was belching a huge column of smoke. I don't think we were told the final casualty count, but judging from the activity here, it must have been substantial. I was told later that there were probably far more burials than could be judged by the stack of caskets. Since the cabinetmakers couldn't possibly make enough coffins to accommodate all the dead resulting from a major air attack, each cemetery had a number of special caskets with hinged bottoms, so that the body could be slid into the grave after family members had departed. The casket was then retrieved for re-use and the hole filled in over the scantily clothed or even naked body. Yes, it would be a shameful waste to bury a body in anything but a nightshirt!

Since the odds of our home being completely destroyed were quite high, we packed a large suitcase full of extra clothing for all three of us and shipped it to my uncle Gerhard in Westphalia. Gerhard, a family physician, lived in a small farming community far from any metropolitan areas and the baggage was reasonably safe there. Should we lose all of our possessions, which often happened when houses were substantially damaged, we would at least have a change of clothes to fall back on. Luckily, we never had to retrieve the suitcase and I was able to pick it up intact after the war.

On September 8th the radio started blaring again; this time the news commentator boasted about the appearance of another new "reprisal" weapon against the allies. The message went something like this:

"Our inventive scientists have developed another wonder-weapon named the " V-2". This is a gigantic rocket-propelled missile, which will be launched right here in the homeland. The missile will ascend all the way into the stratosphere and then, in a giant ballistic trajectory, will find its way to strategic targets in London or elsewhere with pinpoint accuracy. The explosive load is far greater than that of the V-1; therefore this weapon will surely do its part to insure the victory of the Reich."

Sure enough, from that day on I observed almost daily launches of the V-2 in a distance. The slender and ominous-looking missiles ascended majestically skyward, leaving behind jagged trails of white smoke as they disappeared westwards toward enemy territory. However, their activity didn't seem to change the overall war picture very much.

The air raids became more frequent and deadly and the number of bombers visible in the sky increased from week to week. The British night raids also increased in intensity, but so did the German defenses. One day three impressive Flak guns of 105mm caliber appeared at our repair factory mounted on railroad cars. As we went over to inspect them, the gun-crew members were quite cocky and confident.

"We'll show you guys how to shoot down some of those *Amis*. You know, we hardly ever miss with these cannons!"

"How can you guys be that good. We've seen batteries of 88-s fire for twenty minutes without knocking down a single plane!"

"It's not the caliber, sonny, it's the quality of the equipment. See that gadget over there? That's a radar tracker that's hooked directly to the aiming mechanism. All we do is set the fuses, load and fire; the guns do the rest."

We were duly impressed as we'd never heard of automatic radar coupling before. The next day the gunners proved their point. A pair of P-38 Lightnings suddenly appeared out of nowhere. The big guns let out a roar as the first salvo screamed skyward. It came unbelievably close to the planes. The pilots immediately started evasive maneuvers, curving and banking in an erratic and zigzag fashion. In spite of these crazy movements, the second salvo scored a direct hit on the lead plane and sent it tumbling. The third salvo blew the other Lightning right out of the sky even before the first plane crashed. My feelings were impersonal again, returning to the cold realities of war; we cheered for the expert crew and returned to our own gun battery.

Both the heavy bomber activity as well as the low level *Jabo* attacks increased steadily week by week. Kaiserslautern was no longer being spared and we had to constantly stay alert to avoid being injured or killed. On a nice sunny Saturday in September I was home on an overnight pass to enjoy *Mutti's* cooking and baking. In spite of the sparse and lean ingredients available she still somehow managed to inject flavor and aroma into her creations. She had just pulled a piping hot cake from the oven. The cake was concocted from a mixture of flour, potatoes and milk and sweetened with saccharine. When eaten fresh, such a cake was very tasty, but as soon as it was left overnight, it became soggy and mushy. What an excuse to stuff myself while the cake was still warm and fresh!

I had just helped myself to a second slice and was telling *Mutti* about the new radar-controlled guns that I had seen when the sirens began wailing. Having changed my foolhardy attitude somewhat, I immediately led the way to the air raid shelter in the nearby *Wehrmacht Kaserne*.

As we sat down on one of the benches leaning against the wet stone wall, Mutti remarked:

"Jochen you are really making me happy with your changed sensibility toward the air raids. You used to make me so nervous when you wanted to watch the activity rather than go into the shelter with me. Thanks!"

"Well, I used to think they would never bomb Kaiserslautern, but lately I've been proven wrong. The city really looks pretty bad. Soon they're won't be enough housing left for the survivors to find shelter in!"

Suddenly the earth reverberated with a massive explosion, then another and another. The light bulbs suspended from wires attached to the roughly hewn ceiling, began swaying to and fro. Stone dust and chips began dropping from the walls and ceiling and cries of "Oh God" and mumbled prayers could be heard. Several more blasts resonated on the outside of the shelter and then silence reigned again. Soon afterward the *All Clear* sounded and we carefully came out of the shelter into the sunlight. The nearby three story stucco barracks had received multiple bomb hits. Two of the buildings were almost demolished and a third was ripped open with flames erupting from the remains of the top floor. A military fire crew was already pouring water on the flames and soldiers were hurriedly pulling rifles and ammunition from the burning building.

As we wound our way through the rubble-strewn compound, we caught sight of our duplex apartment two blocks away. Mutti shouted:

"Oh my God, Jochen, our roof is gone! What are we going to do? Our things will get all wet if it rains!"

"I replied: "Don't worry so much, *Mutti*, it looks like the building isn't badly damaged. I'm staying overnight anyway, so I'll have plenty of time to do something with the roof."

As we drew closer I could see that most of the clay tiles had been blown off the roof on our end of the building and were scattered about in the woods. We could easily look into the attic through the exposed rafters observing our storage boxes and suitcases stacked up along the walls.

Mutti cried out: "Look at the windows, Jochen; all of those in the front of the house are completely gone. Whatever am I going to do?"

"First of all, let's be thankful that the whole house isn't wrecked and that our possessions are still intact; it could be much worse! There's a glazier over on the Friedenstrasse. I'll remove the frames after I fix the roof and we'll borrow a hand wagon from the neighbor so you can haul them to the glaziers. When they're done, maybe old *Herr* Kirchner from upstairs can help you put them back on their hinges again."

My first task was to borrow a long ladder from the *Kaserne*. I then carefully picked up all the unbroken tiles and laboriously lugged them up to roof. They went back in place quite easily, as each tile had a ridge, which nested into the rafter stringers. Luckily, the sandy soil around the house had cushioned the falling tiles and very few were broken.

After several hours of tugging and hoisting, the job was done. I jammed a piece of canvas into the hole left vacant because of broken tile and said:

"Now, *Mutti*, this wasn't so bad after all, was it? At least the house will stay dry now. We'll close the Rolladen[1] tonight and tomorrow we'll unhook the windows so you can haul them to the glaziers on Monday."

Looking up from the pile of broken glass she had carefully swept up, *Mutti* said:

"I don't know what I would do without you, Jochen; you're always taking care of things for me. I hope they won't call you for your *Luftwaffe* enlistment soon; you'll probably end up far away from here."

Not knowing what to say, I changed the subject, since I knew that I'd be gone by winter at the latest.

The next day brought another brush with our pesky friends the *Jabos*. I had taken our enameled steel two-quart milk pitcher and hopped on my bike for the half-mile ride to the milk store. The first leg of this shopping jaunt took me on a sandy, well-worn path through the woods and past the *Kaserne*. Just as I was abreast of the rear gate I heard the growl of a Thunderbolt radial engine. As I looked up the plane was already thundering over the pine trees on top of the hill. Luckily I felt trouble approaching and dove headlong over the handlebars and into the soft sand, the milk pitcher hurtling end over end into the bushes. At the same moment a single bomb exploded on the parade ground as I was still in mid-air and I could hear the bomb fragments tear through the branches above my head. A shower of pine needles settled on me and my bike as the P-47 pulled up sharply and disappeared over the autobahn bridge. Whew.......my first really close call!

Later that afternoon we unhooked eight window sections and stacked them on a wooden cart. It was quite a task for my mother to

---

[1] Wooden tambour shutters

drag all that weight to the glaziers, but I had to return to duty that night, so she was on her own again.

When I visited home a week later, she had re-installed the windows with a neighbor's help and restored the apartment to its former organized and tidy condition.

Mutti said to me: "Jochen, I wish this terrible war would come to an end.....the air attacks are really taking their toll. I talked with my friend Karola Geissler on the telephone yesterday. She was sobbing as she told me what happened to her daughter Ruth last week. It seems that Ruth, who is about your age, was sent to Dortmund with 55 of her schoolmates. The girls were operating searchlights and listening devices during a hellish night raid. Their position received a direct hit by one of those British "super-bombs" and Ruth was one of only 5 survivors. They let her come home to recuperate but the poor girl can neither eat nor sleep she's still in such shock. I wish they didn't make young girls take on such hazardous duty!"

Less than a month later, written orders were received at battery headquarters that would drastically change our para-military careers. A large segment of our group of *Luftwaffenhelfer* were to be discharged and inducted into the *Reichsarbeitsdienst*. During peacetime all young people, both men and women, were required to serve in this labor service for a six-month period. It was Adolf Hitler's clever method of reducing unemployment, constructing highways and bridges and imparting military basic training and marksmanship to Germany's youth. The young girls were used extensively for crop harvesting and domestic functions. As the war progressed and young men were desperately needed to replace front line casualties, the one-year term was repeatedly shortened to meet these needs. At first the term was cut to four months, then to three; when our turn came up in September of 1944, we were told that our enlistment would last only two months.

I was among the group to leave for the National Labor Service. As we made preparations to be discharged, rumors began to circulate in the barracks.

"Did you know that 50 replacements of underclassmen from our *Oberschule* are coming next week to replace us?"

"Now they're saying that the entire battery is leaving Kaiserslautern to guard the airfield at Lachen Speyerdorf!"

Both rumors turned out to be the truth. The day after our departure all guns and personnel (new and old) were loaded on a train by night and transported 40 kilometers to the East, where new positions were dug into a hillside adjacent to the fighter base.

Somewhere in the background, some guardian angels must have been hard at work because, exactly one week after we vacated our positions, the repair shop was plastered with dozens of heavy bombs, several of which leveled our primitive gun pits beyond recognition!

During the two-day leave between assignments. Friedrich and I had a serious discussion. Both of us were sitting in his model airplane filled bedroom when he remarked:

"I've been thinking, Jochen, about our enlistment in the Luftwaffe. One of my friends from church enlisted in August with the intention of becoming a pilot. Would you believe that he's now with the *Division Hermann Göring*[1] doing infantry duty and they think they'll soon be sent to the Russian front. It seems that the Luftwaffe has enough pilots and planes but not enough fuel to fly them. Boy, I don't want to end up in the ground forces, do you?"

"I agree, Friedrich; I hope we didn't go through all that glider training for nothing! I have an idea; I heard about a special program for rocket planes and I think they're looking for volunteers. Why don't we check it out?"

Without further ado, we walked downtown to the office of the *NSFK,* the National Socialist Flying Corps, which was the political entity controlling all para-military aviation activities, including all of the Hitler Youth Glider Schools. We were in luck as the *Sturmführer* was very happy to see us. He replied to our inquiry:

"You fellows came to me just at the right time. There is a special training program going on at a number of glider schools. This involves pre-training to fly the Me-163 rocket fighter. They have found out that glider pilots lend themselves quite well to pilot this bird, especially since one has to glide home from around 10,000 meters after the rocket fuel has been spent. Are you interested in signing up?"

---

[1] A Luftwaffe Division trained for ground combat

Friedrich said: "What do you say, Jochen? Shall we give it a try?"

"It'll be better than doing infantry duty at the front; let's do it!" I replied.

The *Sturmführer* said: "I'm really proud of you fellows, volunteering at a time like this. A lot of people are beginning to doubt our ultimate victory; it'll be guys like you that will help Germany come out on top! Now for the details: I'll send your flight records along with the *Sonderlehrgang*[1] applications to Headquarters right away. If they consider you to be qualified, you'll get an acceptance notice within a few weeks. You'll then be notified of the next glider school openings. There is one condition, however; I'm aware that you both have been accepted as Luftwaffe officer candidates. "You'll have to obtain releases from that program in writing so I can submit them along with your applications. For some reason they don't want to conflict with any officer training programs; probably because it would delay your flight training and subsequent availability for combat. Is that OK with you?"

We both nodded in assent, saluted smartly and walked away, ready for the next adventure and hoping fervently that we'd be accepted.

---

[1] Special Course

12

After a brief leave of two days, I packed a few personal items and was on my way again. This time a 40 kilometer train ride took us to the *Neustadter Weinstrasse*, a fertile strip of farmland along the eastern edge of the *Pfälzerwald* hills. When we approached our destination village of Edesheim, row upon row of harvest-ready grapes filled the entire countryside, as far as my eyes could see. The *Arbeitsdienst* barracks were but a few kilometers from town and we soon reported for duty. Several of my *Luftwaffenhelfer* comrades were included in this conscription group, so we felt at home right away. The accustomed routine of being fitted with uniforms, shoes, helmets and gas masks went quickly the next day. We did, however, notice the effects of the ongoing war and the subsequent supply shortages. Most of the uniforms in the distinctive brown color denoting that the wearer was a member of the *"Arbeitsdienst"*, showed signs of considerable wear. The selection of shoe sizes was quite limited; with my usual lack of aggressiveness, I ended up with a pair that was half a size too small. Exchanging them for another pair the next day, I was stuck with shoes much too large. My problem was finally solved three days later when the correct size was requisitioned from the headquarters supply department.

As a novel twist, we were each issued a shiny, chrome-plated spade, the distinctive mark of the *Arbeitsdienst*. As we experienced later that day, the spades were meant to glisten brightly in the sunlight as the *Arbeitsdienst* men performed "Shoulder Arms" and "Present

Arms" with spades instead of Mauser rifles! This established a snappy "drill team" atmosphere and added flavor to many of Germany's propaganda films.

Our days started very early with a short breakfast, then an immediate march to the parade ground. It didn't take us very long to realize that the *Arbeitsdienst* tradition of working on projects had completely given way to military training! A constant routine of infantry-type activities filled out our day; close-order drill, rifle handling, map reading and marching, marching and more marching. It turned into such a grind that the twice-daily air raids became a welcome break in our schedule. Luckily, the enemy airplanes ignored us and merely passed overhead, carrying their cargoes of destruction to other targets.

After three days of sweaty infantry training, I was called to the Troop Commander's office. As I walked up the steps, I met a colleague from the next building responding to an identical summons. As we saluted smartly, the group leader said:

"You both seem to be alert young fellows; how would you like a special assignment?"

"Yes sir, what do we have to do?"

"We need a daily courier to carry communications back and forth between this camp and our District Headquarters near Karlsruhe. You can take turns going on the courier run on alternate days; that way you won't miss out on all your training. You'll be traveling by train and bicycle and will have a whole day to complete the round trip. Under normal conditions five or six hours would be sufficient, but with the *Jabos* as active as they are, you may be lucky to get home before dark."

We both agreed to the new assignment, eager for adventure and the chance to avoid some of the boring training.

My turn came first. Outfitted with a bicycle and a road map, I embarked on my first courier run. Cycling to the rail station I waited for the 6:00 AM train to Karlsruhe, about 50 kilometers to the south. Arriving at Karlsruhe, I retrieved my bicycle from the baggage car and pedaled about eight kilometers to District Headquarters in Eggenstein. After exchanging mail I proceeded to kill several hours of time until my return train was scheduled to leave Karlsruhe again.

On one trip, exhausted, I took a long nap after lunch and woke up just in time to catch my train. On another day, I went to a movie theater in Karlsruhe to watch a film about *U-Boot* action in the North Atlantic. To accomplish this interruption without losing my valuable bike to thieves, I detached the easily removable handlebars, tucked them under my arm and took them into the theater. A bicycle without handlebars was useless even to most clever of thieves!

One morning I was awakened before my usual 5:00 AM call by screaming alarm sirens. I thought: "What an unusual time for a raid, just before daybreak; I wonder what's going on?"

My question was soon answered when a heavy bomber, probably a four engine Lancaster, thundered overhead at low altitude. Evidently crippled and limping toward home, the plane jettisoned its bomb load as it flew over the little town of Edesheim. Several loud explosions erupted as the plane disappeared toward the west. As I dressed hurriedly and gulped down some bread and coffee, I could hear the "Ooooga, ooooga" of fire engines as they responded to the fire and rescue calls in the smoking village.

After picking up my mail pouch and bicycle, I pedaled toward Edesheim just as day was breaking. Arriving at the railroad station my heart sank; one of the bombs had fallen right in the center of the double tracks directly in front of the station platform. Instead of the usual perfectly aligned tracks, there was a huge crater with twisted steel rails protruding in all directions and splintered wooden ties scattered throughout the track area. There would be no trains coming through here today!

Adhering to our strict instructions not to allow anything to distract us from our courier functions, I cycled past the working fireman and headed toward the highway to Karlsruhe. Today the courier would be traveling solely by pedal power! Passing the pile of rubble that had only yesterday been a grocery store with living quarters above, I was quite surprised to see several undressed mannequins grotesquely sprawled amid the smoldering debris. I mused to myself:

"Why would a grocery store have mannequins?"

In took only a few seconds for me to realize that they were human corpses, stripped stark naked by the vicious force of the bomb blast!

The courier run went without incident that day, except for my extremely sore calves from constant pedaling to get back to the barracks before dark. I made it just in time to view the completely repaired railroad tracks, ready for the next train to go whizzing through.....talk about organized rebuilding!

As I had been told, my alternate days were spent with my comrades in the regular camp routine of infantry training. We were soon in excellent physical shape and took pride in our accomplishments. The food was much better than we were accustomed to in the *Flak* barracks; they were most likely fattening us up for combat duty!

On another day, enemy aircraft messed up my courier run in a different way. On my return trip from headquarters a high-level bomber attack on the city of Karlsruhe put everything to a standstill. Apparently there were several formations involved, as we were confined to the shelter for many hours. When the "All Clear" finally sounded, the center of the city was in shambles. Picking my way through the rubble-strewn streets to the rail station, I almost collided with a overhead trolley wire swinging to and fro in the breeze. As I quickly veered to one side, sparks suddenly spewed forth as the wire short-circuited against the car tracks.....another close one!

Unable to cycle safely at night because of the blackout conditions, I returned to Headquarters to sleep and complete my trip the next day. That was no simple matter, either. No trains were running the next day and the Rhine River bridges were all seriously damaged or blocked with rubble. Repair crews were constantly harassed by *Jabos* so that there was no crossing possible for some time. Not wanting to be delayed another day, I consulted my trusty road map and decided to travel south about 20 kilometers to the next crossing point shown: a cable ferry. Arriving at the ferry dock a few hours later I wasn't at all surprised to see a waiting line-up of horse-drawn wagons, a produce truck and a few dozen bicycle riders. The ferryboat was tethered to a heavy overhead cable by its own cable with a pulley on the end. As the ferry was cast off from shore and held at an angle to the stream direction, the strong Rhine River current soon seized control and propelled the vessel to the other side. There, after unloading and reloading, the angle of attack was reversed and the ferry slid back across the river again. Soon my turn came to cross the river. I boarded the craft amid horses, wagons and people and was taken across. I was on my way again, using the road map to find the best route back to the barracks.

The middle of October brought another surprise development. One morning our Group Leader called for an *Appell* and addressed us as follows:

"*Arbeitsmänner*[1], I have just received direct orders from Headquarters that our entire camp is being transferred to a location at Herrenalb in the Black Forest. Preparations will begin immediately by loading all equipment and supplies into railroad freight cars for transport. Then we'll all travel with our personal gear by bicycle to the new camp, except for a guard detail accompanying the train. It will be an arduous trip by bicycle, as you'll be carrying all your belongings in your rucksacks, including your blankets and shelter halves. Our truck will be following along in the rear, ready to pick up anybody who peters out on the way. I hope there won't be many of you in that category!"

No reason was given for the sudden move, but we drew our own conclusions. The western allies had pushed back the German army across the borders of the *Vaterland*; there already was fierce fighting around the cities of Aachen and Metz. As long as our unit wasn't needed, why not get us across the Rhine River and out of the way?

With horses and wagons commandeered from local farmers to supplement the group's one and only cargo truck, we spent most of the next day transferring camp equipment to a line of rail cars parked on a siding next to the station. It was almost like an evacuation, as everything was packed to go; the entire inventory of uniforms, gas masks, helmets, bedding, rifles, ammunition, kitchen equipment and anything that wasn't nailed down found its way to the train station. By nightfall the loading procedure was completed and we dropped onto our bare mattresses for the last nights' sleep at Edesheim.

At sunrise the next morning we rolled up our blankets and finished packing our rucksacks. Shouldering our heavy loads, we soon

---

[1] Basic rank in National Labor Service meaning "Workmen"

learned, by trial and error, how to keep our bikes in balance and pedal down the highway at a reasonable speed. Breakfast and lunch consisted of black bread and salami issued from the mess hall the day before and washed down with cool water taken from village fountains along the way.

Somehow we managed to cross the Rhine and pass through the city of Karlsruhe without air raid interference and proceeded southward toward the Black Forest. The countryside gradually changed from flat farm and wine country to rolling hills with quaint villages nestled in the valleys. Soon there were no more fields and we were in the dense woods of the Black Forest. Coasting down some of the winding roads I felt that the my whole world was at peace and that the war and air raids were a thousand miles away.

We arrived at the charming town of Herrenalb just as the sun went down. The *Arbeitsdienst* camp was located about two kilometers beyond the city limits. As we rounded the last bend in the road we could see the barracks nestled in the valley traversed by a clear mountain stream. Dense woods surrounded us completely and the colorful autumn foliage added a picture-postcard touch.

As the last tired and sweaty *Arbeitsman* pulled his bike up to the main building, our troop leader called us to order:

"Men, you've shown good spirit and discipline today. Other than the five fellows who almost passed out and had to wait to be picked up by the supply truck, you all came through our 80 kilometer trek OK. As you may have heard, the railroad cars with our supplies, equipment and bedding won't be here until sometime tomorrow. Since this area is served only by narrow gauge tracks, they have to exchange all the undercarriages at the rail yard in Karlsruhe so that the cars will fit on the tracks. You'll have to make do tonight and sleep in your blankets.....you may as well get used to such things anyway; you'll all probably be somewhere on the front lines by Christmas! I'll see you all in the morning.....Group dismissed!"

There was mounting evidence of the steady allied advances into Germany; we spent the next day making our new quarters less visible to the enemy. We stretched endless yards of camouflage netting between and over the buildings to help them blend into the forest surroundings. All items with the least bit of shine were painted a dull dark green and special care was given to the blackout curtains in all rooms. Even the tiniest sliver of escaping light could attract a destructive cluster of unwelcome bombs, so we weren't taking any chances.

Our ambitious group of 120 sturdy young men had the camp completed just in time to begin unloading the train, which had meanwhile arrived at Herrenalb. Again using commandeered horses and our only truck, we spent the rest of the afternoon and most of the following day transferring the trainload of gear to our new camp. The constant tugging, lifting and hauling was cheerfully done, as it included our bedding and kitchen gear, which was dear to our hearts. What better pleasures are there for seventeen-year-old boys (men) than eating and sleeping?

Within three days we were all settled in. The infantry routine began once more, this time in earnest! From dawn until dusk we marched and drilled until we were ready to drop. At this point we wore our gas masks often to become accustomed to the difficult breathing and talking while wearing them. Gobs of sweat accumulated in our face valves as we ran in circles around the parade ground. The crowning blow came one day when we were digging foxholes while wearing our gas masks when an ice-cold October rain started pelting down. With lots of grumbling and cursing, we managed to finish our entrenchment and were dismissed to return to the barracks. The next morning 12 boys out of our group of 120 reported for sick call!

I had been trying to ignore a bothersome pain in my fingers and toes ever since we left the camp in Edesheim. However, it soon became painful enough that I also went on sick call to the local *Lazarett*[1] As the gray-haired *Stabsarzt*[2] examined me, he immediately said:

"Young man, you're starting on a good case of rheumatic fever. We're confining you to bed at once; I'm sure you won't miss that fancy infantry training they're putting you through over at the *Arbeitsdienstlager*, will you?"

---

[1] Military Hospital
[2] Captain in the Medical Corps

In my youthful and stupid enthusiasm, I replied: "Yes Sir! I really will miss being with my comrades; are you sure you want me to stay in bed?"

"Young man, please listen to me. You definitely have rheumatic fever and I don't want you to take any chances. If we can nip this thing in the bud you should be OK, but if we don't, you might very well develop heart trouble. We wouldn't want that to happen, would we? Besides, you'll be fighting the *Amis* soon enough; there's no need to be in such a hurry!"

The doctor continued: "I want you to check in with the *Sanitätsunteroffizier*[1] in the office over there. Tell him you're to be admitted today and for him to send a report to your unit. Now, I'm going to put you on medication right away. You'll be taking 30 aspirin tablets daily. I want you to crush them into a powder and add just enough water to make a creamy liquid. You should take a small sip every half-hour or so to give your body a steady infusion of the stuff. We normally can control the infection in about week, especially if you stay in bed. Don't let me catch you walking the halls, young man!"

My room was on the mansard floor of the hospital. Two roommates occupied the other beds and there was a table with chairs in one corner of the room. Four small hinged rooftop windows afforded some daylight but allowed a minimum view of the pretty town, as one could only look through them in a skyward direction.

After a few days extreme boredom set in, as my room mates were both mobile and spent their time elsewhere in the hospital. The bitter aspirin concoction did nothing to improve my spirits, and I was eager to get well and rejoin my comrades.

Eight days after my admission to the *Lazaret* the horrible aspirin treatment had run its course; the pain and swelling had disappeared completely and I was certified "fit for duty" again. Returning to the barracks, I was welcomed with:

"How's the *Drückeberger*[2] doing? Must be nice, flirting with the pretty nurses while we're working our butts off digging trenches in the mud! We'll forgive you this time, Jochen, as long as you open that

---

[1] Medical Sergeant
[2] One who shuns work

sweet smelling package that your *Mutti* sent you while you were in the hospital.....how about it?"

Glad to be well again and together with my friends, I cheerfully opened the carefully wrapped parcel and discovered about two dozen *Marzipankartoffel*. Germany is world-famous for these delicious candies made of almond paste and coming in countless shapes, such as fruits, animals or, as in this case, miniature potatoes. Genuine *Marzipan* was an extreme rarity at this time, but my mother cleverly managed to fashion *ersatz Marzipan* by combining farina, saccharine and almond extract, rolling the concoction into tiny round balls and dusting them with powdered cinnamon. Not the real thing, but were they ever delicious! I gave each roommate one of the sweet morsels, enjoyed two of them myself and tucked the remainder into my rucksack for another day. At this stage in my life I'm willing to admit that I woke up in the middle of the night and polished off the remaining lot!

The war news reports became extremely ominous; things weren't going well for the *Vaterland* at all! It was now the middle of November 1944; Aachen had fallen, Metz was almost encircled, the Russians were making steady progress westward and air raids were at an all-time peak.

On November 13th we were discharged and sent home to await conscription into the regular armed forces. I took the train to Kaiserslautern and a few weeks of rest and relaxation. Arriving at the train station, my first impression included a distinct and ominous rumbling toward the West. Would you believe, the Americans had advanced far enough for us to hear the unmistakable sound of artillery, even though the front lines were still more than 50 kilometers away.

What a pleasure it was to be a free man again! No more 5:00 and 6:00 AM wake up calls, no more marching everywhere I went and no more being chewed out for every little infraction. The downside was the change in my daily menu. The food in the *Arbeitsdienst* had been quite substantial even though it wasn't always as tasty as could be desired. Upon arriving at home, I was once more on civilian rations. As I went to the Ration Office to pick up my monthly food coupons, I came to the full realization of the German civilian's wartime plight. Rations had been reduced to less than 1200 calories daily, hardly enough to sustain a sedentary person let alone anyone engaged in any sort of physical activity. Black market trading flourished for those fortunate enough to have items of value to exchange, as faith in the value of the German *Reichsmark* was rapidly diminishing. Luckily, my mother had squirreled away a few reserve staples such as lentils, dried peas and a little extra flour, which she gladly shared with me in her usual unselfish way. Hunger brings out the worst in people, and I hate to admit what it did to me in those days. I remember one incident distinctly; my father was on a rare weekend visit from his assignment in Alsace Loraine and Mutti had baked a round *Apfelkuchen*[1] . As was her usual practice, she carefully measured the circumference of the cake with her sewing tape, dividing it neatly into three equal sectors. When dessert time came, would you believe that I took out the tape and re-measured all three sections to make sure I hadn't been cheated? Only a loving mother would put up with such an insult! My father took me aside later for a little talking-to; only then did I realize how badly I must have hurt *Mutti 's* feelings. I went into the kitchen, took her in my arms and said:

"*Mutti*, I'm really sorry that I didn't trust you in measuring the cake. I don't know what got into me, but I'm so hungry I can hardly wait for the next meal coming up. Please forgive me!"

"It's alright, Jochen, I understand. It must be awful for a growing boy like you to have to survive on these meager rations. I hope this terrible war will be over soon!"

I had been home barely a week, enjoying my new freedom, when the anxiously awaited letter from the NSFK arrived. Mutti said:

"Hurry up and open that letter, so that I know what's happening to you!"

With fumbling hands I tore open the envelope and read:

"Flight Student Volmar, Joachim; you have been selected to participate in a Special Training Program. You are to report to the Glider School at Brünn, Czechoslovakia on January 2, 1945. A one-way railroad pass is enclosed herewith."

---

[1] Open-faced, flat yeast cake covered with sliced apples

Mutti exclaimed: "Thank God, you're going to another school and not to the infantry at the Eastern front. I wouldn't be able to sleep a wink if they sent you there!"

Elated, I hopped on my bike and cycled to Friedrich's house. "Look what I got today, Friedrich! I've been accepted in the Me-163 program and I'm going to Czechoslovakia. Have you heard anything yet?"

He replied: "Yes, I our mailman was just here and I got my letter also; I'm glad we'll be together. Did you know that Friedhard and Fritz Klein have already been drafted? Fritz is in the infantry and Freidhard was sent to an armored division as a radioman because of that aircraft communications course he took with the Hitler Youth. Those guys will be fighting before the year is over!"

"Yes, I'll be glad to get out of here and away from the *Amis* coming closer all the time from the West. I think we'll be OK where we're going as the Russians are still quite some distance away."

We were at home during the entire month of December, just bumming around. Of course, many hours were spent in air raid shelters, but at least we weren't at the front lines. The only boys in our age group we saw about town were either invalids or soldiers home on leave. This made things quite boring and we became anxious to resume our glider flying.

The monotony was broken by an unexpected visit; my friend and classmate Rudi Martens came home on a short leave. He had been drafted into an infantry unit stationed at the Western front somewhere in Alsace Loraine. He filled me in with details:

"We've been pretty lucky so far, Jochen. With the winter weather, both the *Ami* and the Germans haven't been raising much hell lately. There are occasional artillery duels and they send us on patrols almost every day, but no real activity is going on. I hope it keeps up this way; I don't want to get my ass shot up like a lot of my buddies have."

"Sounds like a piece of cake to me, Rudi. Do you know that Friedrich Schwarz and I signed up for the Me-163 rocket fighter program? We're being sent to a special glider course in Czechoslovakia in January; how about that?"

"Boy, you guys are both crazy. I've heard that even the training in those birds is pretty dangerous, let alone the combat situations. I'll stay safely on the ground with my rifle-slinging buddies! However, if this damned war would ever end, we would all be happier. Do you know, those *Amis* are regular guys like you and me.....they even have a sense of humor! A couple of weeks ago our entire platoon was sent on a daylight patrol into the next village. When we came back, would you believe that an *Ami* patrol had visited our tent, swiped a few rations and left us a note that said: *"Thanks for the Pumpernickel"* in English! I wish this war would be over so we can get back into school; I want to get on with my life!"

In some ways I agreed with him; on the other hand, I was looking forward to the adventure of advanced glider training and the thrill of becoming a dashing fighter pilot.

Cloudy and snowy weather had minimized the air raids considerably and we became immersed in preparations for Christmas. *Mutti* was scrounging ingredients and baking a supply of cookies for my trip to the East. Suddenly, on December 16th, our radio became alive with priority news broadcasts:

"A gigantic counter-offensive has been launched this morning against our enemies in the West. Numerous SS and regular Panzer divisions have pushed through American lines in the Ardennes area with great success."

Later that day, a message followed: "Our spearhead offensive is moving ahead rapidly; thousands of Americans have been taken prisoner and German casualties have been light."

As I met Friedrich later that day we discussed this latest turn of events. I remarked:

"Man, this new offensive is really too good to be true. Do you think we can push the allies back far enough to make any difference?"

"I really don't know, Jochen. Those guys seem to have an endless supply line. On the other hand the air raids are keeping our panzers and planes from getting nearly enough fuel to operate on. I have a feeling that this is sort of our last big effort. I hope I'm wrong, but our success just sounds too good to be true."

Day by day the radio reports seemed more optimistic. We all welcomed the breather of the absence of allied air raids and it was a pleasure of getting a few nights of uninterrupted sleep. Three days passed and the news was still good. I had just finished breakfast when the roar of approaching aircraft engines reverberated through our house. With no time to seek the shelter I ran to the balcony to get a glimpse of what might be coming. A moment later four Me-109 fighters roared over the hill behind our house at treetop level, headed toward the West. I hadn't seen a German fighter plane this closely in years. Maybe we *were* making some headway!

How wrong I was.....! As Christmas came closer, the tone in the broadcasts changed. We heard reports like: "Our spearheading panzers have been forced to detour around several pockets of stubborn American resistance" and "German forces have been delayed somewhat in the face of vast material and manpower resources that have been committed by the allies."

By the time Christmas Day arrived, we knew that the German *blitzkrieg* offensive, later to be called the "Battle of the Bulge" had run into difficulty. Hitler's last supreme effort to push back the Western allies was becoming mired in the snow and mud of the Ardennes! The weather had improved and allied air attacks resumed, both at the front lines and throughout the German Reich.

We celebrated Christmas in a Spartan fashion; presents were almost non-existent, although my dad had scrounged a roll of film for my miniature box camera and I had saved up some cigarettes for him as I hadn't yet acquired the smoking habit. A safely kept bottle of cologne filled *Mutti's* needs; to have both of us at home for the holidays was good enough for her. We toasted the future with one of our last bottles of homemade wine and retired early, thankful that no air-raid sirens had wailed on Christmas Eve.

My days at home were numbered, since the glider school was scheduled for January 2nd. Packing a small suitcase with toiletries, underwear, extra dress shoes and a few books, I had a hard time deciding what to take with me. With the mounting ferocity of air attacks and the chances of becoming "bombed out[1]" becoming greater and greater, where would my prized possessions stand a better chance of surviving the war? If stored at home, there was the mounting

---

[1] Term used when a home was destroyed in air raid

danger of air raids or even the entry of allied ground troops into Kaiserslautern. On the other hand, if I took the stuff with me, the glider school might be captured by the advancing Russians. I decided to gamble on my luck with the Russians and packed my photo collection of around 200 pictures, my camera and a number of aviation textbooks. I was ready for adventure again!

13

On December 30th I met Friedrich at the station to catch the late afternoon train to Mannheim. We impatiently paced back and forth on the station platform in the chilling winter wind. After what seemed like an eternity, the stationmaster made an announcement:

"The 15:00 o'clock train to Mannheim has been canceled. The tracks in Homburg have been badly damaged and are impassable at this time. There will be no further trains until late tomorrow at the earliest."

Forever resourceful from past experiences, I told Friedrich: "Let's hurry over to the *Wehrmacht Kaserne* over near my house. As you know, my Mom works there as a secretary and knows all the transportation officers. Maybe we can catch a ride on an army vehicle."

Dragging our suitcases aboard a city bus, we rode as far as the cemetery; from there we climbed the snow-covered hill leading to the Kaserne. My mother, just recovering from our tearful farewell a few hours ago, was surprised to see us again. Apprised of our predicament, she quickly made a few telephone calls. Hanging up with a smile, she said:

"That was *Unteroffizier* Schnelle of the Transport Department. He says that one of the medical officers will be taking a truck to Mannheim sometime tonight. He told me to call the dispensary and he's certain that they'll give you boys permission to ride in the back.

No sooner said than done; *Mutti* made the call and permission was given. Another farewell and we left to meet the medical officer; we were finally on our way!

The late-night trip to Mannheim was agonizingly slow due to two alarms enroute. In both instances, we hastily jumped from the truck and sought refuge in the ditches along the road. The last stop was probably within 20 kilometers of Mannheim. As the enemy bomber formation neared the city and the searchlights let their bright and stabbing fingers sweep methodically across the sky, the crescendo of hundreds of flak guns began rumbling through the countryside. Suddenly one of the four engine bombers was caught in the brilliant beam of the searchlights. As the aircraft tried various evasive maneuvers, more searchlights joined in the focus. The plane was obviously doomed. Within a minute or so of concentrated firing, one of the shells hit home. The bomber burst into flames and started careening earthwards. Abruptly, a tremendous bright flash ensued, followed by a fireworks display like I had never seen before. Apparently all the explosives aboard were set off at once; bombs, ammunition, flares and fuel must have been touched of at the same time, as flashes, stars and streaks of all the rainbow colors arced from the hulk in many directions. At this point there was no more cheering; we were reaching the point of being weary of all the killing on both sides. Our efforts and attitudes were now being focused on survival rather than on participating in the *Vaterland's* glorious victory.

Soon thereafter the raid was over; we climbed back into the truck and motored eastwards again. Luck was with us; after the truck dropped us off at the Mannheim train station, we immediately caught a slow train to Heidelberg. A short wait there put us on an express train to Vienna..... we were finally making some progress!

The trip to Vienna via Munich was fascinating to me; I had never been to southern Germany to experience its world-renowned beauty. The train clanked through the night as we nodded our heads, slipping from one short nap to another. As daybreak came, we were approaching the city of Munich situated at the northern edge of the Bavarian Alps. The towering, snow covered peaks glistened in the early sunlight, giving the panorama a picture-postcard appearance. We pulled into Munich's Main Station, popped into the restaurant for some coffee with rolls and were soon on our way again. Alternately napping and viewing the pretty Bavarian countryside, we sped along the tracks. Unaccustomed to the low incidence of air attacks in this part of Germany, we had a smooth and uninterrupted trip to the city of Vienna. Arriving there around midnight, we changed trains and were soon headed north toward Czechoslovakia.

The late morning brought us to the town of Brünn (Brno), our final destination. We showed the stationmaster our travel orders and were directed to a small airport just outside of town.

Lugging our suitcases we trudged up a narrow and winding road to the glider field which overlooked the striking little city, nestled in a valley covered with a light dusting of snow. As we approached the neat and well-maintained wooden barracks, we could hear the familiar sounds of a launch in progress.

The booming voice of an instructor filled the crisp mountain air with "Get Ready" and then "Staaart", which was immediately followed by the rapid "putt-putt-putt" of the launching winch engine. Suddenly a sleek "Grunau Baby" soared steeply into the sky, straight as an arrow. The pilot soon reached the limit of the launch cable and pulled the release.........The plane lurched slightly in its new-found freedom but quickly stabilized into a smooth flight pattern. What a thrill to watch! It had been over six months since I'd been up in the air and I could hardly wait to get the feel of a flying glider again.

Friedrich and I marched into the Orderly Room, gave snappy salutes and blurted :"*Heil Hitler*! We are reporting for assignment to the glider school!"

We were astounded when the *Feldwebel* got up from his chair and bellowed: "What in the hell do you think you're getting away with by reporting to class three days late?"

I told him about the air raids, bombed-out bridges and delayed or canceled trains. His only response was: "It's an honor to have been selected for this school; you should have left home a little earlier!"

The chewing-out went in one ear and out the other, as we were getting used to such exaggerated performances; this seemed to be a common trait found in all German *Feldwebels*! However, when he told us we couldn't stay at the Brno school as the class was filled to capacity, we were dismayed. What now? We had been looking forward to this course for months and months. When was the next class ?

To our chagrin, the *Feldwebel* began writing transfer orders. He said "You're being sent to the Brüsterort School; they still have room for a couple of dummies like you!"

"Where in the world is Brüsterort?" I asked him.

His curt reply was, "It's near Königsberg in East Prussia, just this side of the Russian front!"

We took our new orders, saluted and headed back to the railroad station.

At this stage of the game waiting was the order of the day; it was a pleasant surprise when we only had to wait about an hour for the next northbound express to come along. We climbed on board and staggered along the companionway as the train lurched forward from the station. Shortly we found a compartment with only one occupant, a young *Flak Leutnant*. I addressed him:

"*Herr Leutnant*, do you mind if we join you in this compartment? There seems to be lots of room and we want to sleep a little tonight. We've been riding the rails for three days now and we're pretty bushed!"

"Sure, boys; come on in and sit down. Where are you headed?"

"We're glider pilots and have been assigned to a school near Königsberg."

"Ah-ha, that explains everything; I wondered why you weren't in uniform. At this stage of the game, anyone your age in civilian clothes is either an invalid or a deserter!"

After we had put our suitcases in the overhead racks and settled ourselves on the hard wooden benches, the *Leutnant* told us his tale of woe. He had seen lots of action in Africa and Italy but his 88-millimeter battery had run into some good luck. It was assigned to guard an aircraft factory near Vienna. Even though the target was critical, its remote location in Austria kept air raids to a minimum. Under these conditions it was no problem for the *Leutnant* to obtain a seven-day leave so he could visit his family in Königsberg. He hadn't seen his wife and two children in over two years and was champing at the bit to reach home. We chatted amiably as the train clattered northwards through Poland.

"So you fellows are going to the glider school in Brüsterort? My brother is a *Stuka* pilot and learned to fly gliders at that field before he enlisted in the *Luftwaffe*. I wonder if you guys know how famous that area is, both for gliding and otherwise?"

"We really don't know a lot about it; please fill us in", I said.

"First of all, the tip of the East Prussian peninsula that juts into the Baltic Sea is called the Samland. This happens to be the center of what is known as the *Bernsteinküste*, which is the "Amber Coast" of Europe. It is world famous since there have been countless important discoveries of amber on the beaches there. The supply never seems to run out, as people are always searching in the sand for pieces of amber that have washed ashore. There is a museum in Königsberg that has a large and interesting exhibit of special finds, including a number of pre-historic insects encapsulated in amber. If you get some time off during your course, I would recommend that you take a weekend trip to Königsberg to see the museum and the rest of the historic sights. As you should remember from your history classes, the city has a rich historic background, The philosopher Immanuel Kant was a famous native of Königsberg and the city was the residence of the dukes of Prussia during the 16th and 17th centuries. The castle and cathedral are both historic landmarks dating back to the 13th century."

He continued: "Now, there is also a reason that the glider school is famous. Sometime during the summer of 1943 a well-known pilot named Jachtmann broke the world endurance record for gliders there. You'll find that the seashore cliffs, which are about 40 meters high, provide excellent soaring conditions when the wind is just right. This guy flew above and in front of the cliffs for 55 hours with only a sandwich and a thermos of coffee to sustain him. He was so stiff that they had to lift him out of the glider when he finally landed during the second night. They had placed kerosene flares marking the edge of the cliffs and also a double row of flares to identify the landing strip. The poor fellow said that he was hallucinating so badly during the second night that he saw non-existent caves in the face of the cliff with gremlins peering at him. Quite a guy! I've always thought that you glider pilots were crazy, anyway! Anybody that flies an airplane without an engine has got to have more than just guts!"

Between naps in the dimly illuminated compartment I remarked how strange it seemed to be traveling without blackout restrictions.

The *Leutnant* replied: "This part of the country is still so far removed from both the eastern and the western fronts that they don't have to worry about complete blackouts yet. However, as we get closer to East Prussia you'll notice a difference. Right now the Russians have entered the province from the Lithuanian border and the front line is getting closer and closer to Königsberg. You'll see strict blackout orders very soon. I really don't know what to do about my wife and kids, with the Russians coming closer and closer. I'm sure you've heard the stories about how they treat civilians, especially the women. We just talked to some refugees from Hungary last week; their story is hard to believe. Anyone who is German or even remotely connected to the Germans is considered an enemy. Those drunken bastards show no mercy; even the officers aren't much better. Mass rape by 20 or 30 Russian soldiers attacking the same woman is the order of the day and, if the poor thing survives the ordeal, she's often shot anyway. I heard an eye-witness account in which a number of women were ravaged while the men of the village were forced to hold up lanterns and watch. When one of the men resisted because his daughter was one of the victims, the Russians castrated him and then shot him in the head. Needless to say, the other men became obedient! This is why I don't know what to do about my family."

I commented: "Maybe with all this snow I see coming the Russians will hole up for the winter. That'll give your wife a chance to flee in the spring before things get going again. I wouldn't want to be a refugee in this damn weather!"

"You may be right; I'll see what the radio says in the coming week and then make up my mind. The trouble is, I can't help her escape at all; I have to be back in Vienna on the seventh day or I'll be shot; they're not giving AWOL people any chance to explain. If your papers have expired and you're still away from your unit, they automatically classify you as a deserter and that's the end of it!"

Such was the mood as we pulled into the Königsberg station. Deep snow had accumulated during the entire day and the crews were busily plowing, scraping and sweeping the white stuff from the station and the city streets. We were lucky again; the train for Brüsterort left within 30 minutes of our arrival; soon we were on the last 40-kilometer leg of our 1700-kilometer journey halfway across central Europe just to attend a glider school!

It was still daylight when we pulled into the rail station at Brüsterort. In a stiff breeze, which was swirling the fresh snow about us from head to toe, we made our way to the airfield. Extending almost to the cliff edge bordering the wind whipped Baltic Sea, the smooth and straight airstrip was criss-crossed by huge snowdrifts. We were glad to take refuge in the adjacent headquarters building. Shaking the snow off our jackets, we reported to the *Unteroffizier* on duty.

"You fellows look frozen; I guess you're not used to an East Prussian winter, are you?"

"I replied: "No sir; we didn't expect to come all the up here near Lithuania. We were originally supposed to go to the Brno school, but they were all filled up."

"I'm assigning both of you to room 124; why don't you drop your bags off in the room and then go down to the mess hall to get warm and eat supper with the rest of the guys. Reveille is at 5:30 A.M.; the screening and indoctrination will start at 8:00 o'clock. Dismissed!"

After a hearty dinner of potato soup and delicious white bread, we made our way back to the cozy, steam-heated quarters. The rooms only had two double bunks each, with lockers and a good sized table for studying and letter writing. We unpacked our bags, made up our beds and were soon fast asleep. Extended conversation with our new roommates could wait until morning.

At the *Appell* the next morning there were 90 of us assembled in the main classroom. The *Unteroffizier* called us to attention and saluted the youthful, medal-covered *Leutnant* who entered the room with a slight limp.

The *Leutnant* returned the salute and addressed us: "Welcome to this *Sonderlehrgang*[1] for glider pilots. At ease and be seated! You have all volunteered for this specialized training and were chosen because of your flying ability as well as your attitude and spirit. There will be additional screening at this school, both physical and mental;

---

[1] Special Course

don't be disappointed if you are disqualified, as you have already achieved this honorable assignment. Let me explain what's in store for you. As soon as the weather breaks and we can clear the snow off the runway, you'll be introduced to a newly developed launch method. It is called the "center of gravity" launch method used for winch launching. Basically, a bridle has been fashioned to fit on the *Kranich* as well as on the *Grunau*. Instead of hooking the tow cable up at the glider's nose, it is fastened to this new rigging which places the pulling point at or near the glider's center of gravity. The first time you see such a launch will remind you of launching a kite; the glider will go up at a very steep angle and you'll get lots more altitude from a given length of winch cable."

He continued: "We'll give you a couple of two-seater instructional flights.....then you'll be on your own in the *Grunau*! We'll do a lot of work on precision patterns and spot landings. However, we also want you to have some fun. When the wind is right, we'll teach you how to fly figure-eights above the cliffs and when you get better, you can try flying below the level of the cliff tops. Just don't let those wing-tips scrape the rocks, though; that Baltic Sea water is pretty damn cold!"

Fascinated, we listened intently as the *Leutnant* continued: "I'm sure that you're all aware that you are in an accelerated training program for the Me-163 rocket fighter. Your next *Sonderlehrgang* will take place about four to six weeks from now, depending upon your progress here and available vacancies at the next school. I just hope that this Russian winter that has come upon us will ease up a bit so we can get you fellows in the air. As far as the next school goes, you guys will really be put to the test. How many of you have ever seen a *Habicht?*"

Almost the entire contingent raised their hands as he continued:" You are all aware that the *Habicht* is a terrific stunt glider; in fact, it's the only glider in the world that has been fully certified for aerobatics. It has been tested in dives up to 420 kilometers per hour[1] without showing any dangerous characteristics. Now comes the surprise: the wingspan of a standard *Habicht* is 14 meters; the factory

---

[1] 260 mph

is producing two other models especially modified for your training group. These are called "*Stümmelhabicht*[1] ; one has a wingspan of 8 meters and the other one only 6 meters! That little one is really a bastard to fly but they say it closely resembles the Me-163 in handling characteristics. That's good, as you can imagine the Me-163 is as touchy as they come and has caused quite a few broken backs! Once you become reasonably proficient in the *Stümmelhabicht*, you'll be making one or two gunnery passes from each winch launch before you land. They have installed a machine pistol in the nose for this purpose that will get you accustomed to aiming the entire aircraft at a target."

One of my roommates who was sitting next to me whispered: "He makes it all sound so easy. My cousin is undergoing basic Me-163 training right now. He told me just a few weeks ago that the accident rate in that *Habicht* school is around 20%! I almost chickened out when I heard that, but it's still better than the Russian front!"

The *Leutnant* apparently heard our whispering and barked: "Gentlemen, if this briefing is that boring for you, I can arrange an immediate wash-out for both of you! Either give me your attention, or go to the office and pick up your travel papers!"

As we sheepishly hung our heads, he continued: "I might as well give you the latest details on the Me-163. This fantastic rocket fighter has been modified again and again to make it better and more stable. It now can climb to 12,000 meters in 3 minutes at around 960 km per hour. It only has fuel for about 12 minutes maximum; that's where your glider training takes over, as the entire journey back to earth after combat is a fast glide."

The *Leutnant* concluded: "You will now be given physical exams; we regret that some of you probably will be disqualified. Those who pass, pick up your study books from the office and get to work. You have a lot to learn in a short time. There will be a navigation class right after lunch. Dismissssssed!"

We anxiously lined up for our physicals, which were routine, until we were very carefully measured for height. Anyone shorter than 170 cm and those taller than 180 cm were told to pack their bags and head for home. It was quite a blow to both of us when Friedrich

---

[1] Stumpy Hawk

measured out at 169. After lunch we bade each other good-bye as he dejectedly trudged down the hall toward the exit. Little did we know that we were not to see each other for quite some time.

By late afternoon nine students were eliminated for one reason or another; our total contingent now stood at 90. The instructors used these washouts to their advantage by keeping us in perpetual fear of being cut from the roster. We were now members of an elite group of glider pilots who were about to embark on the unusual and heroic mission of flying the latest rocket propelled aircraft in defense of the *Vaterland*!

Although the blustering winds and swirling snow prohibited any sort of flying, the instructors pressed on with the indoor work. Wake-up whistles sounded at 5:30 A.M. and we didn't have a moment's rest until dinnertime. It became dark by 4:00 P.M. in these northern latitudes; by the time we broke for dinner, did a little studying and wrote a few paragraphs to our parents, we were more than grateful for the "Lights Out" command at 8:30. We studied and crammed with receptive and eager minds; morale was excellent! I don't want to say that we didn't have any fun, either. After dinner we gathered in one of the rooms or in the mess hall and a guitar would suddenly appear from nowhere. Some military songs and a German folk song or two and everyone would slip into in glowing and sentimental mood. Unfortunately, "off-key Jochen" had to mouth the words to prevent my colleague's disapproving glances; I enjoyed the camaraderie just the same.

We were issued snappy, special uniforms with zippered jackets and the *Luftwaffe* eagle embroidered on the front pocket. When it came to footwear, I drew a bad lot again. There were no more size 44 military shoes in stock. I would have to wear my civilian oxfords until a new supply of shoes arrived; in the meantime, if we went outdoors, I would have to wear a pair of rubber boots that the *Unteroffizier* had dug up. I didn't relish the idea, because plain rubber boots get awfully cold in the snow, especially if your feet start perspiring.

The *Unteroffizier* said: "You have two options, Volmar, until a pair of 44-s comes in from Königsberg. You can either wear the boots or I'll give you a pair of regular shoes in size 46.....whatever you want. It'll take about a week or so until we receive a supply shipment."

I tried on the larger size and my feet just floated around inside them.....rubber boots it would have to be!

It wasn't very long until the radio news broadcasts took on a more ominous tone. Nothing catastrophic yet, but we could tell that the much touted Ardennes campaign had petered out. News on the eastern sector wasn't especially encouraging, either. "Strategic withdrawals" from the advancing Russian armies were admitted on a frequent basis along the entire eastern front all the way from Hungary to Lithuania. When we arrived in East Prussia, one of the first new experiences that we encountered was radio jamming. Whenever we turned on a radio for news broadcast or music listening, there was a constant effort by Russian military transmitters to jam the German airwaves. This was done on a random basis so as to be psychologically the most disturbing. One would be listening to a news reporter just nearing the crucial point of a story only to have his voice entirely obliterated by a high-pitched squeal transmitted by the Russians. They would switch from station to station and from squealing to bursts of conversation in Russian and also to a voice in flawless German advising us that the war was almost over and that we should surrender.

The food at the school was quite good and the instructors exerted great effort to speed up our aviation training. The weather was still bordering on arctic conditions, so we couldn't do any glider work but there was much else to learn.

One day the *Feldwebel* announced: "This afternoon we're going to teach you fellows something about hypoxia. I might as well tell you now, anyone that flunks this test will automatically go home. It will be for your own good, since the failure to recognize impending hypoxia can cause you to keep right on flying until you pass out and come crashing to earth."

He then led us to the mess hall where advance preparations had been made. Standing ready at a table in the center of the room stood a large upright steel tank, similar to those used for welding gases. Connected to the tank with a rubber hose was an aviation oxygen mask attached to a soft flying helmet.

The *Feldwebel* continued his briefing: "The air in this tank has been mixed with nitrogen to simulate the atmosphere at 8000 meters. You will take turns sitting at this table, we'll help you put on the mask tightly and you'll breathe this mixture until you pass out. Don't be afraid as this won't harm you. When your head starts nodding, I'll pull the mask off and you'll be OK as soon as you take in a few breaths of normal air. Now, the main point of the test is a follows; I want you to start writing down numbers in a descending order, starting with the number 100. Every time you reach a multiple of 10, you are to write your perceived bodily reactions in the margin. This will tell me how clearly you are noticing the hypoxia impairment."

As the first student took his turn, he was the object of some good-natured ribbing: "Be sure you don't forget to wake up, Franz; you might miss a good supper!"

Franz dutifully put on the mask, the *Feldwebel* cranked open the valve and the test was in progress. The student's chest heaved up and down in rhythmic breathing as he carefully wrote his numbers. I was too far away to read his notations, but he seemed to be acting quite normally. Franz kept breathing and writing for a short while until, all of a sudden, his face turned a bluish gray and he slumped limply on top of his writing pad. The instructor quickly removed the mask and the color returned to the student's face in short order.

Carefully screening the pad from our view, the instructor examined the notations and said: "You'll be OK, son. You noticed right away what was happening and under combat conditions, you would have turned on your spare oxygen or high-tailed it to a denser altitude. Who's next?"

After about a dozen students had taken their turn, the *Feldwebel* pointed his finger at me: "Alright, Volmar. Put the mask on and let's see how well you can tell what's going on in your body."

With helmet and mask secure, I started breathing and writing. Almost immediately, my fingers began tingling; I noted this duly at the count of 90 and continued. At 80 my fingers tingled even more and my face felt signs of becoming flushed. That's about all I remember until I woke up and looked at my notes. I had managed to count a few numbers below 70 when my pen left the page in a squiggly line. I had written "fingers tingling" at all three stages and even tried to write it twice at the 70 count! The *Feldwebel* passed all of us that day.

14

We had been at the glider field barely two weeks, when we could feel the Russian noose tightening. Radio jamming was at its peak and the distant rumble of artillery shelling could be heard almost constantly. On January 20th a major attack was launched by the Russians and we feared that our school sessions would soon be coming to an end. Three days later, things started happening. I was assigned to be "Student on Duty" until midnight and was sitting in the orderly room manning the telephone. Pleasant guitar music drifted down the hall and I occasionally could make out the sentimental words of a folk song. My thoughts drifted to home and family and balmy weather. Suddenly the jangling phone called me back to reality.

I answered in an official tone: "*Segelflugschule* Samland, *Flugschüler* Volmar speaking."

"This is the Garrison Commandant's office at Königsberg. I must speak with your commanding officer at once!"

"Just a moment, Sir; I will summon him right away!"

Striding down the hall I found him in the room with the guitar music, joining in song with the students. I said to him: "*Herr Leutnant*, the Königsberg Garrison Commandant's Office is on the phone and they want to speak with you right away!"

We both hurried to the orderly room where he picked up the phone. I could only hear one side of the conversation, but could easily tell that we would be leaving the airfield soon.

174

Hanging up the telephone, the *Leutnant* said to me: "Volmar, blow your whistle in the hall and have an immediate *Appel* in the mess hall right away. Get everybody down there on the double! I mean EVERYBODY, instructors included......! We have an emergency on our hands!"

It didn't take the 90 students and 10 *Luftwaffe* personnel very long to hurry to the mess hall. The *Leutnant* addressed us immediately: "As you all know, the Russians have been advancing toward Königsberg steadily during the past week. They are now less than 50 kilometers to the East and are moving fast. An enemy armored force has already reached the Baltic Sea west of here, thereby cutting off our escape to Germany by land. Our orders are as follows: All students will proceed by train to Königsberg first thing tomorrow morning. You will be given an assignment to help in the defense of the city against the Russians. They are reserving an entire car for you. Two *Unteroffiziere* will escort you to an assembly area in downtown Königsberg where you will be assigned to the Garrison Commandant for further orders. The *Unteroffiziere* will return to the airfield immediately to rejoin the training staff. In the meantime we will be preparing the airfield for evacuation. We'll blow up the gliders and the tow plane and burn all the important documents we can't take with us. If we're lucky, they'll send a *"Tante Ju"*[1] to evacuate us; if they can't send one, we'll have to take the train to Königsberg and then head for the harbor in Pillau searching for an evacuation boat."

Looking at us in a sorrowful manner, he continued: "I'm really sad that you fellows have to postpone your special training. The way things are looking, you may never get to fly in this war. I wish you all the luck in the world and may God watch over you; you're going to need it!."

The *Leutnant* went on: "Unfortunately you can take only those items with you that you can easily carry on your person under combat conditions, so your suitcases have to stay here. Mark them legibly with your names and home addresses so that they can be shipped to Germany if conditions permit. You already have helmets and gas masks and you'll be issued further weapons and gear when you reach

---

[1] Nickname for Ju-52 tri-motor transport aircraft, "Aunt Ju"

Königsberg. The cooks will prepare a last meal for you while you're sorting and packing; hurry up and get ready, so that you can get and hour or two of sleep, as you are to leave for the station at daybreak."

It was now decision time; what should I take and what should I leave? My favorite American sweater would fit under my flight jacket but my street shoes and American moccasins would have to stay. My military shoes never did arrive so I was compelled to wear my un-insulated rubber boots; since oxfords would never do in these snowy conditions. Luckily I had brought a large fanny pack, a present from my Aunt Waltrudis, which would hold my small camera and the 200 prized photos I possessed. Other than my *Luftwaffe* greatcoat and a warm pair of American mittens, I packed everything else into my suitcase to be left behind. After a helping of pea soup and bread, we retired to our rooms. My short, fitful sleep seemed to have just begun when the whistles shrilled in the hallway for the last time.

The command was issued: "Everybody assemble in front of the building in 15 minutes.....we're moving out in a hurry!"

The snow and wind whipped into our faces as we marched unsteadily toward the village. It was a two-kilometer trek to the rail station but it seemed twice as far in the chilling wind. As we neared Brüsterort we came upon a bustle of activity. Rather than the peaceful early morning, small-town atmosphere we were accustomed to, it seemed like every civilian in town was up and about. Women and children with a mere sprinkling of men (all of them old or crippled) were streaming southward. They were all heavily laden with rucksacks, suitcases, boxes and bundles. There were horse-drawn carts, carts pulled by oxen and small carts pulled by humans. A few sleds and an occasional baby carriage were mixed in the uninterrupted refugee column. Reaching the station, the *Unteroffiziere* had to force a path through the tight throng of a few hundred people lined up on the platform. The crowd was surging back and forth as we made our way to the edge of the platform.

Women shouted "We want to go too.....! Leave room for us!" Some were crying, others were hysterically screaming at their children not to get lost in the crowd; it was a pitiful sight! We positioned ourselves to be first in line as the puffing steam engine pulled up and squealed to a stop.

"No civilians are allowed in the first car behind the locomotive" one of the *Unteroffiziere* shouted. "It has been classified as a military car. We have authority to shoot if anyone disobeys. Out of the way..... make way..... MAKE WAY!"

Reluctantly the surging civilians made room for us and descended upon the other cars. Shouting, cursing and children's cries dominated the scene as we climbed aboard. Suddenly the sound of breaking glass was heard. Looking toward the next car, we could see a woman trying to push her young son into the rail car through the broken window. As the child whimpered in fear, the train started moving and the mother was forced to put the boy down on the platform. Tearful wailing which tugged at my heartstrings accompanied our departure as we slowly headed toward our next adventure.

The train passed through a number of villages on our way to Königsberg, but never slowed down. Loaded to capacity, stopping anywhere would have spelled even more heartache. As we rumbled through each station we saw hundreds of refugees, all in the same sad condition. Those who weren't hopefully waiting for a train ride had taken to the road, either riding on animal carts or just plain walking. After a two-hour run the heavily loaded train squealed to a stop at the Königsberg station; we dismounted quickly and marched in orderly formation to the Kommandantur[1].

Preparations for the Russian attack were visible everywhere. Just as we had seen in the small towns, the streets of Königsberg were jammed with streams of refugees heading away from the Russian onslaught. The *Volkssturm*[2] members, who were either 14 and 15 year old boys or senior males in their sixties, were busily preparing to defend the city. Sandbags and barbed wire were used to cordon off defense areas. There was hustle and bustle everywhere, sort of an organized confusion.

At the *Kommandantur* we were directed to a large building. The place had the appearance of a storage warehouse divided into four spacious rooms. As we gathered around our two *Unteroffizier*

[1] Commandant's Headquarters
[2] People's Guard

instructors, they bade us farewell and wished us luck..... (We were most certainly going to need it!)

At this point an infantry *Hauptman* took charge and addressed the group: "Men or boys, whatever you are, I want you to pay close attention. As you know, the Russians are on their way to Königsberg. In fact, the latest reports say that it's only about 40 km to the front lines right now. You have been assigned to my command to participate in the heroic defense of Königsberg and I hope you'll bring honor to yourselves when the time for combat arrives. These rooms are filled with assorted battle gear; you'll be given a few hours instruction in the use of these weapons and then sent eastwards to support the troops who are engaged in some tough fighting right now. Your unit will be commanded by a Hitler Youth *Scharführer* who has had considerable infantry training. I want to remind you that you are in a front line combat area and that the strictest military discipline prevails. This means that deserters will be shot on the spot..... do you understand?"

With those words we were split into three groups; an army non-com took charge of each group and started the briefing routines. The first area contained long French rifles dating back to the days of World War One. The *Gefreiter*[1] demonstrated the bolt-action mechanism as well as loading and safety procedures. We each received one of these ancient long-guns and twenty five rounds of ammunition. There were no ammo pouches available, so we had to stuff the rounds into our trouser pockets.

The next station was more interesting as it contained machine guns. There was a variety on display; right at the doorway were portable *Luftwaffe* machine guns. These were normally aircraft-mounted on a swivel base and used by observers and navigators to fend off enemy aircraft. In this emergency situation, these machine guns had been pressed into service for ground combat use. Next, there were a number of captured Czech machine guns. As the *Unteroffizier* in this department started the loading demonstration, he picked up an ammo belt, examined the shells and exclaimed angrily: "This damned ammo is for a Polish machine gun; it sure won't help you guys any!"

---

[1] Corporal

Picking up four of the *Luftwaffe* guns with their distinctive, circular double magazines, we moved on to the next department. A half-hour briefing was to make us *Panzerfaust*[1] experts. Here the non-com in charge said: "This is one of the best anti-tank weapons of the century. If you keep cool, let the enemy tank get close enough and take good aim, you'll bag one every time. This is what the fuses look like; don't ever walk around with a fuse inserted as the *Panzerfaust* will go off in a second if you bump the trigger; this baby will not only burn the hair off your head but will take your whole head too! Unfortunately, they didn't give us any fuses. Take the weapons with you and try to scrounge some fuses when you get to the front."

The last room contained an item we'd never seen before. As we walked in, there were a dozen 20-mm cannon mounted on sleds. A 15-minute briefing resulted in more confusion. The 20-mm cannon shells mounted in strips wouldn't insert in the breech at all. After considerable discussion with the *Feldwebel* it was decided that the strips were for a different model cannon. One of the *Gefreiter* said: "I have the answer. I saw a box of empty 20mm strips in the courtyard. Why don't they pick up those and remount the shells on the way to the front?"

Such were the conditions as we were ushered from the building, carrying our assorted weapons. The Hitler Youth *Scharführer* was waiting in front of a large municipal bus, its engine blowing bluish diesel fumes into the snow-covered courtyard. Our newly appointed leader was typical of his kind; somewhat short with a stocky and muscular build, he was probably all of nineteen years old. Even so, he was two years our senior and held the destiny of 90 flight students in his hands. Somewhat fearful and unsure of ourselves but covering these anxieties well with laughter and exaggerated bravado, we prepared to follow his orders. The *Scharführer* stood at the front door of the bus, his visor cap cocked at a rakish angle. His voice, accustomed to issuing commands, exuded authority and displayed a measure of cockiness.

"All aboard, men!" the leader shouted. "They're waiting for us the front. Put those sleds on the roof rack; the machine guns and

---

[1] " Panzer Fist", a bazooka-like anti-tank weapon

ammo can go underneath in the baggage compartment. Take your rifles on the bus with you.....we might need them on the way."

We boarded quickly and the loaded bus chugged into the streets of Königsberg. It was late afternoon but and streets were still packed with moving refugees. As the driver headed eastwards, the *Scharführer* coaxed us into a marching song. Each involved with our own thoughts and fears, we half-heartedly joined in the tune *"Edelweiss"*. This ski trooper song seemed appropriate in the snowy surroundings, but we just weren't in a singing mood. As we traveled eastward along the slippery highway, the bus had to battle a constant stream of refugees coming in the opposite direction. The scene was typical, with hundreds of frostbitten faces staring up at us as we sped by in the opposite direction. One face was like the other, each showing hunger, fatigue and fear as a pair of weary eyes peered out from under a babushka or a scarf wrapped tightly to keep out the bitter cold. Small children were bundled up in sleds or riding uncomfortably in baby carriages stuffed with clothing and household goods. Often the carriages were abandoned at the roadside when it became too much of a chore to push them through the snow; the possessions were then given up and the child carried on the mother's shoulders.

We had traveled about 40km when darkness began to settle in. A disturbing sight presented itself; not only were the civilians fleeing towards Königsberg, but we came upon an infantry company tromping along the road, headed West! The soldiers looked tired and beaten and many of them wore blood stained bandages. This group had been issued white camouflage tunics, many of which were stained with dirt and blood. These guys must have been in combat for a while.

The sound of exploding artillery shells had now reached an intensity that exceeded the noise of the bus engine and our half-hearted singing. The *Scharführer* told the driver to stop the bus while he cracked open the folding door and shouted at a *Feldgendarm* directing traffic.

"Where is the nearest command post. I have a load of reinforcements ready to fight!"

The MP replied: "Drive over to the church on the next street over. There's a Battalion Command Post that was just set up two hours ago. They'll be glad to get some help; the Russians have been battering us all day!"

Arriving at the church with half its steeple crumbling from an artillery hit, the driver parked and the *Scharführer* went inside. He re-appeared a few minutes later and climbed back into the bus.

"All-right, men; they want us to bed down for the night and take a front line position when daylight comes. The Russians are about four kilometers away but apparently have dug in for the night".

We dismounted, grabbed our weapons and took refuge in two houses right next to the church. There was no problem gaining entry, as all civilians had left in a hurry and securing their homes was the last thing in the world they might worry about.

"What do we do about some food, *Scharführer*?" I asked.

"We're out of luck for today. They told me that the field kitchen got lost by the wayside somewhere. There's a supply depot about two kilometers from here that hasn't been blown up yet. I need some volunteers to check it out and see if you can rustle up something to eat."

While my group hauled the weapons and ammo into the yard between the homes, the driver was released to return to Königsberg. Another group departed for the supply depot on their urgent mission to feed 90 hungry teenagers. We stacked the weapons and made ourselves as comfortable as we could. The furniture was thrown into the snow to maximize the floor space for sleeping. We had no blankets of our own so the few that we found on beds and in closets were shared by two or more students huddled close together on the floor.

With my usual luck, I was assigned to the first two-hour sentry shift. Pacing back and forth in front of the houses, I could readily see and hear the front line activity. Things were fairly quiet, though. An occasional artillery round gurgled overhead and the "rata-tat-tat" of small arms fire could be heard some distance away. There would be a bright flash in the distant sky followed by the delayed sound of the cannon causing the flash. The supply contingent came into the yard, each man loaded down with an armful.

I asked: "What did you guys find at the supply place?"

"The damned place was already burning when we got there. The engineers had orders to destroy the depot as soon as possible, but they let us go into one of the buildings that wasn't entirely in flames yet. All we could find were these wheels of cheese. Well have to make do with them until tomorrow".

It had been over 24 hours since we had eaten anything substantial; consequently we attacked the cheese wheels with fervor. Washing down the sharp tasting cheese with a few gulps of wine from several bottles which had mysteriously appeared from out of nowhere, we took the edge off our ravenous appetites. Wrapping our greatcoats around us, we lay down on the floor to catch what sleep we could. Lined up with my friends like cordwood and using my soft cap and mittens for a pillow, I soon dropped off into a restless sleep.

We probably slept for three or four hours but it seemed like only minutes when we were rousted by the *Scharführer*: "Everybody up and outside.....! The Russians are attacking! Grab your weapons and follow me! You might as well leave the 20-mm cannon here, as the shells won't fit. We tried to remount them last night to no avail."

The eastern sky was brightly illuminated with artillery flashes and the clatter of small-arms fire could be distinctly heard not far away. We were herded to the edge of the village along a secondary road, which was deeply cut into a hill. As we approached the railroad tracks, the *Scharführer* directed us to set up a defensive position. What a laugh....we didn't even have entrenching tools for digging into the snow!

Our leader said: "I want all machine gunners to take positions at the top of this embankment. All others place yourselves in this ditch to fire along the road from whence we came. A few of you jump into this other ditch by the tracks and fire along the railroad when you see the Russians crossing."

With pulses racing we waited for the enemy. The sounds of combat drew closer and closer, as did the dawn. Suddenly we heard the much feared and bone-chilling battle cry of the vodka-primed Russian foot soldiers:"Uuuuuuurrrrrraaaaaayyy!" Within minutes a mortar barrage began descending upon our position. The first casualties came from among my friends with machine guns at the top of the embankment. They were peppered into their backs by mortar shells primed to burst on the slightest contact with the surface of the deep snow.

The first man groaned, slid down the hill, rolling over on his back as he came down. Looking me straight in the eye with a sorrowful glance, he murmured "Say farewell to my mother!" and gurgled his last breath. Several others screamed in agony then became motionless where they lay. During this commotion, another buddy and I tried to cover the Russians who were crossing the tracks about 100 meters ahead of us. My friend placed himself in a drainage manhole, which was just the right depth to afford him good protection, and still allowed him to fire freely down the tracks. I laid down in the snow behind him, but when I loaded my ancient rifle, it refused to fire a single shot; the mechanism was frozen tight. Discarding the rifle, I passed my ammunition to the friend in the manhole and looked around for something to do. One of the machine gunners had slid down the embankment toward me, blood spurting from multiple holes in his leg. Resorting to my Boy Scout training from long ago, I cut off his trouser leg with my pocketknife and fashioned a makeshift tourniquet out of his pants; this slowed the flow of blood somewhat.

Cries of *"Sanitäter, Sanitäter!*[1]" brought four army medics from out of nowhere, who hurriedly put two of our still-alive comrades on a hand drawn sled and headed across the tracks toward the rear area. Suddenly I was unable to stand on my feet. Apparently the combination of the frightful events coupled with feet half-frozen through my thin rubber boots had taken its toll; I was momentarily paralyzed and dropped to my knees. Shuffling around in the snow, I watched in horror as more mortar shells burst within a few meters of my position. My friend in the manhole shouted: "Jochen, I need more ammo! Can you find me some?"

His request brought renewed strength to my legs and I started a search for ammo. Rifling through the pockets of one of the corpses, his face already turned ashen gray, I came up with several clips of French ammunition. I passed it to my friend, who kept on coolly plinking at the Russians, reminding me of an experienced Kentucky rifleman.

The intensity of small arms fire increased as the Russians moved closer. The chatter of machine guns and machine pistols joined

---

[1] Medic, Medic!

in with the mortar bursts; soon the *Scharführer* shouted: "Let's get the hell out of here; we can't hold on any more! Everybody get across the tracks and head for the river. Bring the wounded if you can!"

It now seemed that everything happened at once; the bulk of our group scooted across the tracks, including my friend from the manhole. I had just started to run across myself, when a machine gun burst from down the tracks cut down two of my running comrades. One was killed instantly, the other fell into the snow holding onto his gut. He screamed in pain and cried out: "Help me across the tracks, I don't want to be taken prisoner!"

I started toward him when the machine gun renewed its chatter; the bullets whizzed like a swarm of bees through the air between us. In an adrenaline induced rage I shouted to the fellows who had already crossed the tracks: "Come back here, you cowards! Help me get this guy out of here!"

They were sensible.....I was not! Had they crossed back over to help me drag our wounded comrade, we all would have been mowed down. When no one responded, I happened to glance back toward the village. Less than 50 meters distant stood a burly Russian, wearing a fur cap with the typical quilted winter jacket and brandishing a machine pistol. I could plainly see the round drum magazine, which I knew to hold 72 rounds of 7.65 mm ammo.....I made a hurried decision: "Jochen, you had better get the hell out of here!"

Leaving behind the wounded comrade who was flailing around on the tracks and screaming pitifully for help, I sprinted across the tracks. Luckily no fire came from the Russians along the railroad, but, I had barely reached the far side when I heard the distinctive "Buuuuurrrrrpppp" of the machine pistol directly behind me. I felt a sharp hammer-like blow to my right arm, but I kept on running. I ran and ran and ran attempting to catch up with my friends. To head for the river, I had to depart from the flattened road and start trudging through snow at least a foot deep. The firing continued; machine guns, mortars and machine pistols resounded as I struggled through the drifts.

As I worked my way through the snow, I started panting and sweat poured from my face. Off came the helmet, then I discarded my gas mask; finally, very reluctantly, I unbuckled my belt with the fanny pack containing my prized camera and photographs. My treasures slid into the deep snow and I continued onward toward the river. Suddenly a huge black stain appeared in the snow no more than three or four meters away..... a mortar round, fused to detonate at the slightest contact with the snow, went of. Then another and another.....! By some miracle I was spared, as all the shrapnel whizzed harmlessly by.

A lull in the firing descended upon us as I reached the bank of the frozen river. My arm began to throb as I made my way across the flat expanse and climbed up the bushy bank on the far side. Feeling out of danger for the moment, I slowed my pace, regained my wind somewhat and assessed my situation. Luckily, the Russians weren't following directly on my heels as I was one of the last ones to cross the river. My friends were nowhere in sight but some fleeing infantrymen ahead of me were gathering in groups along the highway waiting for someone to take command. Slogging through the ditch and finally reaching the road, I asked: "Is there a dressing station nearby? I've been shot in the arm!"

One of the soldiers replied; "I saw a red cross flag on that barn over there; why don't you walk on over and get some help."

Sure enough, as I reached the barn and pushed open the swinging door, I saw the medics at work. Several soldiers were lying in the straw, their white bandages in sharp contrast to the dingy environment of soiled gray-green uniforms and dirty straw. Other wounded men were sitting up leaning against the stall partitions. The *Sanitäter* were busy wrapping up a young soldier with a massive shoulder wound. I awaited my turn; finally one of the medics looked at me and said: "They're sending them up here younger and younger all the time! How old are you, boy? And where did you get hit?"

I replied while trying to pull off my greatcoat: "I'm seventeen and they got me in the right arm; it hurts like hell but I don't see very much blood at all!"

"Here, let me help you take some of these clothes off".

As we cooperatively stripped off my coat, uniform jacket and sweater he examined my arm. The medic then gave his diagnosis: "Boy, you have a *Steckschuss*[1]; that's why there was so little bleeding.

---

[1] A gunshot wound wherein the projectile has not exited

There isn't much I can do for you here; I'll put some gauze and tape on the entry hole and you'll have to find a surgical facility to remove the bullet."

He helped me get back into my uniform and reached for a bottle of wine and a metal cup that were lying in the straw.

"Here, take a swig of wine for the pain and rest easy on the straw. We'll send you to the rear with the next ambulance."

The wine taken on my empty stomach had an immediate effect. A warm glow and feeling of relaxation ushered me into a deep sleep within a few minutes.

Many months later I met one of my glider student buddies while we were both in a British P.O.W. camp. He filled me in on the missing details of this day. As best as could be determined, out of 90 proud glider pilots, we lost 20 killed or missing in our four-hour combat experience that fateful morning of January 25th. Our friend in the manhole was awarded the Iron Cross Second Class for his cool-headed sniping. The boy, whose pant-leg I cut off, survived but they amputated his mangled leg to save his life. The remainder of the group escaped from East Prussia unharmed. He had no information as to the fate of our instructor staff at the Samland glider field, which was included in an area that held out against the Russians for many months until finally surrendering on VE day on May 8, 1945.

15

When I awoke, probably half an hour later, we could hear the sound of renewed activity coming from the front. The *Sanitäter* addressed us all:

"I don't know what's holding up that ambulance driver. It's been hours since he left here with a load of wounded; he was going to come right back as soon as he dropped them off at a collection center. From the looks of things, I think you guys who are able to walk should try to make your own way from here. Walk or catch a wagon ride.....anything is better than being captured by the Russians!"

We made our way to the road, several of us supporting the soldier with a shoulder wound. As the heavily loaded refugee wagons came along, each one made room for one or two of us. When my turn came, I squeezed in beside a gray-haired farmer who had three children on the seat beside him. As the children huddled together to make room for me, they told me that their mother had succumbed to a Russian strafing attack just the day before. They had all headed for the protection of a ditch but the mother, carrying an infant, stumbled and both were riddled by machine gun bullets.

We didn't have to travel very far to notice major changes in the highway traffic. Instead of disheveled and downhearted soldiers mixed in with the civilians fleeing westward, there were now fresh troops moving forward. Infantrymen wearing snow-white white parkas, many of them armed with the latest sub-machine guns, strode purposefully in the opposite direction. These were apparently fresh and rested troops brought forward in a hurry to halt the advancing Russians. As we reached the next small town, we came upon a village square bustling with activity. *Feldgendarme* were directing traffic and keeping things moving along at a fast but organized pace. At one end of the square were two military ambulances in the process of loading wounded. I thanked my farmer, jumped off the wagon and hurried to the ambulance. The driver, after requesting that I describe my wound, told me to squeeze aboard as the last one in line. I managed to pull myself onto the bench seat and was getting ready to pull the hinged door shut when a soldier appeared out of nowhere.

Clutching his belly with folded arms, he cried:, "Please take me!.....I took a gut shot early this morning and it hurts like hell; I'm about ready to pass out!"

The driver assured me that another ambulance would arrive shortly and helped me load the wounded man into my former seat. He was right; minutes later another ambulance approached the village square from the East. I attracted the driver's attention by waving my good arm back and forth above my head.

As the driver pulled up to me and stopped, he said: "If you're wounded, you had better wait for a different ambulance; we're hauling medical supplies to Königsberg and don't have any room to spare."

Peering over his passenger's shoulder into the vehicle's interior, I said:" I can find room back there somehow, if you just take me to a field hospital somewhere.....I need this wounded arm taken care of!"

"All-right, boy! Hop into the back and we'll drop you off somewhere along the way so you can get taken care of."

I climbed aboard and struggled with some wooden boxes to make room in one corner of the bench seat. What a treat is was to be sitting down and on the way to medical attention! The ambulance slid and bounced along the highway; a drum of gasoline emitted pungent fumes into the ambulance's interior as we moved along, but I was too grateful for the ride to care.

It was late afternoon when we pulled up in front of the *Lazaret* on the outskirts of Königsberg. The last 30-km leg had gone by swiftly with the knowledge that I was getting further away from the Russians and the dangers they represented. I thanked my chauffeur and walked into the hospital.

Checking in with the female clerk at the front desk, I said: "I have a *Steckschuss* in my right forearm and it's been in there since early this morning; I would like somebody to look at it!"

She replied: "The operating rooms are down that hallway and then to your left. You'll see the line-up when you get closer. I'll put your name and rank on this paper; take it into surgery with you and have the doctor fill in the procedure details when he's done. Then you can bring the form back to my desk and we'll see about a bed. How did you get wounded? You're wearing such an oddball uniform and look so young; how old are you, anyway?"

"I'm 17 and I'm a glider student. They sent us up to the front yesterday to help stem the Russian tide and I got zapped this morning. I guess I'm lucky, though; we lost a bunch of our buddies when the Russians came. We were poorly armed and didn't know what we were doing besides. I'm a flyer, not an infantryman!"

With that, I started walking toward the operating area. The smell of ether and disinfectants wafted toward me as I approached a line of soldiers awaiting their turn at surgery. The line moved rather swiftly, as there were four tables in use in the same operating room.

As we waited we were forced to listen to the agonizing moans of a figure covered up on a nearby gurney. Finally, a *Sanitäter* came up and wheeled the figure away.

One of the soldiers in line remarked: "Man, am I glad they're finally taking him in. He's going to the other operating room where they take care of the bad cases. That poor guy is a panzer *Leutnant* and has seven bullets in his body. He was escaping from his burning tank when an *Iwan* machine gunner got him in his sights. I hope he pulls through!"

Finally it was my turn and I was directed to the first table on the right (just like going to a bank teller). My upper garments came off in a flash I was placed on an operating table.

With my right arm strapped down, the doctor said: "Looks like this bullet traversed your whole forearm and is resting down here at the base of your wrist. It's not very deep, therefore I shouldn't have any trouble extracting it. We're very short of Novocain, so we'll just freeze the tissue a little bit so it won't hurt so much. Think you can handle that, boy?"

"Go ahead, sir! I clench my teeth a little".

An assistant sprayed some ethyl chloride on my wrist, there was a quick flash of a scalpel and the doctor held up a shiny 7.65 mm slug. He stuffed a gauze tampon into the opening and slipped the bloody bullet into my shirt pocket to keep as a souvenir. With the words "Who's next?" the doctor looked up and beckoned to the next patient standing in line.

"Doctor, how about the entry wound just below my elbow? Don't you want to look at that also?"

"Oh.....I'm sorry to have overlooked that; we're so damned busy today! Here, I'll put a Band-Aid on it to keep it from bleeding any further! Next patient, please!"

I grabbed my greatcoat and jacket and made my way back to the reception clerk. She said: "Are you ever in luck; there's a bed available in room 137 down the hall. Hurry right down there before somebody beats you to it. I figured such a young boy might need his sleep; am I right?"

"Thank you, *Fräulein*. Yes, I haven't slept for three nights and I'm pretty tired."

The room was normally a two-bedder but a third bed had been crammed in to fit along one wall. One of the room-mates was a soldier with a half cast from waist to neck with arm immobilized on a protruding rack; even though his shoulder was completely shattered, the man was able to walk around and help himself with his good arm. In the other bed was a poor devil whom I shall never forget. This man was minus an arm as well as a leg missing from the hip down. The soldier had already been bedridden for several months and displayed a jaundiced color, giving him the appearance of an emaciated far-easterner. To top off his agony, the poor guy had extensive festered bedsores and had to be shifted about regularly to ease the pain.

However, neither of these could outdo the soldier whose bed I took over. He had just died minutes before and was being wheeled away for burial as I walked down the hall!

After a hot bath with the help of a *Sanitäter*, a hearty bowl of lentil soup followed by a shot of morphine and I had soon forgotten my troubles by drifting off into a deep and peaceful sleep.

The next few days were filled with boredom. It was here that I started my lifelong smoking habit, when I discovered that a cigarette could take the edge off the throbbing pain in my arm, postpone a teenagers hunger pangs and even relieve boredom to some extent. I wandered through the halls, read endless books and newspapers and wished I hadn't been wounded. Even though I was happy to be alive, I was eager to return to my comrades and find a way to "get even" with the *Iwan*.

To this conversation, my roommate remarked: "Look here, my boy; why don't you give up on this hero stuff? You're fortunate to have made it this far, so don't press your luck! If I can get out of this pocket and back to Germany, they'll play hell to get me back in combat again; I've had enough and you should feel the same way. The war is as good as lost anyway!"

As if to emphasize his remarks, the loud gurgling of an incoming Russian artillery shell could be heard. I crouched halfway under the bed as the shell passed overhead and hit another target. I felt so helpless and unprotected in the hospital room, which had a large picture window facing the street. Every time an enemy shell came whistling, I visualized it coming right into our room, bringing with it hundreds of glass fragments. The shelling was sporadic but increased in intensity over the next few days. The radio blared notices of towns over-run in spite of "heroic defense battles" so we were quite aware of the Russians' forward progress.

It was my fourth day at the *Lazaret*; I had been asleep about an hour following my nightly dose of morphine when the dreaded whistles sounded. A *Feldwebel* made the rounds announcing: "All walking wounded get dressed and assemble in the rear courtyard! The Russians are just outside of Königsberg and are moving forward! Get moving.....Get moving.....All walking wounded out of the *Lazaret* as soon as possible! You'll be heading for the Pillau Harbor for evacuation!"

The roommate with the body cast and I helped each other dress as best we could. I slung his greatcoat over his one shoulder and draped a blanket over his unwieldy framework. Sorrowfully, we bade farewell to our bed-ridden friend and followed the *Feldwebel* down the hall.

"*Herr Feldwebel*, I don't have any headgear at all....! Where can I find a hat of some sort?"

He answered: "The supply room next to the operating rooms is unlocked; hurry down there and find yourself a hat!"

Heeding his suggestion, I ran to the supply room as fast I could. There I found just the right thing for a cross-country march: a brown Russian fur cap lay on the first shelf. I tried it on, it fit, and off I ran again, to rejoin the other walking wounded at the exit.

The *Feldwebel* was addressing the group: "Unfortunately none of our staff can accompany you men. We have to stay with the bed patients and also keep the *Lazaret* operating for the new casualties that'll be coming in. Just keep heading West along the canal; it's about 40 km to the harbor at Pillau. Just follow the civilian refugees. Good luck!"

What a motley group we were: soldiers with head wounds, arm wounds and even some leg-wounded with canes were making a try at escape; anything was better than letting the Russians take you prisoner! As we straggled down the street along the canal, we were exposed to an occasional artillery round sent over by the enemy to disrupt German traffic and communications as much as possible. Not being a seasoned combat veteran, I dropped down into the snow every time there was a close one (at least by my standards)!

My roommate soon set me straight: "Jochen if you continue taking cover like that, you'll never make it to the boat. First of all, these delays will slow you down and secondly your uniform will be soaking wet and you'll freeze to death. Pay attention to an old infantry expert like me; I'll tell you when there's a round close enough to worry about!"

After slogging along for several hours, we came to a church in a small village along the road. The priest had stationed himself at the main door and was beckoning us to come inside. A break and a little warmth would certainly be welcome, so we stepped inside. The entire church was jammed to capacity with refugees and wounded soldiers from wall to wall. Several wood stoves were burning brightly giving the occupants an eerie yet comfortable glow. We found a place to sit at a table in the rear and put our heads down to rest. Under the harsh white light of a naked bulb hanging overhead, I found out why my partner had been complaining about his torso cast. The friction caused by continuous walking had worn his skin to a frazzle around his waist and the raw flesh was exposed. I begged a diaper from one of the refugee mothers and fashioned a makeshift lining for his plaster cast but there was nothing I could do for his pain. Even though my arm was throbbing now that the morphine had worn off, it was bearable. Looking at the array of wounded men, I was indeed one of the most fortunate with only a single and clean bullet wound in my arm.

Glancing over at the next table, I couldn't believe my eyes.....wasn't that one of our upper-classmen, Franz Koch, sitting there? It most certainly was! I made my way over to him and we shook hands.

"How in the world are you, Franz? What are you doing here?" I exclaimed.

"Why hello, Jochen; I could say the same for you!.....What are you doing here?"

Franz was a Luftwaffe *Leutnant* and had been in fighter pilot training the last time he was on leave. I immediately noticed his distinctive armband with the lettering *"Division Hermann Göring"*[1] embroidery. He filled me in: "Our training squadron of Me-109-s was just about ready for combat last November when they transferred the whole damn squadron to the Hermann Göring Division to be used as infantry. We had plenty of aircraft but there just isn't enough fuel to go around. We were in combat at the Lithuanian border when I took some shrapnel in my back so they're sending me back to Germany. What are you doing here? That's a strange uniform you're wearing.....who are you with?"

I filled him in on my adventures of the past few weeks, but we both soon rested our heads on our arms and dozed off for a while. Good news roused us quickly as the priest made the announcement: "A motorcycle courier just passed through with a message: they're sending some army trucks to start hauling wounded to the harbor!"

---

[1] Special elite Luftwaffe Division performing infantry functions

We waited and waited..... the dawn appeared and still no sign of any trucks. Warming our hands at the stove for the last time, we trudged into the roadway again. As we joined the bedraggled and slow moving column, we began to wonder if we would ever reach the harbor, by now still about 30 km distant. The roadside was littered with charred ruins of wagons, trucks and carts..... some with dead bodies in them, some just empty hulks, silhouetted against the stark white snow..... the aftermath of Russian strafing attacks. Dead horses and cattle lay askew everywhere, also victims of Russian aerial attacks or of the below zero temperature which chilled both man and beast to the bone!

Suddenly a murmur arose from amidst our column: "Here comes an empty truck! Maybe he's one of those that was supposed to arrive this morning!"

Sure enough, the truck pulled up next to our group of bandaged soldiers. The driver shouted: "I can only take wounded on board. Hurry up and jump on the truck..... we have to keep moving!"

It was a large open stake truck and with some boosting and shoving a large part of our group managed to get aboard. We stood upright, packed in man-to-man like sticks of firewood. At this time I lost track of my roommate and Franz Koch in the frenzy to get aboard; I never saw either one of them again!

The truck lumbered ahead with its heavy load. Progress was very slow and integrated into the jumbled column, the truck had to stop at every slow-down and start up when things got moving again. With each sudden stop, the crowd of wounded crammed into our truck lurched forward in unison but also came to a halt in the same abrupt manner, bringing forth curses and screams of pain. I held tightly onto my arm, which was bent at the elbow to accommodate the sling. However, this did nothing to prevent the sharp pain that seared through my arm from finger to elbow each time we stopped or hit a bump in the road. A short period of bright sunshine and the absence of enemy aircraft did wonders for my mood; it was still a long and arduous trip.

Darkness had settled when we pulled into the town square at Pillau. We jumped off into the crisp snow and the truck immediately took off for Königsberg for another load of wounded.

A number of us found refuge in a vacant house nearby. After a quick serving of stew from the field kitchen parked at the square, we bedded down on the hardwood floor to rest our weary and pain-racked bodies. For a pillow I found a piece of lumber and stuffed it into my fur cap..... anything would do, as exhausted as I was.

January 30th....it was after daybreak when I woke up again, this time abruptly to the clattering of hob-nailed army boots echoing through the vacant building and excited shouts of "There's a boat in the harbor" and "Hurry up, maybe we can get out of this damn place!".

I staggered out the door and down the steps to join the throngs of walking wounded surging down the icy and snow-drifted street.

My arm still throbbed intensely from the hurried surgery at the field hospital to remove the mangled Russian bullet. My body ached from sleeping fitfully on the hard wooden floor; wrapped in my bloody greatcoat, I stumbled tenaciously on through the snow. Today was probably the last chance to escape the rapidly advancing Russian spearhead which had encircled the remaining parts of East Prussia completely; the only exit remaining would be by boat across the Baltic Sea.

Suddenly everybody slowed down and word filtered back through the disorganized throng....."Road block ahead!"

What could be wrong? It couldn't be the Russians already, as there was no close gunfire, only the distant rumbling of heavy artillery drawing closer and closer. "What's the delay?.....we must get to that boat!"

Slowly the green-clad figures pushed and stumbled onward..... Then came the word "Military Police!"

It seemed like an eternity before I could see what was going on; about a dozen burly *Feldgendarme*, their shiny breast shields tinkling ominously with every movement, were lined up across the entire width of the street with their *Schmeissers*[1] at ready. They permitted the tired soldiers to pass, one by one, into the guardhouse at the edge of the street.

"Why are they holding us up at a time like this ?"

---

[1] German machine-pistol

"Can't they hear that the Russians are getting closer and closer by the minute?"

When my turn finally came to enter the guard shack, superheated by a glowing and smelly oil stove, I felt a sudden wave of nausea and dizziness. The abrupt heat and odors of perspiration and foul-smelling bandages was about all I could take.

Brusquely the fat *Feldwebel* in charge said "Take off your bandages, soldier, we have to make sure your wound is genuine!"

I obeyed, holding back a strong urge to vomit, and peeled off the crusted layers of gauze from my forearm. After satisfying the *Gendarms* that my wound was real and rewinding the smelly bandage, I was ushered out the side door onto the street. What a relief to be in the fresh air again!

Not so lucky was a young blond infantryman just behind me, whose wound was merely a first-aid pack wrapped around his head in a not-so-clever deception. This poor fellow was roughly shoved out the back door and prodded into a waiting truck about to depart for the front lines.

I buttoned my coat to ward off the sudden chill after leaving the stuffy guardhouse. "How much further to the boat?"

The waterfront was a real disaster area. Abandoned carts and wagons were scattered throughout, making access to the actual docking area an obstacle course. Once these were overcome, we joined a waiting crowd of hundreds of refugees and wounded clustered around a small ship moored at the quay. The ship was a small German merchantman, perhaps 150 meters in length. A closer view revealed a bomb crater in the foredeck, which had splayed out the upper part of the ship's black steel hull in a grotesque fashion. I hoped that this damage wouldn't interfere with the normal operation of the ship. We probably would be safe unless there were high waves under storm conditions. However, none of this seemed to deter any of the hundreds waiting to board her.

It seemed that as 10 people clambered up the steep gangplank they were replaced by 20 new refugees who joined the waiting throng. Two husky German naval sailors supervised the gangplank entrance. Only minimum hand baggage was permitted and a stack of discarded trunks and boxes began to accumulate on the quay. As the interior areas of the ship filled up, more and more heads began to appear topsides. Even the foredeck around the bomb crater was getting crowded. As the crowd expanded and I was still a long way from the gangplank, I undertook a desperate move. Forging my way out of the crowd, I worked my way to the water edge of the quay. Once there, I cleverly shinnied my way on tiptoe past the front line of waiting refugees. It probably helped that my arm was in a sling and that I was so young, as I was soon at the entrance to the gangplank.

The sailors were just about to slam the gate, when one of them spied me: "One more can't do any harm.....come on aboard, boy!" he said. This time I swore that I felt my guardian angel's hand on my shoulder as I stumbled up the steep gangplank.

Lines were cast off amid the wailing and crying of separated families and the ship moved slowly through the harbor. Chilled to the bone from a whole day of waiting, I decided to explore the vessel. This was a combination passenger ship and freighter. All the holds were filled with a mixture of refugees and wounded; stretchers were scattered in disarray as room permitted when they were hoisted aboard. Cries of small children blended with the agonizing groans of the badly wounded. A few nurses and a *Sanitäter* circulated about rationing the limited supply of morphine available. An occasional covered corpse could be seen, shoved carelessly out of the way to make more room for the living. The permeating stench of blood, urine and feces wafted up the companionway as I turned aside to continue my tour. My progress in exploring the boat was agonizingly slow; wherever I went there were women, children and wounded soldiers..... They were below decks and topsides and even huddled inside the bomb crater!

It was long after dark when we left the harbor for the open waters of the Baltic Sea. As the swells gained in height the ship gained in rhythmic up and down motion. Still uncomfortably cold, I started exploring the cabin area hallways for a place to sit down. No luck, as every inch of corridor wall was taken up by people, sitting shoulder to shoulder along the full length of each hallway. All cabins were also filled to the brim, mostly with wounded soldiers lying in the bunks or on stretchers placed on the floor. Back in the hallway the ship's motion started taking its toll. Retching and vomiting became prevalent and these liquids were soon blended with the urine and feces that sloshed and tumbled down the hallway, synchronized with the motion of each ocean wave. Luckily, I've never been prone to seasickness, although this was the closest I'd ever come!

In a dog-tired state with still no place to sit down, I wandered up to the foredeck and examined the bomb crater. Using my cigarette lighter to light the way, I stumbled around inside the damaged area into what was once the forecastle. Several wounded soldiers were already huddled here on some makeshift bunks made of canvas stretched over a crude lumber framework. I brushed aside some snow and joined the huddle.

After a while the cold got to me again; I started prowling around for a better place of refuge. It was now the middle of the night and everybody was sleeping as best they could. I began checking doorways I hadn't come across before and stumbled upon a pleasant surprise. A door led to the engine room; although noisy and smelling of diesel fuel, the catwalk above the engines was unoccupied! I sat down, letting my legs dangle above the clanking diesel engines, wrapped my good arm around the center-rail and promptly fell asleep.

On occasion, the diesel chattering would awaken me and I would have some flash thoughts and fears, such as "What if we get torpedoed?" "I wonder how long one can stay alive in this cold water?" Then I would nod back to sleep again.

Morning came and I went for a stroll from my newfound refuge. Just down the hall I discovered the galley emitting the tempting aroma of food and coffee. I walked up to the sailor leaning over the stove and said: "Got anything to eat or drink for a poor destitute soldier?"

He replied: "Sure, kid. Here's some coffee and some bread and butter.....just don't show the stuff to anybody else, or they'll be beating down my door. I'm sorry, but we just can't feed all these people. They'll have to wait until we get to Swinemünde!"

Wolfing down my food and drink, I thanked the sailor profusely and returned to my haven above the engines. A short time later, the ship's whistle sounded two long blasts. I hurried topside and saw the Swinemünde harbor entrance in the distance. The blue-green waters of the Baltic Sea were covered as far as the eye could see with small ice floes bobbing gently in the swells. We had completed a 250-km leg of our narrow escape without mishap!

As the ship slowly slid to its docking position along the cobblestone-paved quay, I was overwhelmed with the reception we received. No sooner was the gangplank in place when a horde of *Sanitäter* and nurses made their way to the top and onto the boat.

A *Feldwebel* barked: "All wounded personnel are to disembark first! You walking wounded, there is a hospital train waiting right over there on the siding. Just walk over and climb aboard the cars with benches. We'll carry the stretcher cases over as soon as we can and they will ride in the stretcher cars! Let's get a move on..... some of your buddies may need medical attention right away!"

A long and slow moving line of exhausted wounded men wound its way to the rail siding. I climbed aboard one of the cars and found a comfortable window seat. I had hardly taken my seat when a nurse came up to me and said: "Describe your wound and tell me when it has been inspected last. You fellows sure were lucky.....did you hear about the sinking last night?"

"No, we haven't heard anything! What on earth happened?"

"The 25,000 Ton *KDF*[1] liner named *Wilhelm Gustloff* left Pillau yesterday afternoon with around 8000 refugees and wounded aboard. She was torpedoed during the night and at least 7000 souls perished in the cold water. Didn't you guys hear or see anything?"

"We didn't notice anything while we were on the way over here..... I guess we had a close one!" Reaching eagerly for a sandwich and coffee from the nurse's cart, I could have sworn that I again felt the light touch of a guardian angel's wing brushing across my shoulder.

---

[1] *Kraft Durch Freude* "Strength Thru Joy", a government sponsored cruise ship

16

The train was loaded swiftly; I could tell that the nurses and *Sanitäter* were practiced at their game. None of us in the regular cars were in a hurry to go anywhere. The pleasant warmth, tender care and delicious sandwiches were enough for me to want time to stop for a while, permitting me to enjoy these rare pleasures to their fullest. However, reality took over as the train pulled slowly out of the station. We knew that some of the more seriously wounded comrades should be expedited to a hospital for further care.

Nobody knew our destination; the train commander was apparently under constant supervision by radio and changed routings as he was advised. First we moved south in the direction of Stettin. Soon word filtered through the cars that were headed in the direction of Berlin. Air raid alarms interrupted our progress repeatedly, as we stopped to await "All Clear" sirens. Our direction changed once more and we were now headed on a northwesterly course. This time the word was "Lübeck"..... back up to the Baltic Sea!

With no further changes we finally rolled into the Lübeck station in the afternoon. The transfer from train to hospital was done by crews well acquainted with their jobs. A fairly new school building had been prepared as a temporary *Lazaret* for us. Two hundred beds, unfortunately of the double-decker style, had been set up in the auditorium. The theater stage was set up as a dressing station and for minor surgery; more demanding cases were sent to another hospital.

These folks had thought of everything; a temporary telegraph office had been set up in one of the school offices. I immediately sent off a wire to Mutti, advising her of my escape; a letter would follow soon.

We stood in line and shuffled one by one onto the stage. My wounds were cleaned and dressed for the first time since my surgery a week ago. To relieve the intense pain I experienced while trying to move my arm, a plaster half-cast was fashioned to immobilize the arm. This helped somewhat and, together with a soft clean bed and a full stomach I fell into a sound sleep long before darkness set in.

The next day my re-learning process began: I had to convert my brain and my body to left-handed functions. From shaving to tooth brushing, from showering to one-handed shoe tying..... it all had to be taken care of. Comrades and *Sanitäter* were all very helpful, but with over 200 soldiers, each of us impaired in one or more ways, we had to learn to be self-sufficient.

After a few days in Lübeck, I began to wonder about the absence of air raids. The peace and quite was so unaccustomed, that I asked a *Sanitäter*:

"How do you explain the lack of air attacks here in Lübeck? Have the Amis and Tommies forgotten about this city?"

"There used to be frequent raids on this city, as you'll see when they let you out for a stroll. There was extensive damage done and quite a loss of life. However, they declared Lübeck to be a *Lazaret* city and it seems that the enemy is honoring that request. There are military hospitals all over the place and they keep setting up more, just like they converted this school building just last week before you fellows arrived."

Before I ever had a chance to get a first hand view of this damage, I was transferred. The very next day a number of us lightly wounded were given orders to move to Bad Grömitz, a small summer resort about 30 km to the North along the seacoast.

The *Lazaret* was a small resort hotel, which had been taken over for hospital use. It accommodated about 70 patients and was staffed with three *Sanitäter*, half a dozen nurses and a *Stabsartzt* in charge. A nice set-up, except the doctor was an internist with limited surgical knowledge..... not ideal for patients who were all 100% surgical!

The view of the Baltic Sea was idyllic, the nurses cheerful and accommodating, but.... it was still the dead of winter and the ocean was frigid and no amount of tender nursing care could make up for short rations! Boredom didn't help any; it seemed that all we thought about was the next meal!

Many of the patients were in the last stages of healing and would soon be shunted to the front lines again. I had only been in Bad Grömitz a few days, when one of my new comrades was pronounced "fit for combat" by the doctor. My friend had received an extensive shrapnel wound in the shoulder, which had finally closed up and was healing nicely. It was a consensus of opinion that the man was being discharged pre-maturely but the doctor was the boss, so our friend bade farewell with his orders returning him to duty. Two days later the poor fellow re-appeared with a fresh bandage on his shoulder. While lifting his rucksack at the *Frontleitstelle*[1] his wound burst open again, sending him back to the *Lazaret*!

Now it was my turn to experience the internist's skill; I had been in *Grömitz* about three weeks, when the *Stabsartzt* said:

"Well, Volmar, the arm is looking pretty good; I think we'll take the half-cast off today and in a week or so we'll send you off and running again!"

"*Herr Stabsartzt,* something isn't right inside my arm. Sometimes I wake during the night up screaming in pain when the arm twists into a certain position..... can't you do something?"

The doctor mused: "Well maybe we should take an X-ray and see what things look like inside. We don't have a machine here, so we'll send you to Lübeck tomorrow and have a film made."

With my orders in hand, I made my way to Lübeck by train. Winding my way through rubble-lined streets I came to the large *Lazaret* where the X-Ray facilities were. After waiting in line for an eternity, my turn finally came. Two exposures of my forearm were made and slid into the developing tank. I wasn't at all surprised when, a short time later, the technician informed me:

---

[1] Forward directing center for personnel in transit

"No wonder you have pain, soldier..... look at this film! The bullet traversed your arm lengthwise and shattered the ulna into about 30 little pieces. The fragments will eventually bond together, but they should put the arm in a full cast so it can heal properly!"

Thanking the *Sanitäter*, I took the film and returned to Bad Grömitz. The next day I was given a full cast and another month's reprieve from returning to the war. The cast was quite cumbersome compared to the half cast, as it extended from my fingers all the way to my armpit and held my arm at a firm 90 degree angle. Until now I had stubbornly insisted upon dressing myself and struggled valiantly with my half cast to get into my shirt with the missing sleeve, which had been cut off at the front line dressing station. Now I had to ask for help. The pretty blond nurse whose assistance I had rejected all of these weeks was finally allowed to help. After forcing my cast through the ragged shirt, she would brush up somewhat amorously against this bashful young *Flugschüler* who responded in his youthful discomfiture..... with no response at all!

The little town of Grömitz was a tidy little summer resort with clean water, pebbly beaches and nothing else to offer during off-season times. The population stood at minimum, the small movie house was closed and there were very few young ladies in residence. One day my roommate and I did find a pair strolling along the beach. Since we were restricted to the *Lazaret* most of the time and had very short liberty, we devised a clever plan to see more of these ladies than the German *Wehrmacht* should know about. At "Lights Out" we retired to our room like good, rule-abiding patients. As soon as things quieted down and the *Sanitäter* on duty had retired to his quarters, we climbed out of our beds and quickly fashioned dummies out of bedding and spare uniforms. I even placed my dark brown Russian fur cap on the pillow to resemble a shock of hair. We then quietly sneaked out the French doors of the dining hall and made our way to the beach. Sure enough, the girls were waiting and we took a nice stroll in the moonlight and returned to the hospital later, undetected. I must admit that those walks were just as innocent as could be; the youthful bashfulness didn't step aside until a few months later. I often wondered if the medic had forgotten that my hair was blond or was he really just a good-hearted guy?

It was now March and the Americans had overrun Kaiserslautern where my mother was living. With all communications cut off by the front line, I only could hope that she had survived the combat operations as the city was captured. At the same time the Russians were steadily pushing back the German troops through Poland and Czechoslovakia with the destination Berlin in mind. It looked as if I was about to become the victim of a squeeze play!

After four weeks had elapsed since my cast had been installed, the *Stabsartzt* called me into his office. He said:

"Volmar, I think we're about to send you on to better places; you've been pretty bored around here anyway, haven't you?"

"Yes sir, I would like to be discharged as long as my arm doesn't hurt any more" I replied. "I've been throwing pebbles into the ocean almost every day to keep my upper arm in shape, so I think I'll be alright!"

With a large pair of snips he clumsily crunched away at my cast until it parted and permitted the *Sanitäter* to peel off the cast and expose my forearm, slightly withered from disuse. The doctor pulled and twisted a little and, satisfied that the arm was reasonably mobile, ordered my discharge.

I had no extra clothing or gear, so I was allowed to scrounge around the supply room for a pack of some sort and for a shirt to replace the one I was wearing when I arrived, which had the right arm cut off at the shoulder. I found a battered rucksack and a faded blue shirt to go with my glider student garb. The shirt had a bullet hole right in front, but that would be concealed by my zipped jacket.....I was on my way to another adventure.

My orders sent me to the *Frontleitstelle*[1] in Hamburg, about 50 kilometers to the West. I thanked my lucky stars that it was in the direction of the American and British forces rather than eastwards toward the Russians. As the train rumbled into the outskirts of Hamburg I observed some of the worst destruction I had ever seen. Instead of the intermittent ruins I was accustomed to from other cities I had seen, this pattern of desolation was almost without interruption. We sometimes rolled along for a few thousand meters where there was

---

[1] Front-line Replacement Center

nothing but piles and piles of blackened rubble. There was an occasional break where the crews had cleared a street or an alleyway to allow traffic to pass through, but the landscape was mostly useless debris. Now and then there was a lone building still standing, But those generally had all windows shattered and their bare openings stared at us like the hollow eyes of some evil monster. A feeling of deep sadness overcame me, as I saw an old woman standing next to a child's wagon and pawing through the wreckage, probably in a hopeless search for a useful article left unhurt in a recent raid. My thoughts turned to *Mutti*: had she survived the American advance? Was her home still intact or was she living in a shelter or hut somewhere?

The *Feldgendarme* at the shrapnel-scarred Hamburg station directed us to a waiting army truck, its wood-burning generator ejecting puffs of smoke skyward as we waited for the truck bed to fill up with an array of military personnel. There were rugged infantrymen, black garbed panzer drivers and others clad in the distinctive *Luftwaffe* blue. Soon all of the waiting men had scrambled aboard and the truck rumbled off through the ruins. Ruins and more ruins; it seemed that was all that was left of this once bustling seaport!

The *Frontleitstelle* was housed in an old *Wehrmacht* barracks that somehow had escaped destruction. We were given bunk assignments and told there would be an 8:00 AM *Appell* the next morning.

The return to the military routine I had escaped during my stay at the hospitals was announced abruptly when the *Appell* whistle sounded in the hallway. Trudging outside to the parade ground, we assembled before a one-armed *Feldwebel*, who barked:

"Everyone listen closely as I don't want to repeat myself. I will call out various military specialties and want those of you included to step forward right away and assemble in groups over here. You will then step into the office to get your orders and travel vouchers.....panzer gunners.....105 millimeter personnel.....*Luftwaffe* ground crew.....truck drivers.....infantrymen!"

The selected men stepped forward, leaving about a dozen of us standing in the ranks. The *Feldwebel* said:

"The rest of you are the lucky ones today. Go back to your rooms and be happy that you've gained another day of reprieve from the war. We'll announce more categories tomorrow."

The same procedure took place the next morning and again there was no demand for anti-aircraft specialists, let alone for glider pilots. Tired of sitting around doing nothing, I went up to the *Feldwebel* after the *Appell* and said:

"*Herr Feldwebel*, isn't there anything you can do to find a place for me to go? "I'm tired of sitting around here with nothing to do."

"Look here, son; let me give you some advice. Every day you gain by hanging around here is a day less that you'll have to spend in some stinking foxhole at the front. Why don't you just stay here and let your arm heal all the way?"

"I just don't want to sit here all day and be bored stiff, *Herr Feldwebel*. Can't you find an assignment for me with one of the Flak batteries here in Hamburg?"

"If that's the way you want it, son, let me see what I can do. Come with me to my office and I'll make some telephone calls."

Within a few minutes he found a 37-millimeter battery in the harbor district that could make use of me. Thanking the *Feldwebel*, I took my hastily written orders and directions to the battery and departed. Was this another adventure I was embarking on?

Traveling on an array of streetcars and busses I arrived at the gun position. The 37 millimeters were the same Russian pieces I had been trained for, but everything else was entirely different from the cozy battery I had left behind at Kaiserslautern. The guns were concealed in pits dug into the shifting sand near the Elbe River. A wooden barracks building, pock-marked with shrapnel hits, was nestled behind a hill covered with scraggly grasses. Bomb craters were visible as far as the eye could see and the loose sand swept wind-blown around me as I made my way to the office.

"*Flugschüler* Volmar reporting for duty, *Herr Unteroffizier*" I said saluting somewhat lamely with my wounded arm.

"Why in the hell did they send me a flight student when I need experienced gunners?" he shouted.

"Don't worry, *Herr Unteroffizier,* I'll make myself useful. I'm a trained loading gunner on these Russian pieces."

"That changes things a little; I need a loader on gun number three; one of my *Luftwaffenhelfer* went to the hospital with diphtheria and may not be back for a while; you can take his place for the time being. I suppose I should be happy that you showed up, as you look nice and strong. Most of my crew are either 14 year old little guys or 65 year old feeble men. They do the best they can but can only endure so much physical stuff and they poop out on me. Come with me and I'll walk you down the hall and find a bunk for you."

As we entered the room, a motley group sprang to attention. I immediately could see what the *Unteroffizier* meant when he described his crew. We could have been standing in a grammar school classroom, as most of the boys were rosy-cheeked and pint-size. Two gray-haired men completed the assortment as they slowly and casually stood up in a mere semblance of "attention".

"At ease, men! I've brought you a new loading gunner for gun number three. Make yourself at home, Volmar; you can find some blankets in the storeroom next to the office.....I'll see you later."

As I threw my rucksack on a vacant bunk, one of the boys introduced himself:

"My name is Hans Schroder; what's yours?"

"Glad to meet you; I'm Jochen Volmar. How long have you guys been in this desolate gun position?"

"We were drafted as *Luftwaffenhelfer* last Fall and came here right after our training. We've had some pretty hefty raids and have taken a few bomb hits right in the positions. Thank goodness the raids have slacked off a little since the British front is moving closer. We've had seven fatalities in our battery this year and I came damned close myself last month. We had a real close bomb hit and I was buried alive in my foxhole for about 10 minutes. When we take you out to show you our position, you'll see how the foxholes are constructed here; it's this type of construction that saved my life. Because of the loose sand, we have to line each foxhole with upright timbers to prevent cave-ins. Well, I was crouched in my foxhole while the Tommies dropped a carpet of bombs across this entire area. All of a sudden the explosions started getting closer and closer; then one hit right next to me, pushing in the sides of my hole. Luckily the timbers came together with my helmet in between. Here I was, buried alive in the sand and unable to move. Somebody heard my screams and they proceeded to dig me out of the mess. Believe me, I never want to go through anything like that again."

I replied: "It looks like the big bombers have been going elsewhere; maybe they'll leave us alone for a while. I've never been in a really big bombing raid and I don't want to start now!"

My prediction held true; not a single night raid took place in the week that I was assigned to the battery. This was very fortunate for me, however. When I tried to pull back the massive spring-loaded bolt to insert the clip of 37-millimeter shells, my right arm just couldn't handle it. Clumsily, I reached across the cannon and pulled the bolt back with my left hand. This would be extremely awkward in a high speed-loading situation, so I hoped we wouldn't be firing in the near future.

Radio news broadcasts became more revealing as the days went by. No matter how well the announcers tried to explain the "strategic withdrawals", they had to admit that the allies were gobbling up the *Vaterland* in huge bits. The Russians were rapidly approaching Berlin, the Americans had encircled the Ruhr and the British had spearheaded toward the city of Bremen, a mere 90 kilometers from our present position. The futility of the situation was emphasized by the distant rumbling of heavy artillery, which became somewhat more distinct each day. A week had barely passed when the *Unteroffizier* called our three gun crews together:

"As you can tell from the cannon noise that's getting closer every day, the British are closing in on Bremen and they'll be heading directly for Hamburg thereafter. The *Hauptman* just called me on the phone with instructions to prepare our platoon to move out later today. The entire battery is being transferred to a new location."

We hastily packed our personal gear and started getting the guns ready. With picks and shovels we attacked one wall of the gun pit and fashioned a crude, earthen ramp so that the cannon could be rolled out. The wheels were lowered on the gun and ammunition boxes piled high on the gun carriage. We were soon ready to pull out and took turns looking down the road for the trucks or tractors that would pick up the guns. After about an hour we could hardly believe what appeared rounding the curve in the road: three teams of farm horses came clomping through the sand toward our position!

The *Unteroffizier* said: "Sorry, guys, but all they could find to move us were these horses. Let's get busy and hook up the guns so we can get the hell out of here!"

With all of us pushing and pulling on the guns and the farmer shouting loudly and slapping the leather reins, the horses managed to pull each gun out of its pit and onto the road. A short time later we joined the other eleven horse-drawn guns of our battery, led by the *Hauptman* chugging along in our one and only vehicle, an ancient and battered supply truck. Again we were on our way to a new and unknown adventure. This time we were trudging along a country road, keeping pace with our rubber-tired guns, moving southward in the direction of the cannon fire, rumbling ominously in the distance.

Late in the afternoon the column came to a halt at the edge of a small village with the command "Platoon Leaders come forward for a briefing!"

Grateful for a chance to rest, we flopped down in the grassy ditch awaiting further instructions. In a short time our *Unteroffizier* returned to exclaim:

"As of right now, we're taking on the dual role of anti-aircraft as well as anti-tank duty. Our three guns will be placed over there facing the road and the other platoons will dig in closer to the village. We don't have any armor-piercing shells, so I want you to aim at the tracks or at the peep slots; that's the only way you'll be able to inflict damage. Let's get going right away; we want to be set up before dark!"

Brandishing picks and shovels, our group of children and seniors began the arduous task of cutting a gun position into the compacted clay. The hole ended up being 15 feet by 15 feet with a depth of over four feet to afford us at least some protection from enemy aircraft or tanks. It was well after dark when we finally pushed the gun into its new home and cranked up the wheels to make the cannon ready for action.

The *Unteroffizier* called us together: "You did pretty well, fellows.....that's one nice hole. Now, first thing in the morning I want you to cut a supply of branches from trees and bushes to give us some camouflage. They have some bread and soup for us over at that farmhouse and also a nice surprise for you. Now that we're in front line combat, you can each have a bottle of *Schnapps* warm you up tonight when you crawl into the straw."

I slurped down my soup and followed with a few healthy swigs of the clear and harmless looking liquid that came forth out of my *Schnapps* bottle. In a few minutes my head was spinning in an unaccustomed alcohol stupor and I snuggled into the comfortable straw for a good night's sleep.

We were aroused with the customary whistle blasts accompanied by the announcement:

"Everybody on the move.....grab some bread and coffee at the field kitchen and bring your packs over to the gun positions.....we're moving out again!"

Incredible as it seemed, we took down the guns and hooked them to a new team of horses that had appeared in the meantime. For the next three days this fiasco continued.....dig a gun pit, spend the night and then move on to the next village; then dig another pit, go to sleep and move on the next day!

On the fourth day we pulled into a small village right on the Elbe River. We dug our pits into the dike at the river's edge to give our guns a clear field of fire across the river, which was only about 400 meters wide at this point. Our gun crew slept in a confiscated house behind the dike and we took turns walking into the village to pick up rations from the field kitchen. We kept a constant watch across the river and stretched a camouflage net above our entire position, which gave us a feeling of some security, especially from air attacks, as the net blended in perfectly with the blossoming fruit trees in the yard. As two days passed, we began to think of the gun pit as our semi-permanent home and planted some flowers on the riverside rampart.

Rumors abounded as we wiled away the hours in the mild and pleasant spring weather: "The British have crossed the Elbe already just a few kilometers upstream"......"The Tommies have already encircled the entire area around Hamburg; it won't be long until we're captured, too!" The approaching heavy gunfire confirmed the seriousness of our situation, but we had no idea of the enemy's strength or direction.

Suddenly the farmers and horses appeared again and we were told to hit the road again. Sometimes by day and sometimes by night, we moved away from the river in a large circle around the city of Hamburg. An air of confusion took over as orders were countermanded by opposite orders within minutes and more and more bedraggled troops and refugees were moving along the highway.

One incident comes to mind that utterly disgusted me and was one of the final coffin nails in my Nazi ideology took place in a small farm village along the way. A troop of SS infantrymen was marching along in the same direction as we were. Two women were cycling along with the other refugees, their backs and bicycles laden with vital possessions in search for escape from the horrors of front line combat. Suddenly two SS men pounced on the helpless women, pushing them aside and knocking their bags into the street. Smirking haughtily, they exclaimed:

"You girls can walk the rest of the way!.....We need these bikes worse than you do!"

Always accustomed and living up to the adage: "Women and children first!" I was appalled but could do nothing, as the bullies were heavily armed and cycled rapidly away.

Enemy air activity intensified and there was almost constant *Jabo* traffic in the skies. Soon we were hiding all day and traveling only by night. We were getting almost no sleep and constantly on the move. With no time to dig in, we would hastily set up an anti-tank position at a curve in the road, take turns as lookouts while the others took a nap in a nearby barn, then the horses would re-appear and we would roll down the highway again. Some of the young ones suffered the most and could hardly stay awake as we moved on through the night. Whenever possible, I would lay one of the boys across the cannon fenders for a short nap. I held onto his greatcoat to keep him from falling off as we plodded on to our next stop.

One afternoon I assumed guard and lookout duty with our guns pointed down the road toward the British lines. It was a gloomy day with a slight drizzle settling on the countryside, steaming with pleasant April warmth. A slight wandering of thoughts to a past enjoyable glider flight led me to lapse into other daydreams; suddenly I was shaken back into reality. I was lying face down in the soft mud after drifting off into a sound sleep and losing my balance. Brushing myself off as best I could, I resumed my responsible guard post, hoping that no one had observed my indiscretion!

Just before my relief arrived, a group of *Arebitsdienst* boys came past my post, trudging rearward. I shouted at them:

"Where have you fellows been? You look all beaten up!"

"Man, those Tommies shot the hell out of us about 3 kilometers up the road. Their artillery shells were fused to explode right above our heads. If it weren't for our rucksacks we would have had many more casualties. Look at my buddy ahead of me; his gas mask and mess kit are all shot to hell!"

Shortly thereafter we hitched up our guns and also fled toward the rear; the Tommy was getting too close for comfort at this late stage of the game. Our main thoughts now only revolved around self-preservation.

As my pocket calendar showed May 2nd, we re-entered the city of Hamburg. By this time we realized that all was lost and that the war would soon be over. The battery pulled into a small, tree-lined park and we sent the farmers home with their teams. A radio report admitted that the British had entered the city of Hamburg and that Russian tanks had rolled into Berlin..... we prepared to surrender.

We took refuge in a nice air raid shelter equipped with canvas covered bunks, a rare treat compared to the accustomed straw of the past few weeks.

17

The next morning I walked over to my platoon leader and asked:

"Herr Unteroffizier, should I remove the bolt from my cannon and bury it as we've been taught so that the gun will be useless to the enemy?"

"Volmar, I don't think it'll make a damn bit of difference! The war is lost and it would be a shame to ruin that nice 37-millimeter piece. Who knows, we may join up with the British and Americans and end up shooting at the Russians with that cannon. Just hold off and see what the Tommy says when he gets here! Tell your gun crew that anybody from Hamburg or vicinity who wants to sneak home may do so; the rest of us will stay here and wait to be captured.

As the Hamburg boys shouldered their rucksacks and said farewell, my friend Hans said:

"Jochen, why don't you come home with me for a few days until things quiet down? You can rest up a little and then head for your hometown Kaiserslautern. That's better than being taken prisoner and spending time in a P.O.W. camp."

I accepted his offer gladly and together we waved to our comrades and headed off into the ruins. We walked for almost half a day, passing through completely devastated areas as well as some where the houses were quite intact with flowers blooming everywhere. We had to be constantly alert for British patrols and roving command cars that were moving about at all times. Whenever the Tommies came near, Hans and I ducked into a courtyard, alleyway or behind a pile of rubble until the danger passed. It was almost dark when we reached his parents' house situated in a rural and undisturbed suburb. Hans' father was somewhere on the Russian front and his mother was living by herself. She embraced him tearfully:

"Thank the Lord, am I happy you're home, Hans! I haven't heard from you in two whole weeks since I cycled down to your position and found it vacated."

Hans remarked: "I'm glad to be home and I'm glad this whole thing is finally over! I had no way of sending word to you; they kept us on the move all the time and the telephones were out of order wherever we went. I've brought a friend to stay with us for a few days until it's safe for him to start walking home to Kaiserslautern."

"Sure your friend may stay with us; he can sleep on the couch in the living room. You boys look exhausted; let me heat up some soup and you can go to bed and get some rest."

While we were eating an announcement was made over the radio:

"Attention, all Germans in Hamburg and vicinity. This is the British Army of Occupation with a bulletin. All military personnel are to give themselves up to the nearest British outpost. A strict curfew will be enforced from 10:00 P.M. until 7:00 A.M daily; no Germans are allowed outside of their homes during these hours.....our troops have orders to shoot violators on sight.

Somewhat disillusioned yet grateful that the fighting was over for us, we went to bed. The next day a strange hush settled over the countryside; it didn't take us very long to realize that the incessant rumbling of front line cannon fire had completely ceased and there were no longer the pesky *Jabos* darting about the sky. The announcement of Hitler's death was followed by hints of peace negotiations and reminding all German soldiers to surrender rather than needlessly risk their lives.

On the morning of May 7th the official announcement of the total German surrender came.....the war was finally over! Rested up and anxious to start my journey home, I contemplated on the best course of action. If I surrendered to the British in Hamburg I could be faced with spending months in a P.O.W. camp. If I started walking dressed in uniform, I would soon be snagged by the Tommies and locked up anyway. Accepting a pair of shorts that Hans offered me from his father's wardrobe, I stuffed my uniform into my rucksack and took on the identity of an innocent teenager. By this time my roomy, blue *Luftwaffe* rucksack was harboring a collection of treasures obtained by hook and by crook since my escape from East Prussia. An extra pair of shoes, a hospital blanket, a two pound tin of margarine, several small tins of meat as well as my greatcoat and other articles of clothing, both military and civilian. It had now attained the weight of 80 pounds and had to be kept well balanced to permit walking on an even keel.

Hans offered to keep me company on my first expedition in the attempt to get out of Hamburg and begin my long journey home. Surprisingly, some of the inner city trains and streetcars were operating and we had no trouble getting downtown. The British used the Elbe River as a natural barrier and had set up roadblocks at all the bridges.

I told Hans: "I'm going to try this railroad bridge; there doesn't seem to be a check-point there. If I'm not back in a little while, it means that I've made it across safely and will be heading for Kaiserslautern. In that case, many thanks for letting me stay at your place.....Good Luck!"

As I approached the bridge, there were several German soldiers peering across the river. I approached them and commented:

"Why don't you fellows go on across the bridge? There doesn't seem to be anyone guarding it."

"It's useless for us to try in these uniforms; the Tommies have announced that all military personnel have to surrender as P.O.W.-s. We're keeping out of their sight until we can get some civilian clothes and some papers. One of our comrades tried to swim across the Elbe yesterday and they nailed him with a Tommy gun right in the water. It's not worth trying."

"Well, I'm going to cross over anyway. I speak English well and in these short pants they might let me through!"

With that remark, I shifted my rucksack and started walking across, carefully balancing my load as I stepped haltingly from tie to tie. I had almost reached the other side when a British officer stepped out from behind a steel upright. He looked very businesslike, wearing a beret and carrying a canvas holstered Webley pistol, the lanyard dangling from his shoulder. and he shouted in a crude semblance of German:

"Halt! Do not step any further. This bridge is closed!"

I replied in perfect English: "Sir, I'm on the way to my home in the Palatinate. I'm not a soldier but just a glider student and I want to go home!"

"Don't act so innocent, boy! You may not be a soldier but you were sure as hell being trained to drop bombs on London, weren't you? Now turn around and go back to Hamburg and don't try to cross this river again until you've been cleared by the Military Government."

Dejected and discouraged, I returned across the bridge and found Hans still waiting for me. He said:

"I saw that Tommy stopping you, so I waited. Let's go to the Rathaus[1] to see if we can get you some papers. I was really in an awkward position, as I had lost my Identification Book while running in the snow escaping the Russians and I had no other legitimate papers, military or civilian. In Europe, especially in crisis times, no one can exist without proper identification papers. My worst nightmare was seeing some officious policeman shout "Papers, papers!" and having none to produce!

The city square with the undamaged Rathaus was filled with people of all descriptions. We made our way through the throng and eventually came upon a policeman standing on the front steps to answer questions. I didn't even bother to ask, as he kept repeating: "There won't be any papers issued until next week when a clearing house will set up for civilians without proper papers. Go back to wherever you came from and come back next week! Military personnel are to surrender to the British immediately!"

Returning home with Hans once again, I racked my brain for a way out of my dilemma. The British were cleverly using the Elbe River as a natural barrier containing thousands of German troops who had surrendered. Eventually when logistics had stabilized and screening

---

[1] City Hall

processes were in place, they would certainly allow free passage, but that wasn't helping me now. There was no way I could embark on my 600-kilometer journey to Kaiserslautern without crossing that damned river!

I spoke with everybody I could who might have an answer; civilians, soldiers and policemen. Nobody was of any help and I was becoming quite discouraged. Wandering with Hans to the local grocery store to pick up a meager ration of lentils for our evening meal, I struck up a conversation with a young sailor in civilian clothes. In reply to my query he said:

"There's a small ferry crossing about 10 kilometers north of Hamburg. I came by there yesterday on this side of the Elbe while I was returning from Kiel. They won't let military personnel across but if you have any civilian papers you might make it as young as you are. The nice thing is that I didn't see any Tommies at the dock, just a German gendarme. Maybe you'll be lucky and slip through."

Hans' mother had asked us to pick up the daily milk ration at the store. Carrying the pitiful allotted pint of skimmed milk, a bright idea came to my resourceful farm-boy mind. I had seen a 3 or 4 cows grazing in a field nearby.....why not procure some fresh whole milk tonight?

It was pitch dark and well after curfew when Hans and I shinnied our way through the barbed wire fence and into the pasture. The cows were black and white but even the white parts were invisible in the blackness of night. Listening for breathing and cud-chewing noises, we slowly made our way to the first cow. My farm upbringing swiftly came to bear as I felt my way along the cow's body to her udder. My soft-spoken words of endearment kept her calm while I positioned the bucket. However, I had forgotten one important thing: it's quite a task to milk a cow while the milker is squatting in a pasture without a stool! Somehow I managed and we sneaked home with half a bucket of rich warm milk to help satisfy our constant hunger. Luckily there were no Tommy patrols nearby; it would not have been worth getting shot to have a few quarts of milk.

I departed at dawn, again saying farewell to Hans and his mother. As a parting gift she pressed two slices of bread and a small piece of sausage into my hand and wished me Godspeed.

A train, a trolley and a long hike brought me to the ferry dock. The boat was only about 40 feet long, a double-decker and for passengers only. When I arrived the boat was just leaving with a full load; heads and arms were sticking out all over. Dressed in my short pants, I joined the group that was waiting for the next trip across. A green-clad German gendarme stood at the turnstile, his eyes shifting to each member of the group.

In a short time the ferry returned and squeaked to a stop to disembark her passengers. As the gangplank was clear and the waiting group surged toward the gendarme, I bravely went along. The only piece of paper I had was a tattered Gun Club membership card, which I flashed toward the policeman as we surged by him and onto the ferry. Thank goodness, I was on my way home!

Using a road map and compass I headed south on the highway toward Hannover. There were many German soldiers and civilians moving in both directions. The only motor vehicles were British army trucks and motorcycles; the Germans were either walking or riding an occasional bike. As I met a soldier going in the opposite direction I would ask:

"Where are you going, my friend.....where did you come from?"

"I'm on the way to my home-town Hamburg and I came all the way from Munich."

My reply would be: "I ended up in Hamburg and I'm on the way home to Kaiserslautern."

Wishing each other "good hiking" we continued on our respective journeys. Sometimes we joined up with soldiers traveling in our direction for a day or so. It was strenuous walking with my heavy pack but I plodded on, knowing that each step brought me a step closer to home.

On the first day I learned a good lesson; I usually walked on the right side of the road and stepped off the asphalt pavement when I heard or saw a vehicle approaching from the rear. This time I didn't step away far enough when speeding British lorry swerved off the pavement and intentionally clipped me as it passed. I lunged forward but caught my balance in time to avoid falling flat on my face.....I said to my walking partner:

"I guess some of these guys are still at war!"

The first night on the road I stopped at a farmhouse and asked permission to sleep in the barn. The farmer wasn't home but a lady boarder came to the door and talked with me:

"I'm sure the farmer will let you stay in the barn. When he gets home later I'll tell him you're out there. Where are you from, young man? You're not a soldier, are you?"

"No ma'am, I'm not really a soldier, just a flight student and an *Flak* helper. I was in East Prussia, then in Hamburg and now I'm on the way to my home in Kaiserslautern."

"You look so hungry; let me give you one of the eggs the farmer gave me this morning. Do you know how to drink a raw egg? Here, let me show you!"

With that she punched a neat hole in each end of the egg with my Boy Scout knife and said:

"Now just hold the egg up like this and suck on the bottom hole. The entire egg yolk and egg white will gently slide into your mouth and down your throat. It's very painless and simple if you ever have to consume one quickly before getting caught in a stranger's chicken-coop! Here's a crust of bread to go along with the egg."

The lady continued: "I hope you make it home to your mother without mishap. Do you know, I had seven children and lost all but one of them fleeing from the Russians last winter. Two of the babies froze to death, three others died in a strafing attack and one got run over by a Russian tank. My last remaining child was a 12-year-old boy and he managed to come all the way to my brother-in-law's farm with me. We were here only three weeks when the war ended. The next day my son was playing over there in the woods and picked up a 20-millimeter shell. If I had only been there, I could have stopped him; he apparently pounded the shell on a rock, which detonated the shell, killing him instantly. He was such a good boy.....why did God have to take him from me also?"

Somewhat accustomed to tragedy, I was still shaken by this sad tale of woe. Also, it warmed my heart to have this lady share her skimpy food supply with me, a stranger.

Each day brought new adventures and experiences. Trekking along the road the next day, I was walking by myself and came upon a cycling father and daughter as they were being accosted by two Polish slave laborers. The Poles were helping themselves to the bicycles and luggage. One of the Poles held the father at bay with a long-bladed knife while the other man started manhandling the girl. It looked like and impending rape to me. Without a second thought I grabbed a piece of birch firewood from the ditch and menacingly approached the group. The knife-wielder turned his attention from the father to me. Now both of the bandits came toward me with knives drawn. I had no choice but to put down my club and raise my hands in surrender. While the men went through my pockets the girl and her father quietly escaped, walking quickly down the down the road. I lost my compass and Boy Scout knife to the thieves, who suddenly jumped on the stolen bikes and headed down the road. A few minutes later their hurried departure was explained, when two British motorcycles pulled up from behind. I described the bandits to them and they sped down the road in hot pursuit. A few moments later we could hear several bursts of Sten-gun fire erupting through the trees. However, when we reached the spot in question, there was no trace of Tommies or bandits to be seen. The Poles had either been captured or had escaped into the woods.

I stopped at the next British detachment quartered in a house along the road. Complaining to the Captain about the loss of my only knife, he sympathetically handed me a large butcher knife to keep. This was to be the pattern on my entire trek home: the war was over and 99% of the enemy soldiers were friendly and generous and realized that it's not men that make war but that the leaders and their political aspirations are responsible.

Another night sleeping in the straw was followed by another day of plodding along the road lugging an 80-pound pack. Suddenly the word was passed along:

"The Tommies are arresting all military on the highway and all civilians with no papers. Better head for the woods and stay off the roads from now on"!

We immediately left the highway behind and made our way through the country. We were in the renowned *Lüneburger Heide*[1] a

---

[1] Lüneburger Heath

picturesque area of pine trees and heather meadows. The pleasant sight and aroma of heather blossoms made our hike pleasant and interesting until it came to an abrupt end later in the day. Suddenly we stumbled upon on British armored car parked behind a screen of bushes.

"Halt and show your papers!" a Sten gun brandishing corporal commanded.

In spite of my fluent English, the Tommies were not satisfied with my scrap of paper and cock-and-bull story about being a flight student. Along with my two companions, I was bundled into the rear seat after undergoing a body search for weapons. I obediently surrendered the butcher knife that had been given to me by the British officer a few days before.

As the armored car bounced along through the rough and bushy terrain, the corporal remarked:

"Sorry to have to take you chaps in, but orders are orders. We've been told to pick up everybody who even resembles a German soldier. They'll probably send you to a P.O.W. cage for screening and then send you to your homes. Here, relax and have an English smoke; nobody is going to hurt you!"

A few kilometers of bumpy ride brought us to Battalion Headquarters in a small village. We dismounted, underwent a thorough personal search, unpacked our rucksacks for inspection and were placed in a room to await questioning. We waited and waited for the interrogation officer. Lunchtime came and we were each given a healthy portion of "bully beef" in our mess kits.

Finally the interrogation officer appeared. He was a stern looking Jewish Captain and displayed an attitude (now understandable to me) entirely opposite of the other officers I had met along the highway.

"Where are you coming from? Where are you headed? Why don't you have proper papers? Where did you learn to speak such good English? Why haven't you surrendered?"

"Sir, we just want to get home.....we don't want to make trouble and we're not hiding anything! I lost my Pay-Book while fleeing from the Russians."

"There have been radio announcements all the time ordering all German military personnel to surrender to the nearest British outpost. Maybe it will improve your hearing if we lock you up in a P.O.W. cage for a while!"

With that remark, he beckoned to the Corporal who had brought us in:

"Corporal, put these three men in a lorry, then stop by Battalion Headquarters and pick up whatever Krauts they've rounded up this morning. I want you to drive the whole lot of them to the P.O.W. cage at Munsterlager. Don't you dare let any one of them slip out of your hands, or I'll have you court-martialed!"

A two-hour lorry ride brought us to Munsterlager. Formerly a *Wehrmacht* facility, this enormous complex seemed to stretch for miles as we were driven through its pine-shaded expanse. Rows and rows of wooden barracks situated in barbed wire enclosures were interspersed with huge, shed-like warehouses. The place bustled with activity.....lorries, jeeps and staff-cars buzzed about. There were MP-s and Sten-gun armed soldiers everywhere patrolling the barbed-wire compounds which were filled to the brim with bedraggled and gaunt-looking German prisoners.

Our lorry finally sounded its horn at the gate of a compound. The British sentry directed two Germans to swing open the large wire gate and the truck pulled inside. We were ordered to dismount with our packs and report to the Camp Commandant. There were about a dozen in our group; what a scruffy bunch of once proud German soldiers assembled in front of the office!

The entire compound was run by Germans; the British rarely came into the gate unless there was a serious problem that the German staff couldn't handle by themselves.

The Commandant was an infantry *Feldwebel* who addressed our group:

"Welcome to Munsterlager, men. As you saw on the way in, there are many thousands of us in this facility. The camp rules are very strict but fair. They are posted on the door of the office and on the door of each barracks building. The food is very skimpy; we are told that there is a tremendous logistics problem as there are now several million German prisoners in captivity; there just isn't enough food to go around. Don't try to escape.....it will just make things tougher on the rest of us. Besides, where would you go? If you're caught without release papers anywhere in Germany, you'll be locked up again anyway. I'm running this camp like a German military unit and we are allowed and even required to take care of our own problems such as discipline, thievery and fighting. Just abide by the rules and you'll manage to endure conditions until we all get out of here."

The facilities were definitely Spartan; no bunks, no tables or chairs and no blankets or supplies of any kind. Each barracks had piles of straw strewn in all areas and we spent our time either lying or sitting in the straw. We were allowed out of doors but were told to stay at least two meters from the wire enclosure, the other side of which was patrolled by several Tommies armed with Sten guns.

Darkness arrived along with our evening meal. A head count of each barracks was the basis of distribution. Six men had to share one eight-ounce tin of corned beef and each of us received four small crackers. There was no breakfast meal and at noon we each devoured a messkit half full of soup along with two crackers. Within a few days I was so hungry and weakened, that I started passing out whenever I stood up from lying in the straw. The first time this happened, I awoke with two cigars missing from my shirt pocket; I soon learned to get up gradually, allowing the blood to stay in my brain. I also learned to keep valuables in deep trouser pockets or hidden elsewhere, like way down inside my rucksack.

Hunger and the lack of smoking materials brought out the worst in everybody; it was every man for himself. Many times I saw fellow prisoners bartering with the guards at the fence, exchanging Iron Crosses, wrist watches and wedding rings for a few English cigarettes or a pack or two of crackers. I had nothing to trade, but had a lucky break anyway. One day an interpreter was needed to accompany a lorry loading detail at a warehouse. I quickly volunteered and spent the afternoon translating orders and helping load rations to be distributed among the various compounds. The driver was a kind-hearted cockney, who gave me a smoke every time he lit one for himself and passed me a candy bar at the end of the day.....I was really living now!

Forever resourceful, especially in matters concerning my stomach, I supplemented my rations in my own way. Since Munsterlager had housed *Wehrmacht* horses in prior days, there was a supply of dried sugar-beet chips on hand at one of the warehouses. These were free for the asking, so we acquired three bags to take back to our compound. We chewed them dry, we chewed them soaked in water, we sucked on them and we spit them out again.....nothing we tried made them very palatable. One day I boiled a portion in water, which resulted in a brownish, molasses-like brine that didn't taste any better than the dried version. Never giving up, I scrounged through the cookhouse garbage can and retrieved a handful of potato peelings, which I added to the slop. The taste wasn't much better, but at least the peelings gave it some substance and maybe some nutrition?

I had been a prisoner for seven tiresome and boring days, when a special *Appell* was announced:

"All civilians are to be released today.....anybody who can prove that he's not a member of the German Armed Forces will be discharged and permitted to go home!"

Jubilant and nervous, I shouldered my rucksack and marched with some others to the neighboring parade ground. Probably 50 or 60 of us were lined up, ready to go. A German-speaking British sergeant started at one end of the formation and questioned each one diligently and asked for a show of papers. Most of the men were allowed to step forward to a table manned by several Tommies, including an officer, who were preparing and signing release papers. Noticing that the sergeant rejected several of my comrades who were in partial uniform, I became apprehensive as he came closer. In a last minute attempt at deception, I hid behind my neighbor, frantically opened my rucksack and changed into my short pants.

My turn to be questioned soon came:

"What's your name and who are you?" the sergeant began.

"My name is Joachim Volmar and I was a flight student in East Prussia. I lost my papers when the Russians chased us and I want to return to my home in Kaiserslautern."

"I guess you look young enough to be harmless.....go over to the table and pick up your release!"

Relieved and elated, I strode over to the table. I was given the valuable release paper and civilian ration coupons for one pound of bread. Thanking the Captain in my fluent English, I shouldered my pack and headed for the exit gate. It was Sunday, May 27th and I was a free man at last, clutching the key to my future, a simple piece of paper with a rubber stamp imprint!

Striding through the main gate and down the road to the village, my first stop was the bakery. Even though it was Sunday, the shop was open with several P.O.W. dischargees lined up ahead of me. My turn didn't come soon enough, as the delicious aroma of fresh-baked rye bread was driving me insane. The one pound coupon entitled me to half a loaf of the enticing bread; I paid for it and opened the wrapper as I walked down the road, heading south toward my home.

Good fortune seemed to be following me again. I hadn't even finished gobbling down the soft, fresh bread when a British lorry started overtaking me. Suddenly there was a squeal of brakes and the truck stopped beside me. I could hardly believe my luck.....the driver was my friend whom I had interpreted for back at the camp. Pleased to see me, he said:

"Hop in, buddy! I'll give you a lift to the fuel depot which is about 20 kilometers down the road."

Elated for not having to hoof it, I climbed aboard and we sped off. Enjoying the pretty spring landscape, time passed all too quickly and I had to leave my free ride. The Tommy gave me half a pack of cigarettes and we said good-bye.

From now on it was hitchhike a bit, walk a bit, hitchhike some more and walk some more. My last ride with a British lorry took me all the way to Celle but from here on there were no more allied rides. Compared to the laxness of the *Lüneburger Heide*, I was now entering an area that had been conquered some months ago and was under strict Military Government rules. The vehicles had "No Riders" signs posted in their windshields and the drivers all had strict instructions not to pick up any Germans.

Progress was slow, but as we advanced further south there were more and more German trucks and eventually even trains operating. Part of the infrastructure problem was the lack of passable bridges. During the last months of the war, Adolph Hitler had insisted on the destruction of as many bridges as possible to slow the Allied advance. Even if the delays imposed upon the advancing troops were minimal, he still insisted on this asinine doctrine, consequently even unimportant bridges went plunging down and had to be laboriously rebuilt. A freight train might take me 20 or 30 kilometers and then stop at the last station before a ruined bridge. Then I would walk 5 or 10 kilometers, maybe sleep in a barn or a haystack and then find another train or a truck to take me on another leg. Within a week I had reached the halfway mark of 300 kilometers. As I neared my *Onkel* Gerhard's home in Westphalia, I decided to stop there for a night's sleep and to retrieve our suitcase containing emergency clothing, which we had sent to him for safekeeping.

Tante Martha and *Onkel* Gerhard, together with their five daughters, were happy to see me. When I mentioned leaving for home the next day, my uncle exclaimed:

"Jochen, you are *not* leaving this house until you've had some rest and some of *Tante* Martha's good cooking to fatten you up.....you look just like a cadaver!"

The advantages of being a country doctor were soon evident. Ample supplies of potatoes, lots of real butter and delicious Westphalian ham were on the table for every noon-day meal, with fresh-baked bread, eggs and lunch meats taking care of breakfast and supper.

Onkel Gerhard even had an automobile, and enjoyed my company as he made his rounds. It was tempting to stay longer, but after six days I forced myself to say good-bye and head southwards again. I knew that my parents hadn't heard from me since March and had no idea where I might be and if I had even survived the war! Hitching our heavy suitcase to the front straps of my 80-pound rucksack, I now really had to balance my load for proper walking, but with my final goal in sight, I hit the road again, walking and trying to hitchhike.

Reaching the Ruhr valley, I saw my first Americans. Roaring along the shell-pocked highway, the drivers stuck to their "No Riders" orders just as their Tommy counterparts had done, so I kept on walking. Another German truck, some more walking and another train got finally got me to Cologne. To my surprise, another natural barrier stopped my progress for a little while. At the Rhine River, we were stopped at an American checkpoint and directed to a large warehouse at river's edge across from the famous Cologne Cathedral. One by one, we were channeled into delousing booths, made to strip down and sprayed with an awful smelling insecticide. Crossing the Rhine by foot, I finally arrived in familiar territory. The city was in shambles and the glass roof of the railroad station looked like a greenhouse after a hailstorm. Surprisingly, the cathedral still towered majestically over the nearby blackened rubble and there was pedestrian activity everywhere.

I jumped aboard a freight train at the Cologne station and headed south again. The 30-kilometer run to Bonn was just like old times as I enjoyed the pretty Rhine River scenery. In Bonn I found the same old streetcar that used to take me to and from the *Beethoven Gymnasium Oberschule* and my grandmother's house in Bad Godesberg. The walk from the trolley stop to grandmother's house was a snap compared to what I was accustomed to and I was soon lifting the familiar brass knocker.

My grandmother threw her arms around me and exclaimed: "Jochen, what on earth are you doing here? I'm so glad you're alive.....come in and tell me all about yourself!"

While I related my experiences in detail, she, in her typical manner, brought forth bread, butter and smoked ham from some hidden source. She was especially grateful for news about her son Gerhard and his family, as she hadn't been in touch with them in over two months. She still had no word from her son, my Onkel Paul. Mail and telephone service hadn't been restored at this point.

Now I was really anxious to get moving again, as I had less than 150 kilometers to go! I bade my grandmother farewell and trudged off to the train station. The first train that came through in the right direction was a passenger train. It was loaded far beyond capacity, with people standing on the running boards and hanging out of the windows. The next train consisted of all freight cars with all doors sealed. What was I to do, keep on waiting for the next train, which might be just as crowded? The freight train ground to a halt for some unknown reason; without hesitation, I climbed onto the bumpers of one of the cars and braced myself for a precarious bumpy ride. The train started forward and I soon became accustomed to the back-and-forth action of the bumpers. Balancing my rucksack and hooked up suitcase, I stepped aside each time the train came to a stop, causing the bumpers to compress with a loud bang. It was a pleasant and sunny day as we chugged along the west bank of the Rhine River, a route quite familiar to me. Evidence of the recent fighting was everywhere. As we passed the shrapnel-scarred towers of the Remagen Bridge, I recalled the radio broadcasts of the fierce fighting that had taken place here just two months before. Moving southward, we suddenly came upon a pitiful sight.....an American P.O.W camp stretched from the edge of the highway through open fields all the way to the base of the hills bordering the Rhine valley. Thousands of German prisoners were sitting on the ground, almost shoulder to shoulder. Other than a few pup tents scattered throughout the fields, there were no buildings or shelters of any kind. The terrain resembled a muddy barnyard having been trampled by thousands of hob-nailed jack-boots belonging to the prisoners. As I fingered the invaluable "Release from British P.O.W Cage" in my pocket, I thanked my lucky stars that I wasn't among those poor devils huddled in the field before me. A year later I was to view the results of these deplorable camp conditions.....a cemetery with an endless expanse of white crosses almost as large as the camp itself was nestled against the wooded hillside!

The train moved steadily along; soon I had traveled 100 kilometers perched precariously on the bumpers. We pulled into the station at Bingen when I jumped off. Striding up to an American MP standing near the stationmaster's office, I said:

"Hey buddy, do you know when the next train is heading toward Kaiserslautern?"

"Look, Kraut, don't you ever call me your "buddy"!.....You guys killed my best friend at Bastogne and I'll *never* be buddies with any Kraut!"

Flabbergasted by the unexpected reply, I apologized and slunk away. The stationmaster wasn't very encouraging, informing me that the rails to Kaiserslautern were still not passable because of damaged bridges. My best bet would be to travel to Saarbrücken to the west and then work my way home from there. He expected a freight train going in that direction around midnight.

A light drizzle started to envelop the station platform as I wandered over to an American guard shack at the far end. Reflecting back upon my previous encounter, I hesitatingly struck up a conversation with the one of the off-duty MP-s inside. I must have reminded this man of somebody back home, as he greeted me warmly and welcomed me into the shack. Within minutes, he had opened a can of "C" rations for me and followed up with a candy bar and a cigarette. This nice soldier couldn't hear enough of my story and reciprocated by telling me about his experiences from "D-Day" until the crossing of the Rhine. At the end of a very pleasant three-hour chat, I bade my new friend farewell and stood at the platform edge hopefully awaiting the promised freight train. Before letting me go, the generous American stuffed two "K" rations and a pack of Camels in my pockets; what a good feeling.....I was almost home and had a full stomach besides!

As the freight train screeched to a stop to change crews, I walked alongside until I found a freight car with its door wide open. Swinging my baggage ahead of me, I climbed aboard and joined the half-dozen other people already inside, lounging in the straw. The monotonous "clickety-clack" as we rolled over the poorly-maintained tracks soon lulled me to sleep. When I awoke, we were just pulling into Saarbrücken; I quickly disembarked to search for a train to carry me on my last 60-kilometer ride home.

This time I ended up in an open coal car; the drizzle had since given way to a day of cheerful sunshine, which helped to make my ride bearable, as I had to sit on a pile of dusty and hard chunks of coal. Whenever the train passed some women and children busily scrounging coal from the rail-bed, I quickly threw some large chunks of the valuable fuel overboard to make their collection job a little easier. As we chugged eastward I became more anxious and could hardly wait until I saw the skyline of my hometown on the horizon. We pulled into the station and I jumped off the train. Something new had been added; this station was guarded by French troops, as the entire area was being parceled off into the French Occupation Zone.

As I was leaving the station area, a French sentry stopped me and checked my papers carefully; if it hadn't been for the British P.O.W. Release, I probably would have been taken prisoner again. The sentry waved me on and I was on my way again with just a few kilometers to go. I walked briskly through the downtown area, drinking in the familiar sights and feeling sadness as I passed each bombed-out building that I had known before. I headed toward our part of town, a northerly suburb beyond the cemetery. Finally climbing up the last path through the woods, I caught sight of U.S. Army vehicles parked in front of our apartment house. Moving closer, I could see that all four apartment buildings had been taken over by the Americans. Where on earth were my parents?

The American sentry was of no help nor was the Sergeant he queried who was standing on the balcony, which had at one time belonged to us. No one had a record of where the evicted occupants had gone.

Since there were no neighbors left to question, I trudged down the hill about a mile to my friend Fritz Klein's home. I was in luck.... his mother answered my knock at the front door:

"Jochen Volmar! It's so good to see you and that you are alive."

"I'm sure glad to be home, *Frau* Klein. Have you heard from Fritz and do you where my mother is? Did she survive the combat? There are Americans living in our house."

"No I haven't heard from Fritz yet; his last letter was from somewhere at the western front in March.....that's when we were over-run by the Americans and all mail service stopped. I know where your mother is living; a lady named *Frau* Kittelberger took her in when the U.S. Army evicted her. Why don't you soak your feet while I hop on my bike and go get your mother?"

With that she filled a basin with hot soapy water and left me with the pleasure of soaking my sore and blistered feet and savor being safely at home. About half an hour later, I heard a frantic shriek from the sidewalk. My mother's voice cried:

"Jochen.....Jochen! I can't get the gate open! Come and help me, please!!"

"I'm coming, *Mutti*....I'm coming!"

In my stocking feet I ran outside to meet her. In the meantime she had managed to open the gate and was rushing toward the house. We embraced joyously and tearfully; I was home at last!

I was soon to find out how lucky I really was, as I came home from the war relatively early compared to many of my friends, family and acquaintances. There was no word yet from my father who was last located in Alsace Lorraine, *Frau* Kittelberger's husband was still among the missing as well as most of my close friends.

Thanking *Frau* Klein profusely for her help, *Mutti* and I loaded my bags on her bicycle and trundled off to her new home. *Frau* Kittelberger, as well as her son and daughter, welcomed me with open arms. What a treat to finally have a real bed to sleep in!

A rigid rule of the new Military Government specified that all returnees were required to report to the CIC (U.S. Counter Intelligence Corps) within 24 hours after their arrival. In strict compliance, I made my way to the *Rathaus* the following morning and was ushered to a Lieutenant's office for interrogation. After a brief question and answer session about my wartime activities, the Lieutenant said:

"Why don't you sit down and relax, Joachim; we have quite a bit to talk about. I want to get to know you better. I still can't get over how you speak such flawless English with a typical American accent."

"Don't forget, Sir, that I learned both languages at the same time when I was growing up in the U.S. I spoke English during the day at school and with my friends then we spoke nothing but German when I came home. I can speak German just as fluently and have no trace of an accent."

"Now tell me, how could a bright fellow like you be taken in with all the political propaganda that was presented? Couldn't you see through some of the stories? And didn't it bother you that the Nazis were killing off thousands of Jews in their concentration camps?"

"First of all, Lieutenant, the only information source we had was the German radio and newspapers. It was a crime to listen to the BBC so we didn't really get any other views on anything that happened. I was pretty much a supporter of the German cause and didn't have any disloyal feelings toward Germany until I saw a few bad things last year. I still feel that Germany was right in opposing the Russians and I wish the United States and England would let us help them in driving the communist Russians out of Europe. As far as the concentration camps go, we knew that there were camps to which they sent Jews as well as politically undesirable Germans. I never heard them called "death camps" until after the end of the war."

"Young man, I think you're being truthful with me. I want you to read this report while I interrogate some of your colleagues in the other room. Let me know your thoughts when you're done reading."

I reached for the loosely bound packet of pages and read the title: *"German War Crimes Report, French Sureté, May 1945"*. Leafing through the pages, I noticed that it was the English translation of an actual transcript of the interrogation of concentration camp survivors. Starting at the beginning, I read the word-for-word comments in amazement and with feelings of horror. As I progressed my feelings changed from astonishment to disgust and shame. Eyewitness accounts of an SS trooper slinging an infant against a brick wall to fracture its skull and of wholesale execution of prisoners by gunfire or gassing made me nauseous. The more I read, the worse I felt. How could humans treat other humans this way and how could atrocities like this take place without word leaking out?

The Lieutenant, having given me ample time to read the entire report, returned to his office. He remarked:

"Now do you understand why we don't want to join up with you guys to fight the Russians? We have to get this whole mess sorted out first and see who's responsible and punish them. That's why we're screening everybody as they return home and we hope to catch most of the war criminals in doing so. I don't think you were a real Nazi, even though you were training to shoot down our bombers. I'm going to find you a job working for the U.S. Army; we can use your linguistic talents. I want you to promise me one thing, though; please pass on some of this horrible information to other Germans so that they realize what actually happened.....OK?"

The Lieutenant picked up the telephone and made a call to the Railway Transportation Officer, Lieutenant Tom Scalley, and procured my first job with the U.S. Military. This was to be the first of many positions I was to hold with the U.S. Army and U.S. Air Force until my return to America in 1951. Would the country of my childhood accept me again?

Epilogue

To spare my readers some guessing and conjecture, I'll briefly depict the post-war events leading up to my return to the United States.

My mother worked for the U.S. Occupation Forces for several years and subsequently returned to the United States.

My father was imprisoned by the French for a short time; after his release my mother divorced him for reasons of infidelity. He subsequently remarried and fathered my half-brother Günther, who I tracked down and established contact with in 1990.

The American armed forces welcomed my services, because of my unique bi-lingual abilities and my insatiable desire to learn (I speak both American and German so fluently that I can pass as either nationality without the trace of an accent). From V-E Day in May of 1945 until June of 1951, I was a civilian employee of the U.S. Government. My first jobs with the U.S. Army included janitor, interpreter, jeep and truck driver, 19-year-old supervisor of 55 German employees and general "jack of all trades".

In 1948 I became an employee of the US Air Force CID (Criminal Investigation Division) which was soon absorbed into the newly formed OSI (Office of Special Investigation). As a part of USAFE Headquarters in Wiesbaden, Germany, this new organization offered unlimited opportunities for an ambitious youth. My functions included crime-scene photographer, fingerprint technician, interrogator, investigator and air police instructor. The Berlin airlift and other cold war operations established the scene for many interesting adventures. Who knows, but there may be another book in my future!

Upon my immigration to the United States in 1951, the U.S. Air Force enticed me to enlist in the reserves with a Staff Sergeant's rating, which I held for eight years while pursuing a successful business career.

Yes, the Statue of Liberty welcomed me to her land of opportunity for the second time........ God Bless Her!

Joe Volmar